Who
Discovered
America?

Who Discovered America?

The Untold History of the Peopling of the Americas

GAVIN MENZIES
Ian Hudson

wm

WILLIAM MORROW
An Imprint of HarperCollins*Publishers*

If you would like to contact Gavin Menzies and the research team, please e-mail them at zhenghe@gavinmenzies.net. Our website, www.gavinmenzies.net, is a focal point for ongoing research into pre-Columbian voyages to the New World. Please get in touch and join us on this great adventure!

P.S.™ is a trademark of HarperCollins Publishers.

HarperCollins books may be purchased for educational, business, or sales promotional use. For information please e-mail the Special Markets Department at SPsales@harpercollins.com.

A hardcover edition of this book was published in 2013 by William Morrow, an imprint of HarperCollins Publishers.

FIRST WILLIAM MORROW PAPERBACK EDITION PUBLISHED 2014.

Map Copyright 2013 Springer Cartographics LLC.

Designed by Jamie Kerner

Library of Congress Cataloging-in-Publication Data has been applied for.

ISBN 978-0-06-223678-4

14 15 16 17 18   DIX/RRD   10 9 8 7 6 5 4 3 2 1

This book is dedicated to my beloved wife, Marcella,
who has traveled with me on the journeys related in
this book and through life.
—GAVIN MENZIES

This book is dedicated to my dear parents, Martin and
Primrose, to whom I owe everything.
—IAN HUDSON

CONTENTS

PART III
China's Explorations to the North

Timeline of World Civilizations

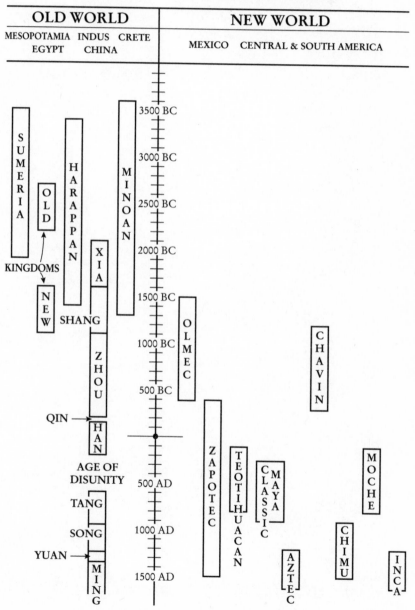

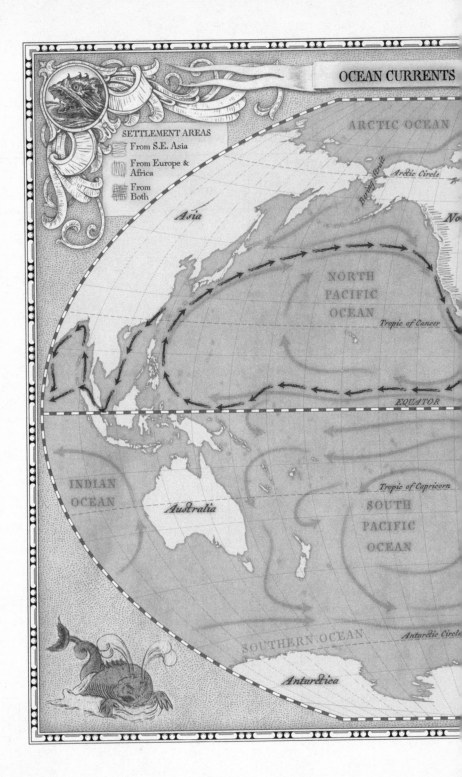

OCEAN CURRENTS

ARCTIC OCEAN

Arctic Circle

Bering Strait

Asia

No

NORTH
PACIFIC
OCEAN

Tropic of Cancer

EQUATOR

SETTLEMENT AREAS

From S.E. Asia

From Europe &
Africa

From
Both

INDIAN
OCEAN

Australia

Tropic of Capricorn

SOUTH
PACIFIC
OCEAN

SOUTHERN OCEAN

Antarctic Circle

Antarctica

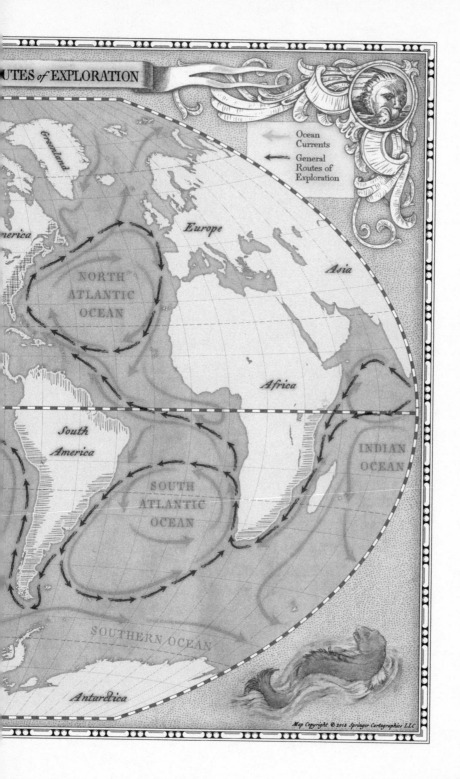

ROUTES *of* EXPLORATION

Greenland

Europe

Asia

America

NORTH
ATLANTIC
OCEAN

Africa

South
America

INDIAN
OCEAN

SOUTH
ATLANTIC
OCEAN

SOUTHERN OCEAN

Antarctica

Ocean
Currents

General
Routes of
Exploration

INTRODUCTION

I have been on the road for more than forty years now in search of a new understanding of early human exploration of this planet. My first book, *1421: The Year China Discovered America,* published in 2002, was the product of my initial work in chronicling China's circumnavigation and systematic mapping of the globe early in the fifteenth century. On March 8, 1421, the largest fleet the world had ever seen set sail from China, led by the great Admiral Zheng He. He traveled with a highly detailed map, dated to 1418, that showed easily the extent of his travels as far as the North and South American coasts. But the annals of the fleet's triumph were destroyed. Not long after the Chinese fleet returned, the empire descended into political isolation, obscuring the written evidence that Zheng He and his fleet had reached the Americas on that voyage. But the Chinese explorers who came to North and South America had left behind unmistakable markers of their presence, seven decades before Columbus reached the Caribbean Sea.

My second book, *1434: The Year a Magnificent Chinese Fleet Sailed to Italy and Ignited the Renaissance,* tracked the fact that China had visited Europe as well. Long underrecognized for their early mastery of technology, including their prowess in seafaring and navigation, the Chinese conveyed a unique cultural spark that fed the Renaissance and ultimately changed the development of modern civilization. Europeans embraced the Chinese ideas, discoveries, and inventions that provided the foundations of Western progress.

My goal in these volumes was to expose readers to the systematic nature of my research, but as an unintended consequence, the books also exposed the fact that professional historians are not willing to adapt to new information. Here was data—gathered from studies of maps, historical records, ethnological comparisons of folklore and traditions, botany, and human DNA—that made such a case for Chinese exploration of the Americas no later than 1421, seventy-one years before Columbus visited the islands of the Caribbean in 1492.

Yet, the well-reported data was taken as fraud and nonsense by some professional historians, in part because I am not a member of their club. I am a navigator and have traveled the world with friends and family, gathering information on the Internet and at home. My network is wide, but nothing has satisfied the critics. Their challenges are often ridiculous and illogical, and when they fail to convince people to go against me, they mount campaigns to ban my writings and public speaking engagements. What are the critics afraid of?

These first two books provided detailed and convincing evidence about Chinese explorations before Columbus. But I am now in the position to provide even more information and a new look at those explorations, taking advantage of an additional decade of research and investigation. More than ever, the record provides broad proof about China in the New World. That is the rationale behind this book—*Who Discovered America?*

Admiral Zheng He was arguably the greatest mariner of the previous millennium, and the proof grows that his fleet of regal vessels visited both South and North America. My conclusion does not stand alone, nor do I claim primacy in my research. I bring along fellow travelers on my journeys in search of new evidence about the exploration of the Americas, and some of the travelers are skeptics themselves. I welcome challenges and I share data with a network of readers and fellow explorers.

With that in mind, we have been gathering a mountain of new data in these ten years since publication of *1421*, so much material that it is now time to publish more evidence of the Chinese exploration of America. In part, the new data is a result of advances in genetics and DNA testing and analysis.

We can now cite genetic information that leads to ironclad confirmation of much of our earlier analysis. I have no doubt that we will have just as much material ten years hence and will be ready to publish once more. Each time the evidence will further cement the case and strengthen the reality before us—China engaged in a remarkable exploration of the globe and reached America long before most Europeans could match their prowess.

The publication of the discovery of Zheng He's 1418 map led to a flood of new data relating to Chinese voyages to North America over the past two thousand years. No reasonable person can deny the facts.

I have organized our new data in sections based on our travels during the first decade of the twenty-first century, providing a basic structure in which we can expand on our evidentiary details—genetic, linguistic, cultural, and archaeological. Taken together, these make a convincing, incontestable account of who really discovered America.

Part I revisits the basic question: Did the early settlers of the Americas arrive by ship or overland? For a century, scientists have clung to the theory that a barren land bridge across the Bering Strait provided access to hunters and gatherers crossing from Asia to the Americas. Could these people have arrived in the New World via a virtually impassable land bridge from Siberia to Alaska? I submit that they could not have. In this section we update our discussion of the strait, which I am not alone in thinking was far too inhospitable for a major migration. Land bridge theorists agree with us that the early settlers of the Americas came from eastern Asia, but they don't take seriously the evidence that we have gathered.

Human presence in the Americas involved not millennia of land-based migrations from Asia to North America southward, but instead a more organized series of arrivals by ship from Asia. We begin to blend in evidence, such as the sudden appearance of diseases and of plants that would not have survived a centuries-long migration across the frozen north. The subject expanded with our trip along the Silk Road in Asia Minor, where we also believe that Chinese commerce and communication by ship had far more importance than is commonly understood. Similarly, we also discuss here the other early great seafaring civilization, the Minoans, whose ships were far more likely to carry their settlers and merchants by sea.

From that basic exposition about seafaring, I turn to the great destinations of Chinese explorers. Part II is devoted to Mexican and Central and South American civilizations and their unquestionable links to Chinese culture. Here we describe new research about maps, about correlations between customs, and about folk traditions that are strikingly indicative of the arrival of a mighty Chinese flotilla.

Part III turns to essential new material about the Chinese arrival in the New World and tracks with our own visits to North America, both in the West and also along the Eastern Seaboard, from Florida northward to Nova Scotia. The footprint of the Chinese, along with the structures, flora, and fauna they left behind, is omnipresent. The information also focuses on Marco Polo's account, well documented, of his voyage when he was an agent of Kublai Khan to North America.

Throughout the book, I return to Admiral Zheng He and his map of 1418, along with the increasingly important evidence that even he was working with charts produced much earlier.

We use the map of 1418, for example, to uncover evidence of Zheng He's voyages to the Outer Banks and North Carolina. Also on the East Coast, we discuss Dr. S. L. Lee's identification of a medallion of the era of the early-fifteenth-century Chinese emperor Xuan De, who appointed Zheng He as his plenipotentiary in North America. By comparing the 1418 map to the evidence, we also debunk charges that it must be a fake.

I agree with scientists who say that the Americas were settled forty thousand years ago if not even earlier, however, not by nomads from the north, but by Asian explorers whose skills were truly legendary. Among our details is material from Charlotte Harris Rees's description of her father's map collection of very old Chinese maps of the Americas dating back three millennia. I also discuss the results of my conversations, among many others, with Emeritus Professor John Sorenson (Brigham Young University, Utah) who, with his colleague Emeritus Professor Carl Johannessen (University of Oregon), has gathered evidence of multiple transoceanic voyages to and from the Americas in the past eight millennia.

After *1421,* and then *1434,* my third book, *The Lost Empire of Atlantis,* was an enjoyable change of pace. In that book, we turned to the Minoan civilization, and described the compelling evidence about the fabled civilization of Atlantis. It is really the chronicle of the volcanic eruption at Thera (Santorini) in 1450 B.C. combined with a devastating earthquake and tidal wave that swept across the Aegean Sea and destroyed the sophisticated Minoan civilization.

Interestingly enough, this present volume had its origins before *The Lost Empire of Atlantis.* My wife, Marcella, and I had set off to Central America and Mexico in 2008 to research new material about the Chinese voyages of the fifteenth century. We traveled for three weeks and amassed a haul of evidence from Mexico and Guatemala. I wrote up this evidence in November and December. Come Christmas 2008, we decided to rest up by spending the holiday at a monastery in Crete. This we did and stumbled upon the extraordinary fact that Minoans from Crete appeared to have carried out oceangoing voyages from 3000 B.C. It soon became apparent that there was considerable evidence about Minoan as well as Chinese voyages to the Americas over the past four thousand years. With the help of Luigi Bonomi, my literary agent, as well as Ian Hudson, my intrepid young partner and cowriter for the current volume, we decided we had enough material for two books. We started with the Minoan voyages and *The Lost Empire of Atlantis* was published in 2011.

I returned to Crete around that time and examined astonishing evidence that men had sailed to the island and set up a base there in 100,000 B.C. Moreover it appeared they had a viable system of navigation because successive voyages had ended up in the same place—at the Preveli Gorge in the south of Crete. So with a group of friends Marcella and I set off on an exploratory trip to Anatolia seeking possible evidence of voyages to Crete one hundred thousand years ago (DNA studies had shown the early inhabitants of Crete had come from Anatolia, not from Greece). We found they were seagoing people who had been sailing the Mediterranean for more than forty thousand years. Moreover, they probably reached the Americas. From this fact emerged this book, *Who Discovered America?*

As always, this book has been a collaboration among friends, colleagues, and fellow researchers. I do want to mention with special delight again that this book is written with the expert assistance of Ian Hudson, a graduate of Eton College and the University of Bristol, who came to work with me around the time *1421* was being prepared for publication. He has been instrumental throughout the publication of our books. He has long traveled with us and produced some of the original reporting. He was also a central figure in setting up our website, www. gavinmenzies.net.

Our goal is for the website to act as a focal point for ongoing investigation into the pre-Columbian voyages of discovery. We are proud of its growth and popularity. Gradually, over the years, we have built up a network of experts from all over the world who were intrigued by the theories initially expounded in *1421*, though of course not all were in agreement. The Internet helped to facilitate an easy interaction, and we were sharing ideas around the world with an immediacy that would have been impossible ten years earlier. Although it was tough, we strived to maintain a 100 percent record of replying to anyone who wrote to us over the years. We think this has really made a difference in keeping the goodwill that we share among our rather large circle of like-minded friends around the world.

In addition to our website, we encourage you to sign up for our free newsletter to keep abreast of our and others' research. We have a database of about ten thousand subscribers, many of whom send us their own content when they can. Join us!

GAVIN MENZIES
IAN HUDSON
London, May 2013

PART I

Across Oceans
Before Columbus

PROLOGUE

Life at Sea

Imagine a fleet of Chinese ships crossing the seas more than half a millennium ago, thousands of miles from the comparatively safe shores of the Asian continent. Imagine as well the isolation, the commitment, and courage to face what cannot be known or fathomed.

The main comparison I have is my service in the British navy submarine service. As early as March 1961, I served as navigator of the HMS *Narwhal*. I recall very well the remoteness and seclusion of cruising at three hundred feet below the surface under a thick Arctic ice cap. Our task was to track Soviet nuclear submarines and produce a report deciding whether patrolling under the ice was feasible for nuclear submarines. If it were, Soviet submarines could shorten the distance between themselves and the Americas—their missiles could hit Texas. Our (future) Polaris missiles could target eastern Russia.

I was navigator of the *Narwhal*. My next appointment was to be operations officer of the HMS *Resolution*, Britain's first

Polaris-missile-firing submarine and at that time, Britain's sole independent nuclear deterrent. *Narwhal*'s patrol area was in the Kara Sea between Jan Mayen and West Spitsbergen. Here the ice was a uniform twelve feet thick, broken every hundred miles or so by polynyas—stretches of clear, unfrozen sea surrounded by ice. During the brief hours of daylight one of my assignments was to find a polynya, so we could attempt to surface, charge our batteries, take sun sights, and receive signals from Faslane Naval Base, our port, in Scotland.

One day, we were cruising in ultra-quiet mode, circling at three hundred feet and searching for the sounds of Soviet nuclear subs, with their distinctive five clover-bladed propellers, driven by two shafts. Suddenly there was a bang and the submarine filled with smoke. As we donned our breathing masks, we needed to surface as quickly as possible. As navigator it fell to me to find a polynya. It was by no means easy.

The Arctic ice cap is not stationary. Where we were operating, the ice rotated counterclockwise unless there was a period of low pressure, when it reversed direction. So, on balance, the polynya we visited two days before should have been carried northeast— that is, farther into the ice toward the North Pole. So I advised the captain that was the course we should steer, accordingly.

We had upward-sounding sonar of ten kilocycles per second. This continuously tracked the thickness of the ice and it showed when this thickness was changing as one approached a polynya. So we watched the upward sonar like hawks. After less than two hours' transit sailing northeast, we suddenly saw the ice change. Shortly afterward the water started to lighten, then suddenly there was clear water 130 feet above us. I immediately called the captain, who came to the control room and took over for me. We were able to surface; we started both generators, charged the submarine batteries, and cleared out the smoke from the submarine.

Now we were safe and earned our entitled "tots" of rum and it seemed appropriate to relax. I had brought a coconut mat and bats, balls, and pads for a cricket match upon the ice. So it was that we placed guards around the pitch to keep polar bears away. I captained the wardroom team and leading stoker Roberts led the ship's company team. The wardroom team duly won.

The Arctic is a bleak, awesomely beautiful, but unforgiving place. The experience of being a navigator there gave me an innate kinship with navigators of all ages. Imagine finally, then, an attempt by an ancient mariner far from home to circumnavigate this Earth, to seek ports of call where one could replenish stocks of food and water, to survive shoals and storms and accidents with no grounding or support system whatsoever.

My time at sea left me with the knowledge of the imposing navigational challenges for any sailor, but it also gave me an appreciation for the triumph of those who sailed before me on their rough-hewn barks. I was easily hooked and enthralled by stories of early Chinese explorations. I began to look at these stories and, using my knowledge of the seas, was led by my research to a new way of understanding the discovery of America.

CHAPTER 1

A Land Bridge Too Far

Decades of research and analysis of the available records convince me that Chinese explorers were the first to reach the Americas. Yet, a seaman to the core though I be, I have long been interested in evaluating the competing theory that many hold about Asian migrations from Siberia to North America across the Bering Strait. Eventually, in 1999, I was able to envision a way to test the case for migration across Beringia, the connector between the continents, a time of glaciers during which humans theoretically could have walked thousands of miles from Asia to America. I devised for myself an opportunity to trace the route under modern conditions when my daughter, Samantha, prepared for her marriage to Pat Murray in Garson, Ontario, north of Lake Huron.

I thought it would be fun and instructive for me to find an amphibious vehicle, drive from our home in London, England, through the Channel Tunnel across Europe and Siberia, then across the Bering Strait when it froze over, and finally through

Alaska and southeast to Ontario. I would collect Samantha and take her to the church in the amphibious car in time for her wedding.

I planned the operation with great care, more than a year ahead of time. We chose an amphibious Bering Strait–capable vehicle made by Dutton Amphibious Cars of Littlehampton. Tim Dutton, the proprietor, arranged for us to have a trial run in Littlehampton harbor—it performed beautifully. I gathered a list of requirements and gear and began accumulating them.[1]

My contact and inspiration for the journey was Commander Tony Brooks, who joined the Royal Navy some ten years after me and became a professional navigator. After he resigned from the Royal Navy, Tony rode a bicycle from London to the Bering Strait across Siberia. We planned to follow the route Tony took, and use his detailed reports to plan each stage. Acting on his advice, we planned to fit our craft, which we dubbed Mariner 2, with an 1800cc Ford diesel engine. George, who owned the local garage in Islington, decided to sell up and come as my co-driver. This brought a wealth of technical expertise to the project. I decided to purchase a second vehicle to accompany us in view of the multitude of spare parts that George considered necessary.

During my time as navigator of the HMS *Narwhal* I had developed a working relationship with the Scott Polar Research Institute, at the University of Cambridge. We carried out experiments on their behalf underneath the ice and briefed them when we returned. Lawson Brigham and Bob Headland, the archivist, provided us with very detailed information about the Bering Strait and eastern Siberia, not least accounts of their journeys through the strait on a Russian icebreaker.

Tony Brooks introduced me to Richard Casey, who had organized and carried out an expedition from Moscow aiming to cross the Bering Strait that was funded by the Russian army—which had provided trucks, fuel and water, icebreakers, helicopters, and backup logistics. Richard and Tony again helped me by introducing me to the captain of a Russian icebreaker who planned to transit from Asia to America, north to south in the Bering Strait, on August 10 and then return north on August 13.

In modern times, the shortest distance for such a crossing is about fifty-one miles, from Chukchi Peninsula in Russia to Cape Prince of Wales in Alaska. We planned to cross the Bering Strait from Cape Dezhnev to Little Diomede (an island in the middle of the strait) on August 13 and from Little Diomede to Cape Prince of Wales on August 14. We would have emergency help if needed.

The Russian army agreed to provide us with fuel for the journey through Siberia. Everything seemed set. I decided to call on the Scott Institute one last time to obtain a final briefing from Bob Headland, who had just returned from the strait.

I was horrified to learn from him how bad things were in Siberia at the time. Two Russian fuel tankers had managed to get through to Pevek the previous autumn but the fuel they brought had run out. Food supply ships had not gotten through and as a result there was widespread starvation in the villages on the Russian side of the strait. The people of Pevek did not even have sufficient fuel for the outboard-motor craft they used to hunt walruses for food. The population had been reduced from ten thousand to one thousand. In Bob Headland's view, if we went through with what appeared an expensive vehicle with food and fuel we would be attacked. Bob advised against proceeding without an armed escort and a fuel tanker.

Until that day I had thought crossing the Bering Strait across the ice in winter or by amphibious vehicle in summer was a realistic possibility. I had no idea just how terribly hard life was. Tony Brooks said the "Road of Bones," which he had used to travel through the Gulag Archipelago, was the most horrible experience he had ever had. Stalin had sent thousands of slaves by ship to build that road. Some mutinied. Hoses were turned on them and they froze solid—hence the bones.

After listening to the horror stories of the past and hearing about the dire situation of the present, I knew that I needed to reevaluate not only my own planned trip but also the issue of the viability of crossing the strait, under any conditions and at any time.

Scientists continue to claim that America was populated by waves of people crossing the Bering Strait from Siberia. Was crossing the Bering strait really possible? For a start there was no food, save for what a traveler could catch. Today's Inuit or Eskimo people cannot catch enough walruses to feed a population of one thousand. They need motorboats to hunt and catch them. Today, never mind in 10,000 B.C., before the Bering Strait was flooded, it is a thousand-mile trek across Siberia to reach the strait—without fruit or berries or trees for wood to make water from ice. Today there is a three-thousand-mile gap between the Russian and American hard road systems, and that is across an endless expanse of boggy tundra, forest, and rivers. It is virtually impossible to trek through the wilderness of Chukotka in the summer due to these endless bogs, rivers, and lakes. The only realistic time to pass through this region is during frigid winter months when all water becomes solid. How do you melt the ice for drinking water without wood to make a fire?

Next followed an obvious question: Why should people head north to ever colder regions, which they would have to do to reach the Bering Strait? Why not travel by sea with the current to America, where life is warmer and easier? And where there are kelp and animals for food? How could they know what to expect when they reached the Bering Strait on foot? Where did they expect to find food when heading north?

The more I thought about the Bering Strait theory of populating the Americas, the more ridiculous it became. If one cannot manage the journey today, when backed by a mighty Russian military machine, how could people have done it with nothing but their hind legs—having to walk in appalling conditions, without food, for months on end?

I concluded only armchair academics could believe in the Bering Strait theory of migration. In my view it never happened—another fairy story to boost the myth that transatlantic journeys were impossible before Columbus.

Sadly, but wisely I am sure, I abandoned my plan to cross Europe and Asia into Alaska on the amphibious vehicle. I decided to attend Samatha's wedding by conventional transport.

After the wedding, instead, I switched focus to a matter related thematically to theories about the land bridge. The spotlight now was a thousand miles away, on an equally vexing theory: the history of the Silk Road, the trade route from China to the West.

This had been another object of my interest and study at least since the 1970s. The link was my interest in the successes and fortunes of Chinese trade and world political power.

The Silk Road was also related to my study of Chinese explorations. Just as the Chinese used their maps and their seamanship to discover America, their maritime skills were also required on the trade routes westward from China to Asia Minor and then to Europe. The Silk Road's land route was supplemented by ships on the high seas.

CHAPTER 2

Along the Silk Road

It is certain that the Silk Road, which was really not a single road, but a series of trade routes across Eurasia, had an impact even more than two millennia ago in China's expansion to the West. But it was the very nature of the Silk Road that made it susceptible to changing patterns of migration, rivalries, and political influence.

Just how viable was the land route known as the Silk Road? No doubt parts of the network were vibrant crossroads for mercantile affairs and cultural and political transit. But as we were able to observe, parts of the route were impenetrable, even now. It is now clear to me that ancient sea routes provided by the Chinese were crucial in the success of what we know as the Silk Road.

As I wrote in my first book, *1421,* it was in December of that year that the Ottoman Empire blocked the land routes of the Silk Road from China through central Asia and on to the Middle East. What's more, the Ottomans controlled the Bosphorus Strait at Constantinople. Separately, the ancient canal that joined the Red Sea and the Nile had fallen into disuse.[1]

With the empire's hegemony and the loss of the maritime alternatives, traders needed to find an additional route—an ocean route—from East to West. This was precisely the moment that Zheng He had set off on his two-and-a-half-year voyage across the globe, thereby changing world history.

My goal, after scotching our journey to the Bering Sea, was to look at this other prominent land-sea conundrum and to evaluate competing theories. Asia Minor was the place to go. We set off for the Silk Road in 2001, exploring the eastern and central portions from Beijing through central Asia, and ending in Samarkand. Traveling this with a team of twelve friends—I like to call them the "Cantravelers"—we planned the trip mostly by public transport, notably by the extremely powerful and efficient Chinese diesel-electric trains.

It was not my first foray along this route. Marcella and I first took our little girls (as they then were) with us across the western part of the Silk Road in 1978. We traveled through Iran and Turkey from Shiraz to Isfahan, then past Lake Van and across Anatolia to Istanbul. It was a lovely summer and we stayed in some magical caravanserais, soaking up Persian and Turkish culture.

This second journey was equally striking, and always exotic. A typical day would start at a railway station where the train had deposited us at dawn. Awaiting us would be a prearranged minibus driver and guide for the day. We would explore the sites, usually long-lost cities, during the morning, have a packed lunch, then continue sightseeing in the afternoon, traveling ever westward. At dusk the driver would deposit us at the railway station for the next night's travel—again westward for some six hundred miles while we slept. Before dinner we would gather in the cabin of the "duty Cantraveler," who would have arranged beer, wine, and Chinese champagne.

Each night one of us gave a talk on an aspect of Silk Road travel—popular subjects including Islam, Buddhism, Chinese and Tibetan monasteries, the Taklimakan Desert, and export of Chinese blue and white ceramics. It was a highly efficient, economical, and educational way of traveling. The trains were clean, the food reasonable, though I disliked noodles at breakfast. Our journey was westward from Beijing to twelve cities: Xian, Lanzhou, Xiahe, Jiayuguan, Dunhuang, Turpan, Ürümqi, Kashgar, Naryn, Bishkek, Tashkent, and Samarkand, whence Marcella and I flew home.

One fascination was awakening at dawn each morning to see a completely different landscape from the night before. For example, we boarded a train at Xian and traveled overnight through the lush Yellow River valley, with farmers in their big hats weeding rice fields, and arrived at dawn at Lanzhou, a dusty plain where the wind blew sand into our ears.

Another surprise was how the Silk Road invariably lay in the foothills of mountains that were still snowcapped in May. By June, rivers are full of snowmelt. By choosing the date of the journey, travelers could find water within a day's camel ride all the way from the South China Sea to Samarkand.

The guidebooks all allude to the Silk Road being almost impossibly tough, across the worst territory in the world; in the deserts goblins would appear among sandstorms to kill and eat travelers. In fact the route lies between the Gobi and Taklimakan deserts—skirting the latter to the north, where one finds pleasant markets full of fruits.

Our goal was to experience a modern version of what must have been a dangerous, arduous ancient journey. We wanted to assess the quality of that crossing, to witness the diversity of culture, the imposing geography, to see archaeological sites and meet the descendants of those who populated the Silk Road. Here are some highlights along the route:

XIAN

First was Xian, more than 650 miles southwest of Beijing. Xian was the capital of the Tang dynasty and claimed to be the greatest city in the world. Today it retains its magnificent rectangular walls, which allow twenty horsemen to ride abreast. There are mementos of Xian's two-thousand-year history in mosques, Buddhist temples, bell and drum towers, the tomb of Qin Shi Huang, who was the first emperor of unified China (who built the famous terra-cotta warrior statues in the second century B.C.), and a host of tombs stuffed with priceless works of art all over the plains surrounding Xian.

The incredible wealth of China during the Tang dynasty can be seen in the superb Provincial Museum—the finest collection of Tang dynasty (618–907) art in the world—a sumptuous display.

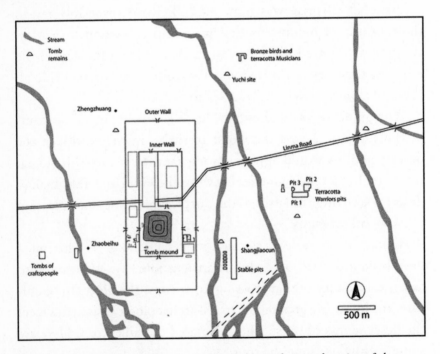

Site plan showing the First Emperor's Mausoleum, showing location of the Emperor's tomb, Terracotta Army, and other elements of the complex.

We had three days in Xian but would happily have spent three weeks there.

XIAHE

We reached Xiahe, several hundred miles to the southwest, after a long, tiring minibus journey from the railway station toward Tibet. The town is set in a scenic mountain valley on the edge of Tibet, at an altitude of about seven thousand feet—high enough to give one a severe headache. The Labrang Lamasery, where we stayed, is one of the most important Yellow Hat Sect monasteries in China. Today just one thousand lamas serve there, compared to four times that in the past. My recollections are of their brilliant vermilion clothes and the stench of yak butter and yak fat candles. On the way back to the rail line we visited the famous Bingling Temple, which includes 183 grottos and an eighty-foot-high statue of Maitreya, the future Buddha.

JIAYUGUAN

It came as a considerable surprise, perhaps a shock, to learn Jiayuguan is where the Great Wall ends. Emperor Zhu Di's father, Hong Wu, built this section in 1372. It has been designated by UNESCO as a World Heritage Site. We spent the afternoon walking along the wall, viewing the dusty desert surroundings.

Before we started this journey I had thought the Great Wall would protect merchants from Mongol attack the whole way from China to the West. I now realized that this was a misconception—the wall stretches only halfway across China, to Jiayuguan.

For thousands of miles, from here to Kashgar, merchants were defenseless against Mongol attack. The same was the case on the stretch from Kashgar across the steppes to Samarkand. How was travel along the Silk Road possible without protection? Indeed, that would be a powerful argument for having an alternative, more secure means of journeying from China westward.

DUNHUANG

Dunhuang boasts perhaps the world's finest Buddhist cave art. Some 492 grottos contain 2,000 sketches and 45,000 paintings—a most romantic city. In the evening we took camels to view the famous lake, surrounded by the "singing sands," an oasis of green trees. I experimented with camels to learn how much weight they could carry through the soft sand at Dunhuang.

TURPAN

The day started earlier than usual. The train pulled into the station at Turpan before dawn. We washed and shaved in the station restrooms, still half asleep. Our morning tour was through the *qanats,* underground tunnels that channel mountain water to irrigate the famous melons and grapes. In the afternoon we visited the ancient Bronze Age city of Gaochang. Dinner was washed down with Turpan white wine. The few museum artifacts were badly presented—a pity, as the collections included dinosaur skeletons. There was no evidence of Silk Road trade, none of the famous Chinese blue and white I had hoped to see. We boarded the train that evening surrounded by merchants selling every sort of grape—raisins and sultanas, as well as currants, white figs, and salted plums. Our overall impression was of dust and dust-colored buildings surrounded by grape-drying rooms.

KASHGAR

The trip from Turpan to Kashgar, 864 miles toward Kyrgyzstan to the southwest, takes most of a day. We arrived on Marcella's birthday, the day of the Sunday market, perhaps the most famous horse market in the world. William Dalrymple's *In Xanadu* describes it as "a fair and a carnival, a masque and a festival." Kashgar lies on the edge of the desert, with the Pamirs to the north and the foothills of the Hindu Kush to the south. The Sunday market attracts thousands of Uyghurs to Kashgar to exchange cereals, vegetables, camels, sheep, and cattle. The minority peoples appear in their colorful traditional dresses. Around the edge of the market, women dunk silkworms into warm water to make silk thread. Ladies in scarlet and crimson mingle between swaths of clothes. Aisle after aisle of colored cloth and spices dazzle your senses and the market is filled with a cacophony of voices, creating an almost magical world.

Outside the market, animals weave between oxcarts pushing their way through tinsmiths, rope makers, butchers, brush makers, cobblers, tinkers, and furriers with furs from the local mountains. Kazakhs and Kirghiz, Uyghurs and Uzbeks barter, gossip, and grumble. Horses are put through their paces before being sold. The noise is deafening. Waiting animals are drowned out by loudspeakers. Men in beards with tanned, brown, and leathery faces share stories and jokes. The air is heavy with the smell of warm animals, manure, and roast mutton.

There were neither Chinese nor Europeans there; only us and the peoples of the area. The goods, the food, and animals were all local. We had not seen an international market since Xian.

THE STEPPES

Kashgar is close to the international border with Kyrgyzstan and marks the end of the Chinese railway system that served us so well along the journey. From there we traveled by truck, or by minibus when there were decent roads. Carol Mellor, Marcella, and I continued ahead, and the rest of our Cantravel friends bade us farewell. I awoke with a moderate hangover—a result of celebrating Marcella's birthday and Frank and Gill Hopkins's forty-fifth wedding anniversary. I distributed Diamox tablets and aspirins from our stores, because these would help to battle altitude sickness. We were about to cross the mountains into Kyrgyzstan.

We saw marmots sunning themselves as the road reached the tree line. They screeched with anger at having to move out of our path. Officials checked our passports and visas no fewer than twelve times before we were allowed into Kyrgyzstan. The customs officers clearly disliked foreigners. They ostentatiously made us wait two hours while they enjoyed their lunch. There were no toilets; a spade was produced to dig a trench. Ladies first!

As we left the mountain border to descend to the steppe it began snowing, which served to dampen the dust underfoot. The snow fell for three hours, until on the steppe the sky cleared to reveal a glorious early summer evening. The beauty of the steppe leaves one speechless. Stretching around us to the horizon was a sea of flowers—purple vetch, bluebells, lady's mantle, brilliant dandelions, yellow ragwort, white mushrooms, campanulas the color of the sky, cornflowers, and swaths of brilliant purple poppies stretch to eternity. Flocks of wheatears and meadowlarks flit across the tall grass, alighting now and then on the tumuli of Mongols who died in the saddle.

By nightfall the Tian Shan mountains were behind us, five fingers high on the horizon. Rather than traveling by truck overnight, we were to take a local flight from Bishkek to Samarkand. The pilot, a fat Russian, was so drunk he had to be carried aboard. He began to shout obscenities and was strapped into his cockpit seat and was hit on the head until he finally shut up. We were relieved when we reached Samarkand, and to our surprise the pilot made a perfect landing.

SAMARKAND

Samarkand is the epitome of central Asia—the imagination is seared by James Elroy Flecker in his 1913 poem "The Golden Journey to Samarkand" and in his play *Hassan:*

> *We travel not for trafficking alone,*
> *by hotter winds our fiery hearts are fanned*
> *for lust of knowing what should not be known*
> *we take the golden road to Samarkand.*

Samarkand is a city of 370,000, the second largest in Uzbekistan. It pretty much lives up to its reputation as a center for trade over the centuries. Our luxurious hotel was built on the site of Tamerlane's former palace and the bar is said to be made of marble from his palace.

We found the mausoleums of Tamerlane (also known as Timur) and his grandson, Ulugh Begh, located in the center of the city, to be sublime. They are built around Registan Square, as are the mosque of Bibi Khanum (Tamerlane's wife), the Shah-i-Zinda burial complex, and Ulugh Begh's masterpiece, the Guri Amir mausoleum. Our visit coincided with festivities to celebrate Samarkand's birth 2,500 years ago. It claims to be the world's oldest city, though Damascus and Cairo make the same claim.

Registan Square is an architectural masterpiece— well-proportioned, elegant buildings tiled in fabulous painted ceramics—majolica, azure, and peacock blue for the most part.

To the great disappointment of anyone hoping to link Samarkand with the Silk Road is the lack of a substantial international market and the absence of historical evidence in the museum— which does have a yurt, old carpets, stuffed animals of the steppe, and a section upstairs linking the city with Stevenage, England. While I was attempting to puzzle out Stevenage's importance, an elegant Frenchwoman, a diplomat, came over to talk to me. She had never heard of Stevenage. She was lonely, bored, and depressed with her diplomatic life in such a far-off post. I couldn't blame her. She invited me back to her home for drinks, which I thought was rather inappropriate!

Samarkand was the end of our journey, a Silk Road expedition that had been of huge interest. The great surprise to me was Jiayuguan, close to the beginning of our journey and some 1,650 miles east of its end.

Chinese protection to Silk Road travelers was limited. The traveler was safe upon entering China at Jiayuguan from the desert by the Gate of Reconciliation. Chinese customs officials there registered the merchant and his goods. He could deposit heavy articles and collect them on his return. Eastward from Jiayuguan, Chinese soldiers protected travelers within the safety of the Great Wall. The Silk Road thus stretched across half of China, from Jiayuguan to Xian.

West of Jiayuguan there was no protection. The traveling merchant would have been at the mercy of robbers. To the Chinese, Jiayuguan was not only the terminus of the wall, but the end of the empire and the end of the Silk Road. Only the barbarians lived beyond to the west.

Sad though it is to relate, the story of the Silk Road as a continuous conduit from China to the West, along which the fabulous Chinese ceramics and silk reached Persia and Venice, is a myth. The Silk Road was a vibrant commercial highway, but the land route ended at Jiayuguan. Goods bound for the West must have come by ship, not over land. And if they came by ship, the sailors needed charts to guide their journey. Once again, all signs pointed to the seamanship of the Chinese, and specifically to Admiral Zheng He and his map.

CHAPTER 3

Plants Between Continents

So much of the evidence about Chinese arrival in the New World depends on Zheng He's 1418 map. The support for the map and its reliability as an authentic document continues to grow. I have lectured about the subject around the world, in each case providing background and describing the latest evidence. As I explain, the map, first of all, is drawn in the shape of a globe and the vantage point is above China. Within ten years, by 1428, European mapmakers were using the document when producing their own maps, which usually had a different perspective: for example, looking down upon Egypt, the Pacific, the Atlantic, or even Greenland. These maps are often outright copies of the 1418 map.

On a beautiful summer's evening, on June 13, 2006, to be exact, I gave just such a talk about the map, in Xian, the old capital of China, titled "Why the 1418 Map Is Genuine." I had been invited by Xian International Studies University and California's Humboldt State University to address their international and interdisciplinary conference "Alexander von Humboldt and Zheng

He, 2006." I was honored to be invited but not sure until the last moment whether my presentation would take place. We had placed the content of my talk on our website and critics, notably at the National University of Singapore and the University of Hong Kong, had mounted a virulent attack in an attempt to prevent me from speaking. They had contacted the chancellors of both universities and many other people of influence who they thought would be of assistance in having my talk scrapped, but to no avail. So it was really a relief that the event went forward.

It turned out that this particular discussion at Xian would lead to a further understanding of the map's importance and its use in Chinese explorations. After the question period, a tall, imposing man approached to introduce himself. It was Carl L. Johannessen, emeritus professor of geography at the University of Oregon. Carl and his coauthor, John L. Sorenson, emeritus professor of anthropology at Brigham Young University, are recognized as leading authorities on the transmission of plants, animals, artifacts, diseases, and much else between continents before Christopher Columbus set sail.

Sorenson's book with Martin H. Raish, *Pre-Columbian Contact with the Americas Across the Oceans: An Annotated Bibliography,* was my "bible" while writing *1421.* Their book lists some six thousand instances of plants and animals indigenous to one continent being found on another—in other words, they must have been brought by ship before Columbus.

Johannessen's presence at the conference meant that we could now establish that the map had in fact been used—there was evidence. Once the map was available in 1418, Zheng He's fleet set sail. Johannessen showed how the outcome of the voyage could be described in terms of what was left behind in America. He and Sorenson had collaborated on a new book, *Biology Verifies Ancient Voyages,* and offered to share information from it with me. The prospect was so exciting that I canceled my proposed visit to the terra-cotta warriors at Xian the next day. Some may say that shows a curious sense of priorities, but such was my enthusiasm.

We met the next morning and Johannessen brought along the preface to the volume. To me, it was like gold. Sorenson's new study offered a chance to expand details about plants and animals that I had summarized in *1421*. Some readers had, quite correctly, criticized me for lumping together plants and animals that in some instances, although transferred from one continent to another before Columbus, could not possibly have been transmitted in Zheng He's era. They were carried much earlier. For example, the skeletons of melanotic chickens indigenous to Southeast Asia had been found by the first conquistadors to reach Peru—but they had also turned up in tombs or burial grounds dated long before the conquistadors arrived. So I was anxious to see if there was any way to narrow the eras in which the plants and animals mentioned by Sorenson and Johannessen had reached one continent from another. In this work the pair do in fact expand on the matter, citing new discoveries and analysis.[1] They describe the presence of about one hundred plant species, citing archaeological studies, writings, art, and similarities in language that existed before Columbus's first voyage in 1492. Most of these plants were not only present, but were cultivated by the local population. Along with the plants, they identify organisms and fauna that are present both in Eurasia and the Americas. Some critics might immediately say that this does not preclude the possibility of either arrival via the land bridge between Siberia and Alaska or of some other natural propagation. But as Johannessen and Sorenson report:

> *This distribution could not have been due merely to natural transfer mechanisms, nor can it be explained by early human migrations to the New World via the Bering Strait route. Over half of the plant transfers con-*

*sisted of flora of American origin that spread to Eurasia
or Oceania, some at surprisingly early dates.*

Their conclusion goes a long way to confirm my thesis in
1421 and today: The Chinese, in sea voyages that took place over
some five thousand years, until the European explorations of
the fifteenth century, brought exotic forms of flora and fauna to
the New World. It is, Johannessen and Sorenson say, "the only
plausible explanation" for their findings.

They further confirmed my analysis of Chinese nautical abilities, both in terms of seaworthy vessels and the skills needed—
navigation and of course the availability over time of increasingly
accurate charts for worldwide exploration. Sorenson and Johannessen believe there were a great many such Chinese voyages over
a period of millennia. "These voyages," they say, "put a new com-
plexion on the extensive Old World/New World cultural parallels that have long been considered controversial."

More than merely controversial, Sorenson and Johannessen's
work does no less than upend existing research on the subject.
Traditional scholars too often dismiss the analysis of such men,
brilliant though it is; such people snobbishly turn away from the
evidence and rarely even entertain the possibility of imported
plants and fauna and human and cultural traits being present in
the New World as a result of Chinese voyages far earlier than
Columbus.

Sorenson and Johannessen analyzed and listed ninety-nine
plant species in the Americas for which "there is what we consider decisive evidence that the organism was present in both
eastern and western hemispheres before Columbus's first voyage.

They clarify that the "decisive evidence" is a result of analysis of plant biology—including pollen testing and DNA analysis.
They also examine the same types of evidence I have also focused
on in my travels—linguistics, culture, and historical documents
of all kinds—to prove that these plants are not native to the Amer-

icas and were transported there from another hemisphere before Columbus and the journey of the *Niña, Pinta,* and *Santa María* in 1492. It is not reasonable to think that the pre-Columbian transference of plants and fauna could have taken place any other way than by sea.

What other explanation could be given? Sorenson and Johannessen agree with me that there is none. "One might hurriedly conclude that certain seeds moved intercontinentally by the action of winds or waves; however, few seeds are equipped to survive long while floating or moving great distances via wind, and no disease organism spreads in such a way." Highly unlikely, I say, and leaning toward the impossible.

In the case of each of the ninety-nine plants mentioned, Johannessen lists "plants with decisive evidence for transoceanic movement." He gives the species' Latin names, their common names, their origin, where they moved to, and when they moved. This was of the most fascinating interest to me because Johannessen separates out transoceanic movement into different eras from 2800 B.C. up until 1492 A.D. From this I was able to separate transfers that occurred before the reign of Emperor Qin (China's first), that is, several millennia B.C.; those transferred in the first millennium B.C.; and those in the epoch of Kublai Khan and Zheng He.

Beyond the question of flora, there are a number of organisms that need to be considered and evaluated; many of these, we will show, would not have survived centuries of an arctic passage. I have selected one of these connections out of the thousands given in Sorenson and Johannessen's books—that is, the presence of the hookworm, the parasitic nematode that has plagued humanity for millennia and continues to be a problem today, especially for people in poor countries.

The presence and study of the hookworm species *Ancylostoma duodenale* in the Americas involves one of the more traceable migrations from Asia. Hookworm infestation has long been traced to Asia, and later to Africa. The parasite had been thought to have been introduced to the Americas via slave trade from Africa beginning in the sixteenth century. That long-established assumption of a logical source could be abandoned following studies I have cited previously, and which Johannessen refers to again. Work by Samuel Taylor Darling in 1920 and Olympio da Fonseca (a fully published version in 1970) showed that hookworm had infested Amazon Indian populations prior to the arrival of Columbus in the New World in 1492.

"If a date for the parasite in the Americas before European discovery could be proven," Johannessen writes, "then the only explanation for the parasite in the New World would be that it had arrived anciently via infected humans who have crossed the ocean."

The argument that Europeans brought this disease to the Americas was further weakened in 1973, Johannessen tells us. These studies found the presence of hookworm in a Peruvian mummy dating to 900 A.D. Other studies of mummies and fossilized human excrement also indicate this to be the case. One study by Brazilian scientists, in fact, traced hookworm to remains found in Brazil and dated to before 5000 B.C.

This alone does not eliminate the possibility favored by many scientists that the parasite could just as easily have been introduced to the Americas via slow migrations of Asiatic people crossing east Asia, then the Bering Strait, and moving down over generations to populate the Americas. The biology of *Ancylostoma duodenale*, specifically its life cycle, does not allow for this possibility, however. "Immigrants who came to the New World in slow stages via Beringia would have arrived hookworm-free because the cold ambient conditions would have killed the parasite in the soil," Johannessen tells us. At an early stage of the worm's life, it requires a temperate climate to burrow into the soil, and subsequently the larvae enter the digestive tract of the human host.

Science then leads one to conclude categorically that the parasite must have arrived in a rather direct way, by ocean voyage from Australia, the Pacific Islands, or the Asian continent itself. As Johannessen tells us:

> Ferreira, Araújo, and Confalonieri (1982) say, "Transpacific migrants from Asia by sea must be one component of the ancient American population." Fonseca (1970) asserts, "shared species of parasite . . . make it inescapable that voyagers reached South America directly from Oceania or Southeast Asia." Ferreira and colleagues (1988) agree: "We must suppose that [the human hosts for the parasite] arrived by sea." Araújo (1988) confirms, "The evidence points only to maritime contacts."

This conclusion is profound in and of itself. If the hookworm infection arrived with Asian seafarers at some moment prior to the arrival of the European explorers, it follows that physical presence includes the transmission of culture, plants, other fauna, miscegenation, and all that follows from the mingling of groups and their habits.

But the presence of this particular vector is not the only categorical biological evidence of Chinese travel to the New World. For example, Johannessen tells us another hookworm-type creature—*Necator americanus*, similar to *Ancylostoma duodenale*—has also been identified by scientists in Brazil. For the same reasons of incubation and propagation, ocean travelers must have delivered it to American shores.

Johannessen also lists several dozen other organisms that either could not have been the product of migrations across the Bering Strait, or are suspicious and uncertain enough in kind to require further examination.

Another nail in the coffin comes from the theory of evolution propounded by Charles Darwin and his successors. Here Johannessen refers us to the esteemed late American biologist Stephen

Jay Gould, who, steeped in Darwin's theory, wrote in 1994: "I regard each species as a contingent item of history. . . . [A] species will arise in a single place [and time]."

In my opinion anyone who has read Johannessen's and Sorenson's books, yet still believes Columbus discovered America, is in need of psychiatric help. But that is much the same feeling I have when I consider the evidence surrounding other ancient civilizations and their maritime exploits, so often minimized by historians and scientists.

CHAPTER 4

European Seafaring, 100,000 B.C.

Scientific studies increasingly offer an entirely new perspective: We should not be surprised to read about the capabilities of seafarers such as the Minoans, or comparatively recently, Admiral Zheng He's voyage long before Columbus arrived in the New World. Genetic testing, particularly, shows that migrations within Europe also could be traced for thousands of years, maybe even tens of thousands of years, and that these migrations would have depended on building boats and crossing the seas.

The trail starts with an international group of geneticists who discovered through DNA analysis that a section of Crete's Neolithic population (that is, pre–Bronze Age) reached Crete from Anatolia—modern-day Turkey. Professor Konstantinos Triantafyllidis of Aristotle University of Thessaloniki has published the findings of this research group, which was led by geneticists from Greece, the United States, Canada, Russia, and Turkey. According to Triantafyllidis, the analysis indicates that the arrivals of these new peoples coincided with a social and cultural upsurge

that led to the birth of the Minoan civilization around 7000 B.C.
Specifically, the researchers connected the source population of
ancient Crete to well-known Neolithic sites in Anatolia.

Triantafyllidis's research deals with the debate about the origin of Neolithic farmers in Crete and the Greek mainland, which
are the earliest such sites in Europe. One side in the debate claims
that the population came from Anatolia. But there are also questions about the ability of such colonization to take place via ships
on the Aegean Sea. He reports:

> To address these issues, 171 samples were collected from
> near these known early Neolithic settlements areas in
> Greece together with 193 samples from Crete. An analysis of Y Chromosome hectographs determined that the
> samples from the Greek Neolithic sites showed strong
> affinity to Balkan data while Crete shows affinity with
> central/Mediterranean/Anatolia.

In addition, Triantafyllidis writes:

> Haplogroup J2b-M12 was frequent in Thessaly and
> Greek Macedonia while haplogroup J2a-Ma10 was
> scarce. Alternatively, Crete, like Anatolia, showed a
> high frequency of J2a-M410 and a low frequency of
> J2b-M12. This dichotomy parallels archaebotanical evidence, specially that white bread wheat (Triticum aestivum) is known from Anatolia, Crete and Southern
> Italy; [yet] it is absent from earliest Neolithic Greece.

Quite separately, a group of prestigious international researchers led by Thomas F. Strasser and Eleni Panagopoulou had
found that Neolithic man had settled in southern Crete at least
100,000 years ago.[1] Crete has been an island for five million years

so this finding by reputable, well-known scholars can only mean seafarers reached Crete by sea more than 100,000 years ago. The DNA research of Triantafyllidis and colleagues shows these early seafarers probably came from Anatolia (Asia Minor).

Was it really possible that the Cretans came from a seafaring Anatolian stock that had left Anatolia from Crete 100,000 years ago? I decided to do my best to find out if this was feasible.

First I collated evidence on the Neolithic Anatolian sites after reading a number of books on Anatolian history. Professor J. G. Macqueen, in *The Hittites and Their Contemporaries in Asia Minor,* has a very good summary of Neolithic and early Bronze Age sites in Anatolia.

There are thirty-four of these sites, from Troy in the northwest to Kultepe (Kanesh) in the east, from Bogazkoy (Hattusas) in the north to Mersin in the south.

The sites may be reached by road quite easily, although it would be a long road journey of around 2,400 miles. I calculated that if we drove for 250 miles each day and allowed six hours for each site visit we could view the majority of the sites in fourteen days. A group of friends agreed to join Marcella and I, which greatly reduced the costs.

After dealing with as much of the logistics as possible in advance, we left Istanbul on April 18, 2011, for Anatolia and followed the planned route, returning to Istanbul on April 30, traveling about 2,200 miles. We returned with a magnificent haul of books, maps, photos, videos, and other material from museums on the sites. There now follows a snapshot of our visit.

TROY AND THE DARDANELLES

The Greek poet Homer immortalized the Trojan War first in the *Iliad,* then in its aftermath, the *Odyssey.* Homer's monumental works are recognized not only as epics but as the earliest surviving accounts of Western civilization. They rival the world's great religious literature in their sweep and power. Homer's theme is the epic struggle for Troy, where Paris has taken Helen, wife of King Menelaus of Sparta. Troy is besieged and eventually sacked by the Spartans. Homer's account is of a pointless war fought over Helen, an exceptionally beautiful but promiscuous woman.

Homer's detailed descriptions appeared to place Troy near the entrance to the Dardanelles.

In the nineteenth century, Heinrich Schliemann, a brilliant German businessman with a fine sense of intuition, read Homer's accounts and deduced the precise position of Troy. He started a dig in 1871 and scored a bull's-eye. His first trench sliced through the middle of Troy. However, he had also cut through nine layers of previous Troys—Homer's was in layer six. The previous layers were of pre-Hittite Troy, dating back to 3500 B.C., while Homer's (Troy 6) existed c. 1740 to 1300 B.C., when Troy was known to the Hittites as Wilusa.

En route to Troy we had visited Gallipoli, a promontory that guards the entrance to the Dardanelles. Though a devastating earthquake left it destroyed and virtually abandoned in 1354, Gallipoli is more famous for the World War I invasion of the peninsula by Australian and New Zealand (Anzac) forces in 1914, an effort to open up the Dardanelles to military shipping with which to battle Germany and its allies. Eventually, the Anzacs were forced to retreat and the victorious Turks held the day, cementing the career of Turkish general Mustafa Kemal Pasha, the father of modern Turkey.

We arrived three days before Anzac Day, April 25, which memorializes the sacrifice of the many thousands of men who gave their lives to capture this small promontory. Their gravestones are inscribed with heartfelt messages from their parents to their beloved children, buried at Gallipoli. I was overcome by the futile tragic deaths of so many young soldiers and wept. Gallipoli was, like the Trojan War, appallingly futile, a disgrace to European civilization.

The one redeeming feature was the message sent by the victorious Ataturk to the bereaved:

> *To those heroes that shed their blood and lost their lives . . . you are now lying in the soil of a friendly country. Therefore rest in peace. There is no difference between the Johnnies and Mehmets to us, where they lie side by side here in this country of ours. . . .*
>
> *You, the mothers who sent their sons from far away countries, wipe away your tears: your sons are now lying in our bosom and are in peace. After having lost their lives on this land, they have become our sons as well.*[2]

We arrived at Troy in pouring rain, soaked and dispirited. After Gallipoli I had lost interest in Troy and wanted to return home. However, the site immediately captivated me—having been excavated and labeled under the direction of a series of extremely gifted archaeologists who followed Schliemann, it is a fascinating scene. Today one can stand on a tower at the apex of the site and view from above layer after layer of the nine cities, each built on top of its predecessor.

There are also well-documented exhibits describing Troy as a center of international trade that stretched from Sicily in the west to Egypt in the south. Clearly merchants must have plied the Mediterranean at the time of Homer's Troy (1700 B.C.). Other maps show that the area of Troy's ancient settlement is huge. As the late Manfred Korfmann wrote, in his wonderful book *Troia,*

> *Measurements taken in 2003 revealed that this [Troy] covered an area of 300,000m²; thus Troia reached dimensions more than fifteen times as great as had ever been suspected.*
>
> *[S]uch evidence certainly seems to corroborate the existence of the large site recognized by the poet [Homer]*

in the extensive remains still visible at the end of the eighth century [B.C.] and celebrated in his epics.

After we left the site, the incessant rain of the previous three days suddenly stopped and the sun burst through to reveal the countryside around Troy in its full spring glory—carpets of flowers and trees in blossom in a kaleidoscope of soft colors. This part of northwest Anatolia has volcanic soil rich in minerals. The mountains bring rain, and for most of the year the sun is pleasantly warm. The climate and geography are ideal for agriculture and forestry. Trees and shrubs flourish—oleander, sandalwood, myrtle, carob, and pine, as well as chestnut, olive, fig, and almond trees. Today the main commercial crops are sunflowers, plums, and figs. Oak forests provide wood for shipbuilding.

Even today the area is famous for hunting—fallow deer, wolves, foxes, bears, wildcats, and leopards. Game birds abound—wild ducks, partridges, pigeons, woodcocks, and francolins. The sea is rich in bream, mackerel, gray mullet, gurnard, bonito, and sea bass, while rivers have perch, carp, eel, and trout. Troy was well supplied with water—an aqueduct had been cut through the rock to bring water into central Troy in the third millennium B.C. So Troy from 3500 B.C. was at the heart of a large metropolis, a center of seaborne international trade and near to the Dardanelles, a strait that connects the Black Sea to the Mediterranean. Trojans even had a system of writing from 1130 B.C.

ANCIENT CITIES IN AEGEAN AND MEDITERRANEAN ANATOLIA

We had been traveling for five days and were on schedule, with no illness, fortunately. All the museums had been open and the hotels provided clean rooms and delicious Anatolian food. On this leg we were traveling beside the Aegean Sea—later it would be the

Mediterranean. Our aim was to visit cities that flourished under Greeks and Romans to see whether they were—like Troy—built on layer upon layer of older cities, stretching back to the Bronze and Neolithic ages. To put it another way, were they in existence when Europeans from Anatolia were setting sail for Crete, thousands of years ago?

The plan was to visit Izmir, Ephesus, Bodrum, Antalya, Perge, Aspendos, and Side as major sites, as well as a number of smaller ones. It was a warm spring, with fourteen hours of daylight each day—ideal traveling conditions, yielding the full prospect that we would complete this leg of the program on schedule.

We started at the Anatolia Museum, one of the finest museums I have seen anywhere. The walls and floor are of white marble, the showcases of exhibits are brilliantly lit, and photography is permitted.

The museum provides an overview of 200,000 years of settlement, and it houses artifacts from the Karain Cave, which is located about twenty miles northwest of Anatolia and provides evidence of Neanderthal dwellers in the region. The first human-made stone tools found in Karain are 200,000 years old.

Examples of Paleolithic tools made of stone and fragments of bone are on display. Artifacts of the Early Bronze Age include daggers, spearheads, razors, ladles, bowls, pots, and animals, which are the same as their Minoan counterparts. The third millennium B.C. Bronze Age razor is identical to those I have seen in museums in Crete, Thera, the Orkneys in Scotland, and at Stonehenge.

By the time we had visited ten archaeological sites and museums along the Aegean and Mediterranean coasts of Anatolia, we realized they had several common characteristics: exquisite classical Greek architecture, surrounded by fertile land, near the sea or a river, and each built on the site of a much older city. Perge is dated by a bronze plate found in Bogazkoy referring to "Parha" (Perge) artifacts from the Aksu River, on which Perge was based.

Recent excavations have provided evidence for the establishment of the city in the "fourth–third millennium B.C." Ephesus is of course mentioned by St. Paul. Even earlier, the artifacts exhibited in the Selçuk Ephesus Museum date as far back as the "7th millennium B.C. spanning the prehistoric, Mycenaean, Archaic, classical, Hellenistic, Roman . . . periods." Ephesus Museum exhibits finds from the southeast part of the city that "date the environs of Ephesus back to 8200 B.C." Bronze artifacts include a second millennium B.C. sword—identical to those found all over the Minoan trading empire, from the Great Lakes in the United States and Canada, all the way to Thera.

The museum at the ancient ruins of Aphrodisias, 130 miles from Izmir, adds additional information. Early Neolithic settlers came to the region around 6000 B.C. and settlements continued in the area through the Copper and Iron Ages.

As earlier described, Paleolithic man reached Crete more than 100,000 years ago but was present in south Anatolia 100,000 years before that. Furthermore, we have now learned that the inhabitants of Crete have the same DNA as those of Anatolia, as found by Triantafyllidis and his colleagues. So people must have traveled by sea from Anatolia to Crete—which has been an island for five million years. Even stranger, these seafarers must have had a system of navigation, since successive waves of human migrants to Crete in 100,000 B.C. pitched up in the same place—the Preveli Gorge in southern Crete.

How could they navigate accurately 100,000 years ago? A glance at a modern map provides the answer. The island of Rhodes, which lies between Anatolia and Crete, can be seen from the Aegean coast of Anatolia. The island of Karpathos, between Rhodes and Crete, is visible from Rhodes. Crete is visible from Karpathos. Seafarers from southwest Anatolia to Crete were thus in sight of land all the way. The sailors simply island-hopped— Anatolia, Rhodes, Karpathos, Crete.

Moreover, the prevailing wind in summer, known as the

meltemi, is a strong, rotating monsoon wind that blows from northeast to northwest in the eastern Aegean. This wind would have carried them from Aegean Anatolia to Rhodes, from Rhodes to Karpathos, and from Karpathos to Crete—a relatively easy voyage. According to the historian Diodorus, Karpathos was a Minoan colony and remained part of Minoan civilization until the end of the Bronze Age. Rhodes has extensive evidence of Paleolithic man and also of Minoan civilization.

After Aphrodisias, we were on schedule and halfway through our journey. I was anxious to find out what aspects of Anatolian civilization the first Europeans had taken with them to Crete, not least the technology of copper and bronze (we know Minoans had been smelting copper from 4500 B.C.). The next leg of our journey was thus northward into central and northern Anatolia. In planning this I relied extensively on J. G. Macqueen's book *The Hittites and Their Contemporaries in Asia Minor.* Macqueen has pointed out that the countryside was even more lush and fertile five thousand years ago than it is today. Huge quantities of trees were felled to smelt copper and tin to make bronze—a subject covered in more detail in my book, *The Lost Empire of Atlantis.* This denuded the forests. Macqueen has summarized the evolution of Anatolian civilization:

> *In recent years it has become clear that Anatolia was an area of vital importance in human development in the Neolithic period, even before the development of metalworking. The discovery that animals and crops could be domesticated, which was first made in the Middle East between 9000 and 7000 B.C., has been described as a "Neolithic Revolution," but its importance lies not so much in its immediate effect (the establishment of settled agricultural villages) as in its enormous potential as a basis for further advance, given the right stimulus and the right conditions. An agricultural village does*

*not grow automatically into a town, but one result of
its formation is an increased demand for materials such
as flint and obsidian, which are necessary to make cul-
tivating tools and other equipment . . . in this way trade
becomes increasingly important and those communities
which happen to have vital materials on their doorsteps
are in a position which they can exploit to the full. . . .*

Macqueen described such a settlement as archaeologists have
found on the Konya Plain in central Turkey. A thirty-two-acre
settlement known as Catal Huyuk flourished with an industry of
copper smelting, lead, and bronze production about 6500 B.C. It
is considered by some scientists to be the first example of urban
dwelling in world history[3] and the largest of its kind ever found.
Writes Macqueen: "A community of this type has been partially
excavated in the Konya Plain . . . covers an area of 32 acres and
is by far the largest site of its age so far found. It was occupied
from before 7000 B.C. . . . [T]hough then prosperity was based on
obsidian, the inhabitants of Catal Huyuk were also acquainted
with the use of other local materials which were to be of infinitely
greater value in the later history of Anatolia."

Anatolia, Macqueen tells us, had become in the latter part of
the third millennium B.C. "a land of small city states, their rulers
living in castles, their economies based primarily on agriculture,
but their real wealth and importance residing in their metals and
metal products."

ANATOLIAN METALS

The Minoans' ancestors were the first Hittites, whose capital,
Kanesh, was at Kultepe, about twelve miles northeast of Kayseri.
Kayseri's archaeological museum exhibits finds from the Kultepe
archaeological dig, including cuneiform tablets that tell us much

about the Hittites. These describe that copper extracted from the Kultepe mine or found lying on the ground was sold in the metal bazaar at nearby Kanesh. Assyrian metal traders had their own quarter at Kanesh, under license from the Hittite overlords. There were additional copper mines at Derekutugun, some two hundred miles north of the Kultepe mines and near the Hittite religious capital Hattusa (Bogazkoy).

While Bronze Age Anatolia was rich in copper, Mesopotamians had neither copper nor tin in commercial quantities. Hence the development of Assyrian merchant colonies set up to purchase Anatolian copper to take back to Mesopotamia. These were called "Karum." Each had its own organization and administrator, and lived in accordance with its own laws and regulations.

THE MINOANS' INHERITANCE

By the time later Minoan voyages sailed to Crete from Anatolia around 5000 B.C., they had a rich legacy to take with them. By that date copper was being smelted at Kultepe. As we have discovered, Anatolia had many harbors in its Aegean and Mediterranean coasts, with a long maritime tradition.

Anatolia had developed cities such as Catal Huyuk, incorporating rudimentary town planning. They were technologically advanced cities where smiths were making the most of their local resources and were already turning out copper jewelry. Hittites by then had a cuneiform method of recording their history. In short, Minoans came from what was at the time probably the world's most advanced civilization, the world leader in metallurgy. With these advantages it should come as no great surprise that they were smelting copper in Crete by 4500 B.C.

We learned about and studied this material in the first twelve days in south and west Anatolia. For the last four days of our expedition we traveled through the Taurus Mountains into central and then northern Anatolia. Our concentration was on the Minoan use of tin in the Bronze Age.

Until 1984, historians did not know the source of tin for the ancient Bronze Age civilization of the Near East. Yet bronze was widely available in the early Bronze Age and tin was extensively used from at least 2200 B.C.[4] Where it came from was a mystery—many historians thought it came over land from Afghanistan.

In 1985, Aslihan Yener, an associate professor at Bosphoros University, found mines and a mining village in the central Taurus mountains. The mine is at Kestel/Kultepe, in the Taurus foothills at Kestel, sixty miles north of Tarsus. Yener found the tin had been mined underground in a system of small shafts. A cemetery holding bodies of children was found in the center of these mines, so it is almost certain children worked there. Ore was extracted by lighting fires on veins then cracking these with cold water. The ore was next washed before being ground and smelted in covered crucibles. Workers blew air through reeds to increase the firing temperature of the smelter. About fifty thousand stone tools were found in the tin mines; carbon-dating determined their age from 3290 B.C. to 1840 B.C.

Several hundred people lived in the Kestel/Kultepe site and produced about five thousand tons of ore during the one thousand years of operation—enough tin to make thousands of tons of bronze and hence a colossally valuable resource. The mines were reached through the so-called Cilician Gates, a pass in the Taurus Mountains that connects the coastal plain, near modern Mersin, with the Anatolian plateau. (Today the road is the E90—wide and modern.) St. Paul and before him the Persian emperor Cyrus and Alexander the Great traveled this road. Before them the Minoans would have carried tin to the coast through this pass. Modern Mersin still has a fortress that once guarded the start of the road.

Today the journey from the coast through the pass takes just over an hour before one arrives at the treeless Anatolian plateau—treeless probably because of the huge amount of wood that was once harvested to make charcoal to refine the tin and copper. As previously described, Kestel/Kultepe stopped producing tin in 1840 B.C.—for reasons unknown. To maintain tin production Minoans had to find another source. I submit this was what took them on their overseas quests. Their "voyages of discovery" were to find tin to enable them to keep producing bronze, the economic basis of their society.

In sum, the evidence is clear that Europeans reached Crete via southwest Anatolia, Rhodes, and Karpathos before 100,000 B.C. Anatolia, whence they sailed, had been populated since 200,000 B.C. Those who sailed to Crete were the same people who then inhabited Anatolia, as DNA studies have shown. The Anatolia they left was a cradle of the world's civilization, with cities as large and as old as those in Mesopotamia.

Later, Minoan sailors in around 5000 B.C. took Anatolian copper and tin to Crete, where they smelted it to create bronze. They thus had the raw materials to make bronze—which neither Egypt nor Mesopotamia had. Minoans could use bronze as soon as tin was found (in 3290 B.C.). Their later voyages of exploration were possibly to find tin after the Kestel/Kultepe mines became exhausted in 1840 B.C. Minoans in Crete came from a rich Anatolian civilization, which by the seventh millennium B.C. had towns with storied houses and a settled way of life.

It is humbling to see the extent of Minoan civilization so many thousands of years ago and it raises the question, What would have happened if Minoan Crete had not been devastated by the 1450 B.C. volcanic eruption at Thera and the resulting tsunami? At that stage Minoans were at least 1,600 years in advance of the Chinese in shipbuilding and 3,000 years ahead in being able to calculate longitude. How would the Minoans have employed their oceangoing prowess when they were far more capable than the Chinese in sailing the world's seas?

CHAPTER 5

Mastery of the Oceans
Before Columbus

Chinese seamanship is all the more remarkable when it is compared with the skills and shipbuilding capacities of other civilizations at similar periods in history. All evidence shows that China had the capacity to send massive fleets from Asia to the Americas at least from the time of Emperor Qin in 220 B.C.[1]

Chinese ship development is lucidly described by Professor K. Gang Deng of the London School of Economics in his 1997 book, *Chinese Maritime Activities and Socioeconomic Development, c. 2100 B.C.–1900 A.D.*[2] As in the Mediterranean, the earliest known evidence of primitive ships was from early Neolithic times, around 6000 B.C. These were carved from logs—a heavy and inefficient method of transport on water, limited by the length of the tree and the ability to hollow out the wood with primitive flint tools. These basic vessels were described in *The Book of Changes*, one of the Confucian classics, as being in use by the time of Huangdi, the first king of China. This claim is supported by carbon-dating. Six primitive oars unearthed in 1973 at a Neolithic site were dated to be about eight thousand years old, meaning they were created approximately in the era of Huangdi.

Bronze saws made it possible to build boats from planks. This meant much longer boats, which were no longer limited by the height of a tree. Plank boats with crossbeams to hold the sides together are depicted on inscriptions on bones and tortoise shells (an early form of Chinese writing) dating back 4,500 to 5,000 years—that is, to 3000 B.C. That these Chinese boats could carry out limited coastal sea voyages is supported by the skeletons of oceangoing mammals, notably whales found at coastal Neolithic sites in China.

The first Chinese seagoing vessel was recorded in the *Bamboo Strip Chronicles* (*Zhushu Jinian*), written in the Warring States period. As Gang Deng writes, "It is also recorded that in the year when King Huang ascended the throne, a large fish that was caught from the sea in the coastal region of Shandong was used for the ceremony."[3] By the Warring States period, metal hoops had been used to strengthen the planks.

> *More records are available for the following Shang period (c. sixteenth–eleventh century B.C.): Prince Jizi was reported to have emigrated from China to Korea by a sea route (Zhang X). Later on in the Zhou period (eleventh century–771 B.C.) the Yi, Wu and Viet tribes living along the east coast of China (Shandong, Jiangsu, Zhejiang Provinces) were reported to be good at building boats and sailing to sea for fishing and trade (Zhang X).*
>
> *... During this period, human muscles were the sole source of energy for the propulsion of ships. Changes in technology seem to have been rather slow: primitive oars were already in use in 6000 B.C., but sail technology was yet to be invented at the very end of the rudimentary*

period. Archaeological discoveries show that the sail did not become functional before the Warring States period, from 475 to 221 B.C. (Zhang X).

We can thus summarize Chinese shipbuilding expertise before 221 B.C. thus: They had ships able to stay at sea and fish and trade—but without sails. In crude terms, Chinese ships could float with the Kuroshio (Black) Current, a north-flowing current in the Pacific Ocean that is analogous to the Gulf Stream in the Atlantic Ocean. Once entering the Black Current off the Asian continent, ships in the period of the Shang dynasty onward could ride along east toward the Americas, but probably could not return, as the westerly current from the Americas to China is too weak. So Chinese voyages to the Americas would be in desperation, to avoid some terrible event at home without the likelihood or consideration of returning—a one-way ticket.

Two other civilizations are well known for ships and sailing: the Egyptian and the Minoan. However, neither one had the same reach as China.

Egyptian drawings and paintings are the first to show seagoing ships—as early as 3000 B.C.—but Egypt never developed into a major maritime nation. This has puzzled me for years. I now think there were two reasons.

The first is that Egypt in the third and second millennia never really needed ships to sail the oceans of the world. Egypt had the Nile, not only a bringer of life-giving water and rich silt but also a majestic transit route linking Africa with the Mediterranean, joining forests of tropical wood with gold mines. Vast herds of animals lived off the Nile waters and the river was full of fish. All the food Egypt needed could be grown alongside the Nile or in the delta.

The Nile has two other attributes. Each year rain pours down on Africa, Lake Victoria fills up, and the Nile starts its annual cycle, once again carrying water, silt, and ships downstream to the delta. At the same time, almost all year round there is a gentle northerly breeze blowing from the Mediterranean into the heart of Africa.

To travel upstream, an Egyptian ship hoists a simple sail and glides along the placid water, where there is never any rain or waves. Once it has reached its destination the Egyptian ship puts away its simple sail, loads its cargo, and floats downstream with the current. Once again it is not bothered by squalls, waves, or other hazards of the ocean.

The second reason is that apparently Egypt has virtually no trees suitable for building substantial ships. The most common wood in Egypt is acacia, which is not suitable for boatbuilding. Trees are small, frequently gnarled, and full of knots. A typical Egyptian ship looked like a floating crossword puzzle, with lots of small planks of varying lengths, all cobbled together. A ship of this type has no real chance of coping with long ocean swells. There is no proper keel, and the boat, made of short planks, hogs and sags. Egyptians got around this on the Nile by using ropes to counter hogging and sagging but this is hopeless in a heavy sea. So until 3000 B.C., Egyptians in effect limited their maritime endeavors to the placid Nile or Red Sea, leaving the way open for the tough Minoans, with their big, flexible cedar trees, to achieve maritime supremacy.

(It must also be noted that a great deal of research has been carried out concerning the possibility of pre-Columbian voyages to the New World from sub-Saharan Africa. That material is beyond the scope of this book, but we have added links to this research on our website.[4])

MINOAN SHIPPING AND COMMERCE

Minoan shipbuilders were becoming increasingly proficient at their work in the same epoch as the Egyptians. The ships shown

on the Thera fresco and the Uluburun wreck are highly sophisticated. (Please read *The Lost Empire of Atlantis,* chapter 2, for
more information.) By the fourteenth century B.C. their ships had
sails that could be raised and lowered in a hurry and adjusted to
tack into the wind. The hulls of the Thera and Uluburun ships
were based on an extremely advanced design. Not only were the
cedar planks held to the keel and each other by thongs of oak
placed in chiseled rectangular holes in adjacent planks; the thongs
were also positioned in such a way that they provided an inner
oak frame at right angles to and inside the cedar planking—giving
a very light, flexible, yet strong hull that would not hog or sag.
This is a very expensive and time-consuming method of ship construction that relies on very sharp chisels and saws. The product
undoubtedly gave the Minoans early oceangoing capacity, which,
coupled with the sails, meant Minoan ships could certainly have
reached the Americas and returned by 1450 B.C., a thousand years
ahead of the Chinese, whose first sails came after 475–221 B.C.

But this is not the only advance Europeans had over the
Chinese—they had sails long before 1450 B.C. The vases known
as the "Frying Pans" dated 2800–2300 B.C. show oared ships with
high prows and sterns but powered by oars, in some cases two men
to an oar, with twenty oars a side. That means a crew of at least
eighty men—these were big ships. Sometime between 2800 B.C.
and 1450 B.C., Minoan ships had sails—but how far back?

D. Gray in Seewesen (cited by Avner Raban—please refer to
bibliography) shows fourteen early Minoan and middle Minoan
seals (that is, from the Prepalatial period, or 2800–2000 B.C.),
each of which depicts a ship with mast and rigging. Masts and
rigging denote sails. As Avner Raban wrote, "Oars appear only
on some, but mast and rigging are never omitted. This difference
may reflect a particularly Cretan development of sail power as
an alternative to human propulsion. Such a change also implies a
new emphasis on sea transportation and commerce in the function of the vessels."

Minoan seals depicting ships with masts and rigging.

So it seems to me one can push back the date when Minoan ships had sails to 2800 B.C.—more than two millennia before the Chinese. We can also push back the dates when Minoan ships could have sailed the Atlantic to the Americas to 2800 B.C. This could explain why coca and nicotine were found with Egyptian mummies and how plants indigenous to the Americas were present in the Middle East in 2800 B.C.

The disastrous earthquake and volcanic eruption at Thera (also known as Santorini) in the Aegean Sea in 1450 B.C. now takes on another dimension. Minoan civilization vanished under a saturation of volcanic ash that buried towns in a sea of mud, blocked out the sun, and destroyed crops. Ports were submerged by a huge tsunami. Europeans no longer had dominance of the seas—the way was open for the Chinese to come from behind and overtake the Europeans in their mastery of the oceans. This the Chinese did in their usual methodical and cautious way.

Gang Deng makes it clear that, though not immediately after the Minoan collapse, over the period of several hundred years Chinese maritime prowess grew, as did the rate of development in creating more and more advanced ships, methods of propulsion, and the ability to navigate the seas.

> . . . Some significant progress in ship design was made in the western Han dynasty (206 B.C.–24 A.D.). The "multideck ship" (Louchan, literally "turreted ship") was developed during this period (Zheng G). Ballast was used to improve the stability of these tall ships; multiple watertight holds were developed to minimize the "free surface effect" and to improve both watertight integrity and the strength of the hull. . . .
>
> . . . The multideck ship was seaworthy. For instance, it is recorded that during 138–108 B.C. Emperor Wu Di (140–88 B.C.) sent his fleet of Louchans across the sea to "East Viet" kingdom.
>
> . . . It is also documented that during 41–42 A.D. the Eastern Han General Ma Yuan commanded a large fleet of multideck warships in his campaign against Cochin kingdom. . . .
>
> . . . During 399–411 A.D. Sun En and Lu Xun led a large-scale rebellion whose base was established on islands off the east coast of China, with over 100,000 soldiers and a large fleet of Louchan (Sima Xin). . . .
>
> . . . An early document shows that in the three kingdoms period (220 B.C.–80 A.D.) some oceangoing ships in Guangzhou were forty-six to fifty meters in deck length with the capacity to carry 600–700 passengers (Li F).

By now Chinese ships had sails. By the Qin dynasty (220 B.C.) a regular sea route between China and Japan was established. On one trip, several thousand Chinese emigrated, led by a Taoist priest, Xu. On this trip it is believed they started from the Shandong Peninsula, traveled along the Sino-Korean-Japanese coasts for 1,750 miles, and eventually settled near Wakayama, in southeast Japan. Since sail technology had been known by the Qin dynasty, it can be safely assumed they relied on wind power.

A written description of the use of sails, including the word for "fan," appeared in the dictionary *Shi Ming* (The Origins of Words) in the Eastern Han dynasty. In a poem "A Song of Guancheng," from 115 A.D., Ma Rong (79–166 A.D.) writes, "Link the supply ships and open up the tall sails. . . ."

The first naval battle using sailing ships took place in 208 A.D., along the lower reaches of the Yangtze River.

The rudder is first shown in a pottery model of a Chinese ship excavated from a tomb dated to the first century A.D. This model is now in the Kuangchow Historical Museum. By 260 A.D. Chinese ships had staggered masts, enabling multisail ships. By now Chinese ships had watertight bulkheads—a typical medium-sized junk had fifteen bulkheads and thirty-seven rib frames.

By the second century A.D. Chinese ships could carry large numbers of passengers and substantial cargo in relative comfort and safety across the oceans of the world. China by the second century A.D. had caught up with European ship technology of 1450 B.C. Chinese ships could sail to and from the Americas with the Black Current and return—it was no longer a one-way journey.

PART II

China in the Americas

CHAPTER 6

The Genetic Evidence

Zheng He's mighty fleet benefited from great shipbuilding, and the courage and daring of its commanders and common seamen. All had an understanding of the capricious seas and took advantage of the charts and maps entrusted to them. Some of the Chinese ships were under the command of Hong Bao, the prominent admiral and diplomat who sailed with Zheng He. They would have made a striking spectacle, sails billowing before the wind as they ranged majestically from Australia, through the South Seas, and on to South America.

The fleet would comprise mostly Chinese sailors—China even then was a huge country with many minority peoples. The sailors might be giants from the Amur River in the north or much smaller people from Hainan in the south. There might have been women on board—a number of these would have been pregnant. Some of the sailors would have contracted diseases before the fleet set sail—others would suffer from benign disorders passed on to them by their forebears. In the hot and humid conditions belowdecks the sailors' hammocks would have been rife with fleas and bedbugs. Mosquitoes would thrive in the water tanks. Down in the holds there would be pigs, dogs, and horses, each having its own parasites. The food on board would include seeds from fruits, vegetables, or grains. The fish and shellfish in the holds would have their own genetic signatures. There also might be ships from other nationalities—Japanese or Korean—attached to the fleet, complicating matters further.

Now imagine that one of Hong Bao's ships was either wrecked or badly damaged. It would beach on a Pacific island, where the sailors would seek shelter ashore. With them came their animals, food, diseases, disorders, and parasites. They might have been at sea for months and those without access to women aboard ship might have been driven by the need for sex—as perhaps were the women on the Pacific island itself.

Fast-forward six hundred years: We come across that island, perhaps as scientists, even tourists. If we consider the possibilities, then we certainly shall find the genetic legacy of a ship of six hundred years ago—a time capsule.

This is exactly what we have done. There have been huge advances in tracing genetic inheritance. We can find from DNA analysis who the shipwrecked sailors of long ago were and what they carried on their ships before disaster struck. We can also determine where they stopped en route to collect food or to trade.

The principal tool is DNA research.[1] The genetic evidence left by the crews of Chinese fleets is overwhelming. In every place in America that I believe they visited, they have left their genetic legacy. Moreover, we can show that the first Europeans to reach places where the indigenous people have Asian DNA found Chinese or Mongolian peoples already there—in other words, the DNA referred to in this chapter does not arise from Chinese settlers who arrived only recently, during the "gold rush."

The "blockbuster" report that seems to show irrefutable evidence of the amount of Asian DNA in indigenous people of the Americas was referred to in a book published in 2006, *Losing a Lost Tribe: Native Americans, DNA, and the Mormon Church.* The author, Simon G. Southerton, an Australian plant geneticist, was once a bishop in the Church of Jesus Christ of Latter-day Saints (the Mormons).

Mormons believe the indigenous people of the Americas are descendants of tribes of Israel who took to the sea, landed in North America, conquered peoples there, then settled the continent. Various theories followed (not necessarily Mormon doctrine) that before the Mormons arrived in America there had been a superior civilized race that had itself been overthrown by violent invaders—it was these violent invaders whom the Mormons were now expelling. Mormons and subsequent European conquerors—Spanish, French, and English—tacitly accepted these accounts of earlier barbaric peoples in the Americas because it gave justification for the European conquest. Southerton's investigation started as a quest to find out who were the barbaric peoples the Israelites had conquered. This could be achieved by DNA research.

More than seven thousand DNA samples were procured, from 175 recognized indigenous Native American peoples ("recognized" means living in designated tribal areas, that is, not living in cities among European descendants or Hispanics).

Analysis of mitochondrial DNA (maternally inherited) and Y chromosomes (characteristic of male cells) was carried out to examine who were their male and female ancestors. The results showed 96.5 percent of indigenous Native American people had mitochondrial DNA from A, B, C, and D founding maternal lineages. Remarkably, those four DNA lineages are found only in Asian populations and nowhere else in the world. Male genealogical studies show that the most common Native American, lineage Q, is closely related to Asian Q lineage, as they share common DNA markers.

In short, Indigenous American peoples are essentially all descended from Asian female and male ancestors.

How did they get there—by crossing the Bering Strait "land bridge" before the ice melted around ten thousand years ago—or by multiple voyages from Asia over the centuries, principally in Chinese ships?

The DNA evidence that follows shows they came by multiple sea voyages from Asia.

My interest in the genetic legacy in its broadest sense was sparked when one of our researchers encountered the work of Gabriel Novick and his colleagues. In Novick's words there was a "close similarity between the Chinese and Native Americans, demonstrating a recent gene flow from Asia." Novick's report, covering twenty-two Indian peoples of the Americas, is clearly and concisely written.

The report shows where the various Native American peoples live. As may be seen, these people are all reached by sea or a great river and these are places where in *1421* I say that Zheng He's fleets traveled—hence the huge significance to me of this report. The accompanying figure shows the closeness of the DNA of the peoples analyzed by Novick and his team to Chinese DNA—as may be seen, the Buctzotz Mayans are so close they may almost be called Chinese, whereas Nigerians (at the top) are far removed from Chinese.

I take several conclusions from the report. By examining Novick's documentation, one can see that the native peoples of Greenland and Alaska have very similar DNA. If the peoples of Greenland were descendants of the first supposed immigrants to North America, who had marched across the Bering Strait on the frozen ice to Alaska, then migrated eastward across North America to Greenland, one would expect the DNA of intervening people to initially resemble Alaskan DNA, then gradually mutate. This is not the case. For the Greenland and Alaska natives' DNA to be so strikingly similar, these peoples must have received their

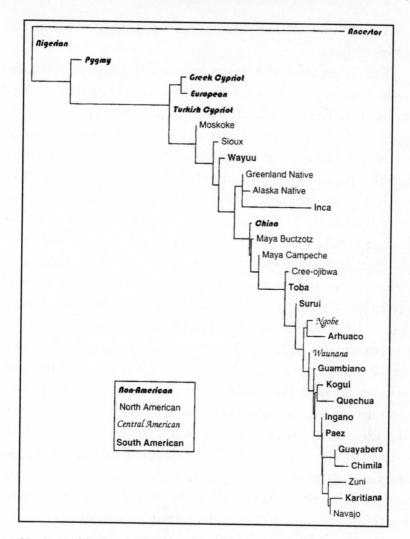

Maximum-likelihood tree illustrating human phylogenetic relationships. The distance between population groups is proportional to the branch lengths on the tree. (Novick et al.)

"recent gene flow from Asia" at about the same time. Alaska is on the Pacific coast and Greenland is in the North Atlantic Ocean, stretching up to the Arctic. The only way that Greenland and Alaska people could have received their gene flow at about the same time is by ship—moreover, from ships that sailed in both the Pacific and the Atlantic. Because of the prevailing winds and tides, these simultaneous voyages must have been conducted by different fleets.

The Greenland and Alaskan natives and the Maya of the Yucatán Peninsula in the Caribbean obviously lived thousands of miles apart. The second conclusion we can draw is that if the "recent gene flow from Asia" had been from across the Bering Strait, one would have expected the intervening peoples between Alaska and the Yucatán Peninsula in the Caribbean to have DNA that gradually mutated from Alaska to the Yucatán as the people migrated southeast. This is not the case. The DNA signature among Buctzotz Maya is far closer to Alaskan DNA than it is to the Indian people who live on either side of the Maya. The Maya on the Atlantic coast and the Alaskans on the Pacific coast must have received their "recent gene flow from Asia" at about the same time, too. Again, multiple fleets would be required.

The same argument can be applied to the Incas of South America's Pacific coast region, since their DNA is closer to the Chinese, the Maya of the Atlantic coast, and the natives of Greenland than it is to the Indian people who lived to their east or north. Novick's team, which finds "close similarity between the Chinese and Native Americans," has sampled the DNA of peoples far distant from each other in the high Arctic, on the Atlantic and Pacific coast, in Amazonia (thousands of miles up that great river), in Patagonia, and in Bolivia, again thousands of miles upstream, on the Paraguay and Parana rivers.

For each of these places to have recently acquired Asian DNA, thousands of miles apart, in different hemispheres, not only would different fleets be required, but they would have to be huge as well.

It seemed to me from reading Novick's report that these huge Chinese fleets must have sailed to North and South America via both the Atlantic and the Pacific oceans. Furthermore, there is a wealth of supporting evidence summarized on our website that Chinese fleets visited each place where Novick and his colleagues found DNA evidence of "recent gene flow from Asia." Because we could also show that the first Europeans to reach those places where Novick's team found Asian DNA also found Chinese people already there, their report was powerful substantiation that huge Chinese fleets had visited the Americas.

We decided to research other DNA studies for more detail and found that, fortuitously, there had been enormous advances in the accuracy of DNA analysis in the past decade. Thirty years ago, there were two principal methods of analysis. The first was mitochondrial, which traced a person's heritage through the mother and her female ancestors. The second involved the Y chromosome, which traces heritage through a person's father and his male ancestors. Then came the bombshell of the Human Genome Project. A number of research companies appreciated that they could use genetics to improve the efficacy of drugs made by pharmaceutical companies. For example, some people of African origin have a different reaction to medicines than have Europeans. Some drugs of the same strength have a vastly more powerful effect on Asian people than on Jewish. By analyzing a person's heritage, geneticists could therefore offer pharmaceutical companies and governments improvements in efficiency and hence lower the cost of prescription drugs.

A number of major American research companies raised considerable amounts of money to invest in research. We analyzed those companies' research and determined that the most cost-effective for us was DNAPrint Genomics of Sarasota, Florida, which indeed was very helpful. The firm's chief scientific officer, Dr. Tony Frudakis, met with me many times over the years and allowed us to use his company's reports.

DNAPrint Genomics devised a novel method of accurately measuring genetic structure by computationally screening the human genome sequence for ancestry information markers (AIM). The results suggest that biographical admixture (a person's heritage) can be reliably read from DNA. Furthermore, their research showed that DNA admixture between American Indians and East Asians (Chinese) is far more frequent than was hitherto supposed. Because DNAPrint Genomics selected the genomes' best AIMs, which earlier methods had not, their results more accurately measured genetic structure. Frudakis discussed the evidence at a symposium in Washington, D.C., on May 15, 2005, that was organized by the Library of Congress and focused on Zheng He's voyages. Frudakis said "there is substantial and statistically significant recently acquired East Asian admixture in Native American Indian peoples of twenty, thirty, sometimes forty, percent."

Research by a number of distinguished geneticists concurs with the DNAPrint Genomics report as well as with the research by Professor Novick and his colleagues. The following material is a summary of their findings. The full text and details are available on our website.

- Professor Noah Rosenberg et al., "Genetic Structure of Human Populations," *Science* 298 (December 20, 2002): "Most Maya, Pima and Colombian groups had East Asian admixture."

- Theodore G. Schurr et al., "Amerindian mitochondrial DNAs have rare Asian mutations at high frequencies, suggesting they derived from four primary maternal lineages," in *American Journal of Human Genetics* 46 (1990): "The mitochondrial DNA (MT DNA) sequence variation of South American Ticuna, the central American Maya and the North American Pima was analyzed. . . . The analysis revealed that Amerindian Populations have high frequencies of MT DNAs containing the rare Asian RFLP hine II, morph 6. . . . In addition the Asian-specific deletion . . . was also prevalent in both the Pima and the Maya."

- Felipe Vilchis, "HLA Genes and the Origin of the Amerindians," Genetica Biomedicina Molecular 2000 résumé GYE 2, Monterrey, Mexico (translated by Ian Hudson): "The results of the philogenetic analysis reported here support the idea that the autochthonous Pueblos based in meso-America and South America had common ancestors, with as many coming from the migratory wave from the north as those that took the transpacific route. . . . Of even more interest, the allelic distribution . . . showed a genotypic pattern that was very similar to that found among Asian peoples . . . which represents a very high incidence in the population that was studied."

- Antonio Torroni et al., "Asian Affinities and Continental Radiation of the Four Founding Native American mtDNAs," American Journal of Human Genetics 53 (September 1993): "The sequencing of 341 nucleotides in the mtDNA loop revealed that the D-loop sequence variation correlated strongly with the four haplogroups defined by restriction analysis and it indicated that the D-loop variation, like the haplo-type variation, arose predominantly after the migration of the ancestral Amerinds across the Bering land bridge."

- Tulio Arends and Emil Gallengo, "Transferrins in Venezuela Indians: High Frequency of a Slow-Moving Variant," Science 143 (January 24, 1964): "In 58 percent of the Upa Indians of Venezuela there is a slow-moving transferrin electrophoretically indistinguishable from Tf Dchi, which to date has only been found in Chinese. This finding is additional evidence for the existence of a racial link between South American Indians and Chinese."

- Fidias E. Leon-Sarmiento et al., "Peopling the Americas," *Science* 273 (1996): "People with the so-called 'new' allele . . . such as the Cayapa Chachi from Ecuador also display an aldehyde dehydrogenase deficiency that is molecularly similar to that found in South East Asia and Japanese people but absent in North East Asians. . . . These similarities add strength to the proposal that ancient voyages could follow the Pacific sea currents that join Japan to South America as well as other routes."

- Fidias E. Leon-Sarmiento et al., "HLA Transpacific Contacts and Retrovirus," *Human Immunology* 42 (1995): "[Marie] Cerna et al. . . . stated that some of the genetic markers on HLA that they found could have been introduced to South America through some ancient transpacific contacts. Such statements fit with our recent investigations on neurological diseases, specifically those related to retro virus; we also suggested that HTLV-1 retrovirus could have been introduced to South America through transpacific contacts. . . . A Colombian aboriginal group living near the Pacific Colombian coast named the Noanama-Wanana is clustered genetically closer to Japanese peoples than to other American natives."

- Peter Parham, in response to "Peopling the Americas," in *Science* 273 (1996): "Another recombinant—of the 4003 which was just discovered in the Guarani and was described as being specific to South America has now been found in Koreans, Japanese and Mongolian. . . . Given this insight the HLA class haplotype B*4003, CW*0304, A*0211 becomes a candidate for having found its way to South America by a route not involving passage through South America."

Reviewing the data, the preceding scientists all reached the same clear conclusion by means of different DNA methods: that the populations of South America encountered by Europeans in the fifteenth and sixteenth centuries were of Asian ancestry and that their ancestors arrived in the New World by sea. The argument that they crossed the Pacific to reach American shores is supported by Katsushi Tokunaga and his colleagues in an article published in *Human Immunology* in 2001: "A 24-CW8-B4B was commonly observed in Taiwan indigenous populations, Maori in New Zealand, Orochon in north east China, Inuit and Tlingit. These findings further support the genetic link between East Asians and Native Americans."

Further evidence provided by M. Hertzberg,[2] Shinji Harihara,[3] Fuminaka Sugauchi,[4] and their respective colleagues support the earlier geneticists' findings that certain North and South American Indian peoples' ancestors came by sea rather than across the Bering land bridge. They also point to the presence of mitochondrial DNA among the populations of the islanders of Oceania, including Cook Islanders, Fijians, Maori, Niueans, and Tongans. I'd submit that a thoroughgoing reappraisal is in order for the Bering land bridge as supposedly allowing the peopling of the Americas by humans crossing the ice on foot—some two thousand miles of it. My belief is that historians who contend that the Americas were populated by sea, by multiple and repeated waves from Asia, are absolutely correct. Zheng He was part of the last and greatest of these waves of exploration.

Finally, on the subject of such migrations, I cite two more startling reports, one by Geoffrey K. Chambers declaring that "Pacific Maoris may have come from China." "The information that has come from several studies in my laboratory turns out to be consistent with a pattern of migration [the Maori people] starting with an ancestral population in mainland Asia. This has been taken up by Dr. Winston Peters, foreign minister of New Zealand, who stated in his address to the Association of East

Asian Countries on July 26, 2006, 'The first inhabitants of New Zealand came from China.'"[5]

The second is even more surprising, a study by Antonio Arnaiz-Villena and his colleagues at the University of Madrid:

> *The Peopling of America sequence may have been more complicated than previously thought; it seems that Mongoloids from China, Mongolia (but not from Siberia) are found to have been both in America or the middle Atlantic (Azores) before Columbus.*[6]

Arnaiz-Villena's study captured my imagination. It led to information that predated the charting of the Atlantic to two decades before even Zheng He.

Studies and new evidence have been accumulating about the Chinese presence in Europe and the New World. Arnaiz-Villena uncovered this surprise: "We unexpectedly found Oriental genes (but Chinese) in the present day Azorean populations, and postulated that the arrival of the genes was before the Portuguese. . . ."[7]

Arnaiz-Villena and his colleagues focused on HLA, human leukocyte antigen, a gene complex related to disease and to the immune system. Their report says HLA is particularly relevant.

Some individuals tested in the Azores showed genetic characteristics "closer to Orientals (continental Asians, like Mongolians and Chinese) than to Europeans and Mediterraneans."[8]

Their analysis goes on to say that the evidence suggested an Asian presence in the Azores before the Portuguese arrival at the islands in 1439.[9]

> *If this were the case, it is most intriguing that the Mongoloid component of the Azorean HLA genetic profile is more similar to the one found in continental Asia groups than the profile found in the American Indians . . . the frequent Mongoloid HLA haplotypes found in the Ar-*

chipelago are Asian continental rather than American Indians.

The Spanish researchers said that since there was no historical record that American Indians or Asians had gone to the Azores after Columbus's first voyage in 1492, it follows logically that "the first inhabitants of the islands may have been Asian or American Indians." [10]

In *1421* I shared my conclusion that Admiral Zheng He's fleet reached the Azores. My principal evidence came from two pieces of information. Columbus reported Chinese bodies had been washed ashore at Flores Island in the Azores. Also, the statue of a horseman on a plinth "with writing [they] could not understand" was found by early Portuguese settlers when they arrived at Corvo Island in the Azores. A report by Jacome Bruges-Armas and his colleagues provides cogent genetic research that clearly bolsters my own analysis.

KANGNIDO

Another enigma surrounding the Chinese presence on the Azores involves the fact that the islands were shown on a map presented to Emperor Zhu Di by a Korean delegation in 1402, that is, thirty-seven years before the Portuguese arrived on the islands. There have been angry disputes with historians who reject the substance of what is found on this famous map, colloquially known as the Kangnido.

I decided it was necessary to establish further proof that Emperor Zhu Di's map actually depicted the Azores, as I have claimed. Since the original map is stored at Ryukoku University in Kyoto, Japan's former imperial capital, I set off for Japan.

I traveled to Kyoto from Tokyo on the bullet train one beautiful spring morning, with snowcapped Mount Fuji over my shoulder, framed by cherry blossoms. The Ryukoku University librarian, Aoki Masanori, took me to the library vaults to examine the map. After passing through one locked door after another, at last deep in the vaults there was the map, wrapped up like a mummy.

Masanori and his assistant delicately carried the map up to an air-conditioned theater. There the swaddling bands were removed and the Kangnido was hung on a rail. Six hundred years later it is still in perfect condition, the Chinese writing as clear as crystal. There were the Azores, off Portugal, with Chinese characters describing them. Although these were written in classical Mandarin, there was no difficulty for Masanori to read them: "Islands with distinctive peaks." Anyone who has seen Corvo from the sea could not expect a more pithy description. Volcanoes rise sheer out of the sea. So there we have it—the Azores on a Chinese-Korean map published thirty-seven years before the Portuguese "discovered" the islands. I had a splendid ride back to Tokyo—champagne all the way!

Obviously a Chinese-Korean fleet had reached the Azores and settled there before 1402, predating Zheng He by nineteen years.

EPIDEMICS, VIRUSES, AND PARASITES

The DNA evidence goes further, allowing us to extend our research into the transmission of epidemics, viruses, and parasites across the oceans before Columbus. We are left with further evidence of Chinese presence. Olympio da Fonseca's magisterial study summarizes the evidence of parasites that are shared between South America and Southeast Asia, and I believe he makes an indisputable case that man brought the parasites from Southeast Asia and Oceania to South America before Columbus.[11]

There is other material as well:

- Ettore Biocca, in "Les Ancylostomas de l'origine des Indiens d'Amérique," *l'Anthropologie* 55 (1950), explains that a species of hookworm that lives on dogs and cats occurs only in the Far East and America. Again, the Bering Strait cold would have killed this parasite.

- Adauto José Goncalves de Araujo, "Contribuição Ao Estudo de Helmintos Encontrados em Material Arqueologico dos Brasil," 1980. "Establishes the existence of ancylostomides among the prehistoric population of Brazil. These originated in Asia and do not survive in cold climates—they would have been killed in crossing the Bering Strait ice bridge. They must therefore have been brought by sea from Asia across the South Atlantic to Brazil."

- Samuel Taylor Darling, in "Observations on the Geographical and Ethnological Distribution of Hookworms," *Parasitology* 12 (1920), surveys the distribution of ancyclostoma species and *Necator americanus* hookworms introduced to America in pre-Columbian times from Asia, Polynesia, or Indonesia. Cold in the Bering Strait route would have killed these hookworms. Again, they must have been brought by sea.

- Fred L. Soper, in "Ancylostoma Duodenale," *American Journal of Hygiene* 7 (1927), describes this parasite introduced to South America from Indonesia or Polynesia—again, it cannot survive in cold climates.

DISEASES

With advanced abilities to analyze the nature of diseases and their transmission, we have additional tools to understand Chinese presence in the Americas. A number of diseases imported to the New World are localized as if specific travelers had transmitted the illnesses directly, rather than over the course of an eon, via a land route.

One prime example is Machado-Joseph disease, an often fatal, autosomal dominant motor disorder,[12] which cripples and paralyzes while leaving the intellect intact. The disease is characterized by weakness in the arms and legs and general loss of control of movement—often manifest as being similar to drunkenness. It is named after the heads of two families, William Machado and Antone Joseph, whose descendants were first diagnosed with having suffered from the disease.

In such autosomal diseases, children of an affected parent have a 50 percent chance of inheriting the defective gene. People at risk who escape the disease will not pass it on to their children or to future generations, since the disease does not skip generations. The disease thus shows a direct link from parent to child, which makes hereditary tracing relatively simple.

I first learned of this disease from Jerry Warsing, who contacted me after reading *1421* and invited me for a visit to his home in Virginia. He had come to the conclusion that a great Chinese fleet had been shipwrecked in 1432 on the coast of Virginia and North Carolina and that the settlers had marched inland away from the swamps near the coast. They had settled in the Appalachian Mountains. In Warsing's opinion, the Ming Ho, Wyo Ming, and Oceanye Ho (Shawnee) were the descendants of those shipwrecked sailors. Warsing came to this conclusion long before my book was published.

Warsing's interest had been aroused when he was asked to carry out historical research into the Mingo and Melungeon people of the Southeastern United States. In his research he found that they had a very high incidence of Machado-Joseph disease.

The disease was first described in the West among immigrants from the Azores to North America, especially those from the islands of Flores and São Miguel. The prevailing wisdom was that the mutation originated in mainland Portugal and was carried to the Azores when the Portuguese discovered the islands in the 1430s. It was then supposedly carried by the Portuguese along the sea routes down the coast of Africa and around to Yemen, India, China, Japan, Australia, and subsequently to the Americas when the Portuguese began to settle in the sixteenth century.

When Warsing dug deeper, however, he found that in fact Machado-Joseph disease had been prevalent in the south-central Chinese province of Yunnan before the Portuguese reached China, and had also been found in places that Portuguese fleets never visited. As a result, he came to the opposite conclusion: that Machado-Joseph originated in Yunnan.

Scientific support for that view is provided by Manuela Lima of the University of the Azores and her colleagues in "Origins of a Mutation: Population Genetics of Machado-Joseph Disease in the Azores." "It was thought that the MJD mutation represented a marker of the Portuguese explorations and discoveries. Beyond going for molecular confirmation of cases does not support this idea, because a large number of confirmed carriers of the CAG expansion typical of MJD have been identified in various countries, making the hypothesis of a unique Portuguese origin virtually impossible."

Every country in which Machado-Joseph disease has been found was visited by Zheng He's fleets; so I concur with Warsing: Zheng He's fleets carried the disease from Yunnan around the world.

TOKELAU DISEASE

The principal work on which I rely is that of Dr. Olympio da Fonseca. His research shows that this highly distinctive infection was found in 1928 among native Indian people of the Mato

Grosso area of Brazil. These people had been isolated from Europeans for many centuries. The endemic parasite disease has such a unique appearance that ancient navigators and explorers referred to it even though they were of course not medical experts. The center of Tokelau's sphere of affliction is the Malay Peninsula. It is also found on the southern coast of China, in Hunan province, on the coasts and hinterland of Indochina, in Cambodia, Thailand, Vietnam, Burma, and Bangladesh. It is prevalent across the Pacific—Formosa, the Marianas, Moluccas, the Gilbert and Marshall island groups, New Caledonia, Fiji, the Samoa and Tonga groups, the Tokelau Islands, the Society and Celebes island groups, the Solomons and Loyalty islands, Sumatra, and New Guinea. Zheng He's fleets visited all of these places and it is my contention that they also sailed up the Amazon and through the river network of present-day Bolivia to what is now the Mato Grosso state of Brazil. Olympio da Fonseca's report on the spread of Tokelau is mirrored by the DNA findings of many other researchers.

ANIMALS AND THEIR DISEASES

A number of visitors to our website have contended that the kunekune pigs of New Zealand, noted by the first Europeans who arrived there, are a Chinese strain. Skeletons of Indonesian pigs have been found in pre-Columbian graves in British Columbia. The wild pigs of Kangaroo Island, off South Australia, are also Chinese. Regrettably, research on the DNA of pigs is in its infancy, but recently Kyu-Il Kim and his colleagues at Korea's Cheju National University have carried out an investigation into H. M. Cooper's (1954) article in the *South Australian Naturalist* about the origins of Kangaroo Island's wild pigs. They say: "Finally, the feral pigs inhabiting Kangaroo Island have D loop sequences of Asian origin. More recent studies into fleas on these pigs have found that the fleas on Asian pigs differ markedly from the fleas on European pigs and that those on Kangaroo Island are indeed Asian fleas."

DISTINCTIVE BENIGN PHYSICAL DISORDER

Professor Mariana Fernandez-Cobo and her colleagues have studied the urine of people with kidney disorders in Cuba, Colombia, and Puerto Rico. Her team has found that although the Timo Indians, the original inhabitants of Puerto Rico, are long since deceased, the type 2A sequence in the JCB genotype 2A from Asia lives on in their descendants. To quote the report:

> While the genotypes of JCB present in Puerto Rico are those expected from the ancestry of the population, the proportion of these different types is surprising. The number of type 2A (Asian) strains, presumably contributed by the long extinct Tectino Indians, far exceeds that predicted by the tri hybrid model based on analysis of polymorphic blood groups and protein genetic markers. If Timo genes make up only 80 percent of the present Puerto Rico gene pool as others have calculated (Haanis et al., 1991) why should type 2A strains make up 61 percent of the JCV strains found in this study?

And in her abstract:

> These findings indicate that the JCV strains carried by the Taino Indians can be found in today's Puerto Rican population despite the apparent demise of these [Taino] people more than two centuries ago. Therefore, molecular characterization of JCV provides a tool to supplement genetic techniques for reconstructing population

histories including admix populations. . . . In Puerto Rico the native Taino population, an Arawak tribe, were decimated by warfare and disease and had completely disappeared by the end of the 17th century, but the JCV genotype (type 2A) of their ancestors brought from Asia has not only survived, but has actually thrived in their living descendants. We suggest that JCB genotyping can be a useful tool to reconstruct human population history, even when the contribution of a founding population such as the Taino has long been obscured.

It seems inescapable to me that there was a massive migration of peoples from Asia to the Americas before Columbus. This does not mean that the DNA of these people or their diseases, animals, or animals' diseases were from Zheng He's fleet. In some cases they may have been carried by Chinese joining the California gold rush in the 1840s and 1850s. However, this argument does not stand up in those places where the first Europeans to reach the Americas found Chinese already there—which is virtually the entire Pacific, Caribbean, and Atlantic coast of North America. A further reason why the critics' argument also does not stand up is found in analyzing the genetic tree produced by Novick and his colleagues. The tree shows close similarity between the natives of the far north of America (on both the Atlantic and Pacific coasts), the Chinese, and the Incas of the South American Pacific coast and the coast of the Yucatán in the Caribbean—all thousands of miles apart, surrounded by different oceans. In my view, to have such close-linked DNA acquired at much the same time means that these people must have acquired their Asian genes from Asian sailors—male and female.

Once one establishes and recognizes the genetic markers in DNA of the ancestors of Native American populations, it is logical to look for the works that the human settlers left behind—culture, architecture, and even the remains of the vessels that brought them to the New World. This is a key part of our search. We now turn to a study of the Chinese people whom the first European explorers met when they first arrived in the Americas.

CHAPTER 7

In Search of Lost Civilizations

The best way to describe the extraordinary scale of the Chinese and Asian influence on Mexican and Central and South American peoples is to take the reader along in a chronicle of our tour of the region. It is not as if the odd piece of ceramic has been found, but instead a saturation of evidence from San Luis Potosi, in central Mexico, right down to Ecuador—an area much larger than Western Europe.

Throughout this huge area the people have Asian ancestors—96.5 percent have Asian DNA. What proportion of these people came by sea as opposed to crossing the Bering Strait will be a matter of debate for a long time. It is incontestable, however, that the peoples of Central America came from Asia, and I say the DNA evidence shows that they came by sea. The conclusion is based not only on the mutation argument, but also on the fact that many of the viruses and diseases they brought with them would not have withstood the cold of a Bering Strait crossing.

It is self-evident, of course, that the indigenous people of Central America are of Asian origin—in their Asian facial structure, bodies, mannerisms, and ways of life. As you will read in a later chapter, the fact that forty-nine acupuncture points are identical in Mayan and Chinese medicine says it all. One or two could be a coincidence, but forty-nine is billions to one against coincidence. Furthermore, it means the use of Chinese acupuncture must have been recorded and spread through written records—one cannot pass down such a complex plan of acupuncture by word of mouth.

Then there are the Chinese customs practiced across thousands of square miles of Central America: worshipping ancestors; killing black chickens; making paper ornaments; the children's tale of the rabbit in the moon; the ceremonial use of jade; the same colors used to denote cardinal points of the compass; red clothes worn at funerals; making alcohol by chewing and spitting grain; the use of Chinese stills; using backstrap looms.

We will cite major archaeological finds, such as the work of Alexander Von Wuthenau, who depicts Asian faces in his book about pre-Columbian peoples of the Americas. Such visages are also seen in the striking Olmec statues at La Democracia and Monte Albán, which we will focus on later.

Olmec and Mayan art in its various glorious forms is almost indistinguishable from Chinese art of the Shang and Han dynasties in all manner of media—superbly carved jade; funerary objects; animal heads on human bodies; jade plugs between the teeth of the deceased; jade face masks made of small rectangular jade pieces; small axes used for money; lions with expressive teeth; Olmec pottery with Shang dynasty inscriptions; the feline cult; concave mirrors; tripod cooking vessels; superb pottery and decorated plates. One or two similarities could of course be a coincidence, but twenty, when coupled with identical customs, pyramid building, and DNA?

Olmec and Maya shared the same astronomy with the Chinese. Ephemeris tables for eclipses in the Dresden Codex are the same as Shang dynasty tables. Olmec and Mayan and Chinese calendars of that era were all based upon the moon, and months alternated between twenty-nine and thirty days. Both civilizations arrived at the same period for Venus's orbit of the sun. Both civilizations used the same (correct) 26,000 year precession cycle. Both estimated a solar year at 365.2422 days and both put the lunation of the moon at 29.53 days—calculations made at a time when Europeans were still hunting in forests.

The increasingly evident links between Chinese seafarers and Native Americans called for additional research. Marcella and I once again planned a journey with our "Cantraveler" friends to Mexico and Guatemala to look for clues about those early explorers and their heritage.

Our search for the lost civilizations of the Americas posed three major difficulties, not least their ages. First, we sought to discover civilizations that lived in tropical America more than four thousand years ago.

The Olmec (c. 1900 B.C.) are a prime example. They predated the New Kingdom of Egypt, the Mycenaeans of Greece, and by centuries the Assyrian Empire of Mesopotamia. The Olmec civilization's age is probably only exceeded by the Shang peoples of China, the Vedic era of India, and the Minoan civilization of Crete. The Olmecs' successors—the Maya and Zapotecs—were older than Macedonian Greece, and began at about the same age (600 B.C.) as the Roman Empire. No silk or paper documents are likely to have survived the tropical heat and damp, neither wooden carvings nor paintings.

The second problem is the extent of the lands of the Olmecs and the peoples they influenced, that is, the Zapotecs, the people of Teotihuacán, and the Maya, who flourished in an area ranging from central Mexico to Honduras and probably as far south as Ecuador—an area larger than the Persian Empire or Western Europe.

Our third problem is the destruction of records. The Spanish bishop Diego de Landa Calderón made a bonfire of Mayan and

Olmec books in 1562 when he was the bishop of the Yucatán. Only four books are known to have survived, being saved by the conquistadors and taken back to Spain. Two of these, the Dresden and Paris codices, fortunately tell us quite a bit about their writing, numbers, calendars, and astronomy. Professional historians become apoplectic when Landa's name is mentioned. In Mexico the Aztec people practiced cannibalization on a horrific scale, involving tens of thousands of captives. It had become a way of life. Landa was disgusted and sought to destroy all possible evidence of these revolting practices, the work of the devil. His big mistake was to equate the Maya and Toltec with the Aztecs. Mayan priests did drink the blood of their victims, but as a religious offering—they also spilt their own blood for the same reason, cutting their arms and penises to do so.

The Spanish conquistadors systematically pillaged temples and pyramids of the conquered Maya and Mixtec to build their own towns. Cholula was stripped of stone to build Oaxaca, similarly Puuc buildings for Mérida. However, not all was lost. Successions of scholars—among them Michael Coe, Charles Gallenkamp, and Jacques Soustelle—have deciphered Mayan writing and their system of numbers based upon twenty (rather than our decimal system). They have also decoded the Dresden and Paris codices, which tell us a great deal about Olmec and Mayan art. Knowledge of the extent of Olmec and Maya influence across Central America grows by the day—it is difficult to keep up with developments.

Before leaving on our expedition through Mexico and Central America, we gathered more than a hundred books and articles to digest. The trip began and ended in Cancún, for a tour of the Yucatán. We drove across the dry, flat, scrubland of the peninsula, visiting Chichen Itza and Uxmal pyramids on the way. These were built by the last Maya and Toltec, sometime around 1000 A.D.—nearly three thousand years later than the oldest pyramids, which we planned to visit later. We then drove south along the coast of the Gulf of Mexico to La Venta, birthplace of the Olmec, created before 1600 B.C. Then into the mountains up the Grijalva River to Palenque, a classic Mayan city stuffed with exotic treasures and founded around 300 A.D.

From Palenque we continued into the mountains to San Cristóbal de las Casas, where there are Indian villages whose people still live much the way their ancestors did. We returned from San Cristóbal by the Grijalva River, descended via the Pacific slope to the lowlands, then climbed the altiplano to Mexico City to visit the great pyramids of Cholula, the world's biggest, and Teotihuacán, with its pyramids of the sun and moon. From Mexico we flew to Guatemala for a visit to the great rain forest city of Tikal, where the Maya had been building skyscraper pyramids for more than one thousand years. To this day they tower over the jungle, monuments to an amazing political system that inspired people for generations.

Our expedition covered not only different geographical areas but also different epochs, illustrated by the Olmec pyramids of La Venta (1600 B.C.) through the pyramids of Teotihuacán and Cholula (started c. 300 B.C.), to Monte Albán, a transitional Olmec/Mayan site, to early Maya (Tikal), classic Mayan (Palenque), and late Mayan (or Toltec) at Chichen Itza and Uxmal. We saw how pyramid building evolved over three thousand years and also how mathematics, art, astronomy, agriculture, and civil engineering developed in that period.

Sometimes Cantravelers split up—while Marcella and I went to Cholula, the others went to Mitla. Some went as well to Labna and Sayil while the rest of us revisited Uxmal. Whenever possible we stayed at jungle lodges built originally for the archaeologists whose dedicated work brought the sites from the jungle to the world's attention. In towns we stayed at haciendas that had been the estates of Spanish conquistadors who carved out their fortunes in jute, or at former palaces of Spanish merchants. None of these were particularly expensive and they provided a charming reminder of the life created long ago by the adventurous but ruthless Spaniards who conquered Central America.

Rather than describe our tour chronologically I have selected three typical days along the way, first in the rain forest at Tikal, Guatemala, then a day in the villages where life was much as it was one thousand years ago, and finally in the marshes of La Venta. The pyramids have a chapter to themselves, as does the art of the Maya and Olmec; two chapters are devoted to DNA of the peoples, and the plants which Olmecs and Maya collected and shipped to the Old World long before the Spanish arrived.

A DAY IN THE RAIN FOREST OF TIKAL

We flew into the airport at Flores, capital of Guatemala's Peten department, in a small aircraft across marshlands from neighboring Honduras. This is the access point to Tikal, the great Mayan archaeological site in the jungle. The road from Flores to Tikal leads through a great national park, part of the huge rain forest (the world's fourth largest) that cloaks Guatemala. Beside the road, every few miles we saw signs warning of jaguars, snakes, or crocodiles. At the Jungle Lodge at Tikal three jaguar carcasses had been dumped quite recently by farmers who shot them for having stolen their cattle. It was dusk when we reached the lodge, but there was enough light to light our mosquito coils, start the ceiling fans, change clothes, and drink chotapeg sundowners on the balcony before dinner. We could hear the roar of the jaguars.

We were surrounded by black jungle, from which erupted a continuous cacophony of noise, largely from howler monkeys that wind each other up like opposing football teams. Suddenly the noise would stop as if by an unseen conductor. But an hour before dawn the howler monkeys were at it again, making sleep impossible. At daybreak, we met our guide, Antonio, a graduate of the University of Florida, whose family have been archaeologists at Tikal for fifty years.

The site is so vast we needed a truck to circumnavigate it, nearly ten miles from end to end. The view from the tops of the pyramids was breathtaking—the jungle canopy far below: one felt to be up in the clouds with the gods. This awesome stone city dates from 600 B.C. to 726 A.D.—dated from inscriptions, the Dresden Codex, and radiocarbon dating of wood used in building. More than one hundred scientists from the universities of Pennsylvania, Florida, and Arizona have been exploring different aspects of Tikal for years. They have bored the lake, extracted snails, and by analyzing the isotopes of oxygen in their shells have dated Tikal's collapse to 869 A.D., a collapse caused by years of prolonged drought. Copan followed, then northern Mexico sites in 909. That was the end of the Maya civilization.

For nearly fifteen hundred years, priests of these Mexican civilizations garnered the collective energy of tens of thousands of people, starting their epic work before ancient Greece or Rome, and continuing to build these colossal structures century after century. They built magnificent edifices, often one on top of another. The structures typically surrounded a central plaza, the focus of ceremonial worship then and now. The most important buildings were nearest the center, the priests having the most favored location.

The surplus labor required for these massive projects could only have come from a very rich environment. Tikal was blessed in many ways. There was (until the widespread droughts in c. 850 A.D.) abundant rainfall—eighty inches a year—and a reservoir that held ten million gallons of water. Sea fish swam up rivers from both the Pacific and Atlantic (Tikal is on the ridge separating them) to spawn. Pheasants and agoutis were plentiful and the jungle was rich in all manner of plants—to be discussed later.

Tikal was also a center of trade, using spondulix (shells) from Ecuador as coinage. Cinnabar (to paint buildings), flint, and jade were exported to Monte Albán and Teotihuacán in the north and to Honduras in the south. Hallucinogens extracted from water lilies, bark, or toad were exchanged for hardwood from Belize. Architectural influences of Teotihuacán were deployed in the pyramids. There were four ball courts (compared to nineteen in Copan); the players were coached and played "away matches" with rivals. An interesting book, *The Graffiti of Tikal,* shows Asian merchants arriving on a three-masted ship. Kings were treated with reverence and were buried inside the pyramids accompanied by great quantities of carved jade (the ruler Pacal with thirty pounds of the stuff!).

However, it was the rain forest that provided Tikal with one thousand years of wealth. More than one hundred medicinal plants were a stone's throw from our hut, varying in size from a seventy-foot-tall ficus to the *guisador,* a small ground shrub. The peoples of the rain forests use 90 percent of the forest for some purpose or other—by shamans for hallucinogens; as palms for thatch; for an endless variety of medicinal purposes; as vegetables and fruit, stimulants and sedatives, aphrodisiacs, soaps, tobacco, for all manner of drinks and vitamin additives.

An astonishing array of trees, shrubs, and their leaves and bark are used for medicine. As with medieval Europeans, people of the rain forest are keen on purges; they use *piñon blanco,* the roots of *chiric sanango,* latex from the *oje blanco* tree (the most powerful purgative of all), and the root of the *piro sanango.* Equally popular are remedies against diarrhea. The young tender leaves of the *cachu* tree mixed with salt and sugar produce an effective remedy against dehydration. Leaves of the *guya abaya,* rich in tannins and potassium, not only cure diarrhea but also have antimicrobial properties. All sorts of remedies are available to cleanse blood—again reminiscent of medieval European man: cafe, a concoction of leaves; quoin—ginger root used all over the world for this purpose; or boiled bark of the puna tree. Interestingly, this bark is now being tested in the United States to discover whether, as claimed, it attacks the AIDS virus. *Shinto vari* leaves cure snake-bites. Abscesses are treated with leaves of the prickly pear, jergon sacha. *Piripiri* bulbs soothe strained muscles. The latex from *sangre de grado* relieves toothaches and stomach pains; the crushed roots of the *guisador* have anti-inflammatory properties and cure herpes sores. *Cedro blanco* and *piñon colorado* resin is used for insect bites.

The rain forest has a diversity of trees for every purpose imaginable. Tall balsa trees provide the lightest wood known to man—with a density of 0.21–0.25, balsa is soft and porous, yet solid. At the other end of the scale is lignum vitae's greenish brown heartwood, seven times as heavy as balsa. In between these two come all manner of woods and canes, flexible for bamboo and cane furniture, with high tensile strength for bows, other wood hard and light for arrows. The dining room chairs and tables at the Jungle Lodge in Tikal were carved from long-lasting ironwood.

The profusion of fruit and vegetables would take several books to describe. A few yards from our hut were wild bananas—bunches hung in our rooms. Yuccas are a delicious alternative to bread and potatoes. Climbing marrows or squashes come in all shapes and colors; cooking oil is extracted from their seeds. Tomatoes are rich in vitamins A, B, and C. Manioc or cassava, with tubers weighing about fourteen pounds, are roasted, dried, and ground to produce sago meal, used instead of rice or with coconut for milk puddings and for thickening juices of wild berries. The juice of the manioc preserves meat. Of all the vegetables of the rain forest, manioc and yucca seemed to be most commonly used at the Jungle Lodge.

A wide variety of beverages are extracted from jungle berries. Cacao (Anglicized long ago as *cocoa*), a thirty-foot tree, flowers throughout the year; the shell of the fruit, which ripens in all seasons, is about nine inches long, resembling a short, pointed gherkin covered with furrows and warts.

Inside the cacao shell are five rows of beans. The shell is

crushed and the wet, fresh beans are fermented to develop their flavor. They are then rinsed and killed to prevent germination. The beans contain fat (cocoa butter) and caffeine, a stimulant. For chocolate, the beans are first roasted and ground, then sugar and vanilla—both available in the forest—are added. Alternatively, a butter is pressed out of the beans to produce cocoa. The tree grows all over the rain forest, in areas up to about one thousand feet above sea level. It yields crops for forty years. *Caucho masha,* a sap resembling milk, is used for baby food and as a tonic when sweetened by *cana negra* ("black cane"), a variety of sugar cane. Herb Louisa—sometimes called lemon verbena—is used today for Inca cola, the popular equivalent to Coca-Cola, sold throughout South America. Mexicans have been drinking cocoa since 1900 B.C.!

Before setting out on this adventure, I had imagined rain forest life would be a battle for survival. When seen at first hand, the richness of the rain forest explains what I had hitherto thought incomprehensible—that the people, where their habitat is undisturbed, may live a perfectly healthy, comfortable, well-fed existence by fishing and by gathering fruits, roots, and vegetables of the jungle. If they fall ill they can apply the remedies derived from the trees and shrubs that grow so abundantly around them.

In 1600 B.C., life in this Garden of Eden was virtually identical to what it is today, or indeed was in 1400 A.D. What has changed is the continued shrinkage of natural habitat. Today the world's rain forest covers less than half the area it did in 1947, only about 6 percent of the Earth's surface rather than the estimated 14 percent of earlier centuries. Valuable timber is being ruthlessly felled as the land is cleared for gold mining or agriculture. With deforestation, fertile soil is blown away or washed into the rivers, with the inevitable outcome—drought, flooding, and loss of wildlife. It is estimated that 20 percent of the world's cultivated topsoil was lost in the forty years from 1960 to 2000. Even today, the rain forest of Peru and Brazil, although halved in area, is substantially larger than all of Western Europe.

As interesting as the profusion of flora in the New World is the evidence that plants were transmitted there from the Old World in the five millennia before Columbus. For this we have to thank Professors Sorenson and Johannessen for their lifetime of work. In the two millennia before Christ, produce indigenous to the Americas was transported to Asia: agave, love-lies-bleeding, spiny amaranth, cashews, peanuts, pineapple, and custard apple. Can one really imagine hunters trekking across thousands of miles of ice and snow to the Bering Strait, taking (along with their wives and children) pineapples and custard apples or Mexican poppies, sweet potatoes, or purslane?

During the Song dynasty, milkweed, kapok, chilis, squash, sage, arrowroot, bog myrtle, tomatoes, frangipani, and morning glory were transported from the Americas to Asia—again it is absurd to believe these were carried across the Bering Strait. A mass of plants including cross-pollination cotton was brought from the Americas to Asia by Zheng He's fleets as well as hibiscus, bottle gourds, yam beans, and potatoes; mulberry trees were taken from Asia to Middle America, as was mugwort to Mexico.

Centuries later, we are still counting further riches. The tropical rain forest yields oils from cedar, juniper, cinnamon, and sandalwood; spices, gums, and resins used in inks, lacquers, and linoleum; tanning and dyeing materials; drugs, poisons, rubber, feathers, hides, fruits, vegetables, beverages, and woods of every description, for almost every purpose.

Our second destination was the colonial town of San Cristóbal de las Casas, nestled in the mountains of the Mexican state of Chiapas. One approaches on a road that wends westward from Tikal, a seven-hour, 345-mile drive through the mountains, a tortuous route with wonderful views of waterfalls, torrents, and cascades. San Cristóbal itself is a peaceful backwater in a pine-clad mountain valley at an altitude of 6,900 feet. The Mayan peoples took to the highlands after Palenque and Tikal were overrun by the Toltec. The Spanish aimed to farm sisal and built beautiful haciendas that line the main street and square today.

We arrived at San Cristóbal on November 1, the Day of the Dead, and found that the ancient Mayan funeral customs of the day are still observed. We visited two nearby Indian villages, San Juan Chamula and Zinacantán, where traditional Mayan culture was in evidence. The villages retain autonomy in certain aspects of life. The elders, for example, can expel women for marrying or having affairs with Europeans. These expelled women rejoice in long black dresses as they walk along the squares of San Cristóbal—exulting in their expulsion. Minor crimes are punished under San Juan Chamula law rather than Mexican.

The main cemetery of San Cristóbal was full of families observing the Day of the Dead. They had brought food for picnics and chatted happily, sitting among the graves of their loved ones; bottles of the deceased's favorite beer and wine were placed on their tomb or gravestone. We felt rather intrusive and drove down to San Juan Chamula, about eight miles away, a unique town that preserves much of traditional Mayan culture.

At San Juan, we were met by our guide, Alex, a well-known figure in these parts. By way of introduction and without explanation or preamble, and rather surprisingly so, Alex exposed the top of his buttocks in the area of the coccyx to show us his "Mongolian spot." He said this identified him as a true indigenous Maya from San Juan Chamula. He had this spot at birth, as his ancestors were Mongolian people from Asia. Alex told us that almost all the indigenous Indians were born with such a spot. I decided to ask him for more information that might lead to evidence of Mongolian or Chinese ancestry among local people.

Alex took me to a local church, where we saw people praying on a bed of pine needles. Here, as I observed the service, I asked questions based on my knowledge of Chinese religious practices. Sixteen of eighteen answers coincided with both peoples, Chinese and Mayan, though both cultures were separated by hundreds of years and thousands of miles.

At the left side of the altar a black chicken was being killed by breaking its neck—not by cutting its throat. I then asked about the Chinese practice of making paper effigies at religious festivals and then burning them. In fact, the same routine is carried out there in southern Mexico. Children, Alex said, make paper effigies that are then placed in a paper bag and hung from the ceiling. They are then given a pointed stick with which to destroy the paper bag.

I went down my list of Chinese practices and he almost always replied with an exact local equivalence:

"Do local people see a rabbit in the moon?"

Yes, Alex told me. "We have a children's story that a wicked prince was turned into a rabbit and sent to the moon."

"Are red clothes worn at weddings?"

"Yes—but not always. People can wear white."

"Do certain colors represent points of the compass?"

"Yes—east is red because that's where the sun rises, west is black because the sun sets there, north is white, from where the rains come, and south is yellow because it is the sunniest point of the sky."

I was startled. He answered yes to most of my questions. I asked him if people there, as in China, make alcohol by chewing and spitting corn.

"Yes, we call it chicha."

I also asked him if the locals around San Cristóbal brew alcohol using European stills. No, he said. "We have much better stills than Europeans. The Spanish were surprised by ours when they arrived."

As in Asia, I found the indigenous people of Mexico were

making complex ceramic from kaolin clay, fine pottery long before the Spanish arrived.

As for clothing and textiles, the story was much the same. Tree bark was used for clothing long before European contact. While the locals do use European looms for their brightly designed dresses and other clothing, they also use a kind of backstrap loom that is quite different from the European system.

Houses, as they are among the Chinese, are built on a north-south axis; bark was also used to make books; Mayans read from top to bottom and right to left; they had mirrors before the arrival of the Spaniards; had nine gods in their Mayan religion, worshipped the rain god, Chac, in their language. They worshipped jaguars, while ancient Chinese venerated the tiger. The only questions that came up with a negative were about the use of dogs as sacrifice and as food, which does take place in China, but not among the descendants of the Maya.

Aside from these remarkable similarities, my fellow travelers and I ventured to say that the descendants of the Maya in and around San Cristóbal and in the traditional Indian villages closely resemble Chinese in stature, proportion, hair, eyes, demeanor, and vivacity.

THE OLMEC SITE OF LA VENTA

From San Cristóbal, almost a mile and a half above sea level, we traveled about two hundred miles northwest to La Venta, in Tabasco state along the Gulf of Mexico. The change in altitude was noticeable and was something to get used to. Some of us were left breathless and had difficulty sleeping at 7,200 feet. We noticed the change when we descended into the tropical areas once again, this time along the coast. As we approached La Venta the air grew warmer and stickier. On reaching the Gulf of Mexico, we were greeted by pelicans, each with its own guano-stained post—a clear illustration of the wealth of fish here. The birds were busy diving into the sea every few minutes, then emerging with their throats bulging as they swallowed fish after fish.

The ancient settlement of La Venta is now the site of modern oil fields. The Olmec used tar from these fields to waterproof their boats. They are also said to be the first people to have used petroleum for fuel—but I have been unable to find confirmation.

The Olmec settled here by 1600 B.C., although this date is continuously being pushed back. That is the same time that Ramses II was building his temples; before the Assyrian Empire and a thousand years before the Parthenon was built in Athens. In short, the Olmec was one of the oldest civilizations in the world. They chose a site on what was then an island just offshore, near some mighty rivers—the Grijalva, Tulija, and San Pedro—that emptied into the Gulf of Mexico. The combination of marshland and sea provided a constant supply of food throughout the year. From the sea, albacore, tuna, and snapper; manatees, turtles, caymans, and Morelet's crocodiles. From the rivers: clams, crabs, and snails. From the beaches, salt. From the marshes: agoutis and armadillos. From the woods: turkeys, bush rabbits, wild pigs, and white-tailed deer. Fruit was abundant—custard apples, soursops, ramón nuts, guavas, and allspice. The famous trio of vegetables—maize, beans, and squash—provided vitamins (maize was boiled with lime to release vitamins), supplemented by sweet potatoes, yams, and cassava.

The Olmec were skillful farmers and hydraulic engineers, building a series of dikes and canals for irrigation to terraced fields and kitchen gardens—all in all a rich environment in which to develop their civilization. The first villages around La Venta emerged around five thousand years ago—scattered settlements with small populations and an egalitarian form of social organization, land being held communally. Between 1900 and 1400 B.C.

social and economic life developed. People began to exchange raw materials such as obsidian, a black or green type of glass used to make a wide range of weapons and tools. People began to specialize; some families became more important than others and more and more plants were grown.

Between about 1800 and 1400 B.C. social and economic life developed to the extent that life was not only about survival—communal buildings were built for ceremonial purposes, as were temples and small pyramids. Over the next four centuries this type of architecture spread fast along the Gulf coast. Around 1300 B.C. the first great monumental work was built at San Lorenzo, near La Venta. As described by "Olmecs," published by the magazine *Arqueología Mexicana*, "social stratification became ever more complex." Over the course of time, culture and economy developed around settlements that became centers of activity in what was to become Mexico. The Olmec emerged in the thirteenth century B.C. and thrived for six centuries, as "the first clearly stratified society in Mexico. . . . Other centers developed at San Lorenzo, Tenochtitlan, La Venta, Tres Zapotes and Laguna de los Ceros, in Southern Veracruz and Tabasco. This 'mother culture,' as the anthropologist Alfonso Casa called it, was the origin of many cultural traditions of ancient Mexico. The people who lived here played a fundamental role in the development of complex societies, and are the direct predecessors of those who built the centers and cities that were to arrive later. . . ."

These ancient cultural groups and their civilizations became great city centers that developed advanced systems of architecture, science (including astronomy), mathematics (including a system of keeping time), agriculture, art, and design. All of their pursuits were fundamentally intertwined with religious practice.

Ancient Mexico, with the development of its cities, flourished 2,200 years ago and amounted to a "revolution" in how human beings lived and spent their lives. "For the first time, large human populations lived in places covering several square miles, radically transforming their environment. Social and economic institutions linked to the existence of these societies often covered wide regions."

In the succeeding chapters we will delve more deeply into the Olmec's achievements, including this amazing revolution in human society. We'll also look more closely at how Olmec civilization became the mother culture of Central America.

CHAPTER 8

The Olmec:
The Foundation Culture
of Central America

The importance of Olmec civilization was rediscovered by Europeans only in the last hundred years, notably by Matthew Stirling (1896–1975). In contrast, Frederick Catherwood drew the world's attention to the Maya a century earlier. Perhaps for that reason Maya culture is relatively well known, whereas more and more of Olmec culture is still being discovered—on an almost daily basis.

The Maya, Zapotec, Mazatec, and Toltec copied and adapted Olmec culture, including their way of life, their art, and their architecture. Their ancient towns can be found along the length and breadth of southern Mexico and Central America. It is essential to consider the similarities among these civilizations and compare their artwork, pyramids, astronomy, and mathematics.

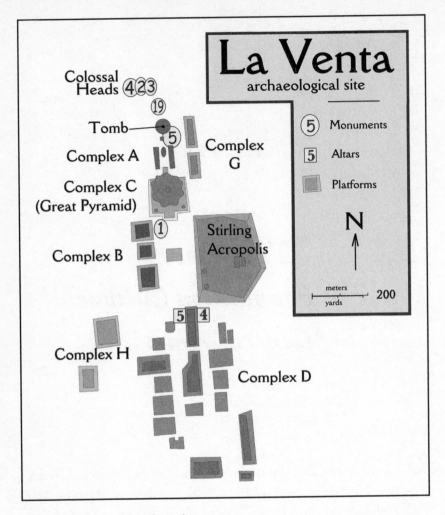

Plan of La Venta archaeological site.

Olmec sites, from about 1200 B.C., were based on a formal-ized layout embracing a great pyramid, a central plaza, a religious area, burial tombs, a domestic quarter, statues, and art. The city was built on a north-south orientation with a commercial center, where sacred and ritual aspects predominated, in the north of the site. (Please see Complex A on the plan of La Venta above.) This exclusive precinct was out of bounds to the common people, usu-ally protected by basalt barriers. At the heart of this ceremonial center (see plan), a basalt tomb was erected that contained a sarcophagus for the ruler, usually including a collection of carved jade ornaments. Often figurines were placed in this central courtyard; at La Venta, sixteen serpentine jade and sandstone figurines were positioned in a half circle, whereas Tikal had carved tablets.

South of this ceremonial area were open public spaces (Complex C on plan). The central pyramid was usually in the center of this central plaza, built of rammed earth and faced with stone, to be described in greater detail in the next chapter.

South of the public spaces were areas for the priests and hierarchy—storehouses and offices supplied with running water and drainage systems.

At the northern extremity of the site at La Venta are three colossal heads, each weighing more than twenty tons, carved out of basalt brought from hills nearly one hundred miles away. It was a great feat to have transported such heavy objects over such a distance.

Workers and tradespeople lived on farms and in villages surrounding the whole complex. These were the people who supplied food for the priests and the artisans who were constructing the site.

The basic layout was copied at other Olmec ceremonial sites—first near La Venta, then at Comalcalco, Tortuguero, Pomona, and Moral-Reforma. Later, more distant Olmec sites are found at Morelos, on the Mexican altiplano; Tzutzuculi and Tonalá on the Pacific coast; and La Democracia in Guatemala.

This essential design was also adopted in Mayan sites and can be clearly seen at Monte Albán, which was in many ways a transitional site between Olmec and Mayan culture. The same principles are seen in the architecture of Tikal, whose central court copies Comalcalco's and whose pyramids adopt La Venta's methods of construction.

The political structure of the Olmec was likewise adopted by the Maya. Property was communally owned. At the top were the priests, headed by a king or leader who induced or coerced the people to build the gigantic structures over the centuries. The common people toiled away relatively safe and secure, well fed and reasonably healthy, but they lived outside the ceremonial centers.

Trade was well developed—roads connected La Venta with Olmec cities on the Pacific coast, with Monte Albán and Teotihuacán on the North, and with La Democracia in Guatemala and Copan in Honduras. Evidence of that trade can be found in Mayan tombs—Olmec objects connected with worship, such as figurines, urns, and statues, can be seen at Monte Albán, and giant Olmec heads at Monte Alto.

The Olmec developed a system of writing that was adapted at Monte Albán and Mitla and subsequent Mayan sites, and a system of counting and mathematics that may also be seen at Monte Albán and later Mayan sites, as will be discussed in more detail in the next chapter. At Abaj Takalik, a site in Guatemala, is a table with both Olmec and Mayan writing on it.

La Venta boasts the first ball court in the Americas, on which the "rubber people" (which is what *Olmec* means in Nahuatl) could play their favorite game with a round rubber ball. The ball court was adopted all over the later Mayan world, reaching its height of sophistication at Copan, where there were nineteen courts. Thousands of spectators could watch the game at the enormous court at Chichen Itza. At Tikal, players became professionals, being trained from an early age and playing "away matches."

The cult of the jaguar permeated Olmec life and was adopted by the Maya. The jaguar was represented in carvings on buildings, in figurines, in statues that had jaguar heads atop human bodies, and in mosaic floors—there are thousands of examples in Mayan, Toltec, Zapotec, and Mazatec sites.

The Olmec were an astonishing people who burst upon the

world and became the Americas' founding civilization at least as early as the New Kingdom of Egypt, long before classical Greece and Rome, even before the Persian Empire. For many historians and archaeologists, they appeared to have emerged out of the swamps from nowhere—or did they?

THE STONES AT LA VENTA

Even before focusing on cultural mores, DNA evidence, or physical appearance, it seems quite clear to me that there is one bit of evidence that would favor Chinese presence in the New World before Columbus. In 1995, Professor Mike Xu, a Chinese-born scholar at Texas Christian University, analyzed engraved writings on excavated stones found at La Venta and compared them with characters prevalent during the Shang era in China, about 1500 B.C.[1] His study offers clear examples of Shang characters—inscribed on Olmec architecture and artifacts. Among the most persuasive evidence is a diagram known as "Offering No. 4" at an Olmec site at La Venta, close to the border of the Mexican states of Veracruz and Tabasco. "16 male stone figurines accompanied by six stones, known as 'celts' on which writing was found[2] (all with noticeably slanted eyes)." The discovery, combined with Professor Xu's knowledge of Shang characters, is for me a veritable Rosetta stone.

The stones are reported as serpentine jade and sandstone, and stand in a semicircle at the burial site. The correlation between Shang writing and the images on the La Venta stones appeared to be exact.

The translation reads: "Let us practice divination at the stone temple over the burial mound and make sacrificial offerings to hear from the spirit of the ancestors."[3]

Research of this kind sometimes involves scholarly politics

and even the power of persuasion. Professor Xu sought help from academic specialists on the Olmec and on their counterparts in China on the Shang period.

Han Ping Chen is perhaps the foremost authority on the Shang in China. He was commissioned as editor of a Shang language dictionary, the first such update in two thousand years. In 1996, he traveled to the United States to view the inscription on Offering No. 4, which was on display at the time at the National Gallery of Art in Washington, D.C.

Chen reported that although some of the writing was impossible to decipher because of aging of the material, what he could read was in fact written in Shang Chinese. He compared the characters he saw with his own dictionaries to confirm the concordance between the writing and the Shang.

However, other Olmec scholars scoffed, saying that Chen's search for Chinese characters on the Olmec celts is "insulting to the indigenous people of Mexico." *U.S. News & World Report* stated, "There are only about a dozen experts worldwide in the Shang script, which is largely unrecognizable to readers of modern Chinese. Of the Americans, Profs William Boltz of the University of Washington and Robert Bagley of Princeton recently looked at a drawing of the celts but dismissed as 'rubbish' the notion that the characters could be Chinese."

After looking at the celts, Robert Bagley was quoted by *U.S. News & World Report* as saying, "it no doubt gratifies their ethnic pride to discover the Mesoamerican civilization springs from China!"

So who is right—Chinese professors Xu and Han Ping Chen, or the American professors Boltz and Bagley?

It seems to me one method of analysis is to compare Chinese art of the Shang dynasty with Olmec art. Over the years I have found countless similarities between Oriental and Mesoamerican art. In the first color section of this book, we have placed several pieces of Chinese art next to similar pieces of Olmec and Mayan

OLMEC	SHANG	CHINESE		ENGLISH
		卜	Bǔ	Divine
		聞	Wén	Hear
		聽	Tīng	Listen Faithfully
		丅	Shì	Spirit Worship
		糸	Mì	Thread Connection
		匡	Xuān	Circulation Name of Tribe
		祖	Zǔ	Ancestor
		厂	Hǎn	Stone structure
		石	Shí	Stone
		官	Guān	Temple Building
		丘	Qiu	Mound, hillock Grave
		皿	Mǐn	Container
		首	Shǒu	Head
		俎	Zǔ	Sacrificial altar

In 1995, Professor Mike Xu analyzed engraved writings on excavated stones found at La Venta and compared them with characters prevalent during the Shang era in China, about 1500 B.C. His study offers clear examples of Shang characters that are inscribed on Olmec architecture and artifacts.

art of the same era. Although they are not all included in these color photos, over the years I have found similarities exist in:

Head of the Lord of Las Limas and the goddess of
   Niuheliang, a Chinese site
Jade bear and jade jaguar

Pottery funerary objects—human bodies and animal
  heads
Terra-cotta soldiers
Jade death masks of King Pacal (Palenque) and Prince
  Liu Sheng
Jugglers and wrestlers
Sculptures of human heads with bulbous noses
Axe shapes used for money
Lions
Olmec pottery using Shang lettering
Orange ceramics
Pottery bowls
Stone necklaces
Tripod cooking vessels
Earrings
Felines
Pottery animals
Mirrors

These paired photographs are remarkable. It is frequently difficult to discern which is Olmec and which is Shang Chinese—
they are so similar.

A civilization that received the same art, architecture, and
writing customs from another civilization is likely to have received the same methods of medicine and curing illnesses.

In 1999, Hernán Garcia, Antonio Sierra, and Gilberto Balám
published *Wind in the Blood: Mayan Healing and Chinese Medicine*. This book is a collective endeavor whose principal protag-
onists are the *curanderos* (native healers) of Campeche and the
Yucatán with whom the authors worked for several years. Several
of the *curanderos*—shamans, herbalists, masseuses, bone setters,
and midwives—worked collectively on it. The authors acknowledge the generosity of these indigenous Indian people in Chiapas
and Guatemala who helped them.

The book, which is heavily annotated and includes a lengthy bibliography, focuses on an array of identical or very close methods of medical treatments of the Maya compared with the Chinese. The chance of these being all coincidence is infinitesimal.

I have selected nine examples to give a flavor of their book, which I recommend highly.[4]

THE BODY

The Mayan view was that the human body is based on a duality of hot and cold, and that this duality exists in equilibrium. The balance between the extremes can be lost because of both internal and external factors. For the Maya, therefore, this is the basic and most frequent cause of illness.

The similarities are of course striking when compared with the Chinese concept of yin and yang. Chinese philosophy focuses on the *Neijing Suwen*—"heaven and earth." The chi and the blood both reflect the interplay of yin and yang. Cold and hot are equally primary forces, water representing coldness and fire representing heat. Yin and yang are commingled and interdependent, reflecting all things in the universe, and cannot be separated. As with the Maya, health is based on a balance of forces. Disruption of yin and yang is akin to a year with spring without winter or winter without summer.

TUCH AND *TIPTE* AMONG THE MAYA AND
THE DAN TIAN OF THE CHINESE

To the Maya, the *tuch* or navel is considered a highly erotic zone. The umbilical region radiates energy, beating with life, and is fundamental to the health of the body. Similarly, Chinese ancient texts refer to the area just below the navel as being "the gate of life"—the Dan Tian. The primordial chi is stored in the Dan Tian, and this is the fundamental material of life. Strong energy in the Dan Tian feeds health and well-being to the organs of the body.

THE RIGHT-HAND SIDE OF THE BODY

The dichotomy between the left and right sides of the body is essential; for the Maya, the right-hand side is associated with health and success, while the left carries the stigma of illness and failure. In China, the right side is yin and the left is yang.

OOL [MAYA] AND CHI [CHINESE]

Mayan and Chinese cultures both refer to the life force of breathing. The ool for the Maya is "wind of life," inhalation. The ool passes through the lungs to the heart, its home. For the heart, the vital energy force of the ool is distributed through the bloodstream. For the Chinese the breath of life is chi; the inhaling breath is the body's vital force.

POINTS AND MERIDIANS IN TRADITIONAL CHINESE MEDICINE AND POINTS AND WIND CHANNELS IN MAYAN MEDICINE

The Chinese view the blood and chi as traveling along the system of meridians, or pathways of life. These pathways connect a series of points both inside and outside the human body. Mayan medicine men—curanderos—manipulated the wind through bleeding and with the application of needles. Each point of entry coincides with a Chinese point—on the left leg, for example, Yinshi

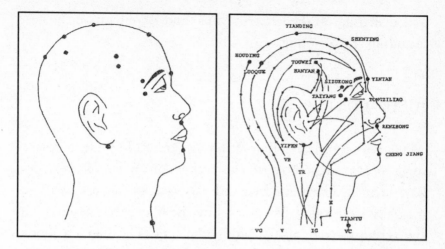

(Left:) *Points in the head and face used by Mayan curanderos and masseuses.*
(Right:) *Meridians and points in the head and face used in traditional Chinese medicine.*

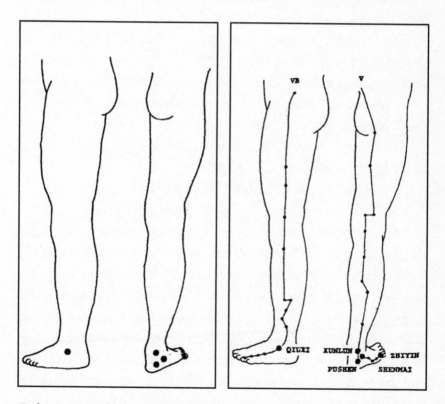

(Left:) *Points in the feet used in Mayan traditional medicine.*
(Right:) *Points in the feet used in Chinese traditional medicine.*

and Liangoiu; on the left arm Binao and Zhouliao; on the head Yianding and Shenting.

HERBOLOGY

Along with our description of the vast array of rain forest plants used in Mayan herbology, the authors of *Wind in the Blood* have identified two hundred and fifty species that are used medicinally to this day. Plants used by the Maya are classified into two groups—cold plants and hot plants. The Chinese book, the materia medica, is called *Ben Cao*. It contains medicinal plants and their uses and a whole lot more. By the year 1082, the Chinese pharmacopoeia included more than 1,558 medicinal products.

The primary Chinese classification divides the plants into those with yin and yang effects.

Plants of a cold or fresh nature have a yin character, while those of a warm or hot nature are considered yang.

MAYAN MASSAGE [*TALLADAS*]
AND CHINESE MASSAGE [*TUL NA*]

Talladas (rubbings) are massages applied with the whole palm, the thumbs parallel to each other and horizontal, spreading the hands across the body with firm pressure—a method used to diagnose and treat muscle problems. When one is performing this massage, various lines are followed, such as the muscles on either side of the spine. Similarly, Chinese massage stimulates the circulation of blood in the capillaries, bringing blood to muscle tissue and joints; it relaxes tense muscles, which also releases emotional stagnation.

MAYAN ACUPUNCTURE: *TOK* AND *JUP*

As may be seen from the diagrams on page 115, Mayan acupuncture has forty-nine points, with each one the same as the Chinese counterpart—an identical but smaller map of points. Mayan *curanderos* use spines and thorns of various bushes, spines from the tails of manta rays (xtoon), and porcupine quills. *Jup* involves pricking the skin at the selected point, either puncturing the skin or using a less sharp spine (such as the spur of a wild pheasant), in which skin is not punctured but merely bruised.

Chinese acupuncture is much more sophisticated and formalized than the Mayan. It has been continually improved by Chinese doctors for centuries. Until the Tang dynasty there was no general agreement on the names and functions of the points. Then the famous doctor Zhenquan ordered a codification of the system, which had been handed down ad hoc from father to son. In 1026, in the Song dynasty, another revision was undertaken to establish the exact function and location of each of the points, which were then displayed on a life-sized bronze model.

Acupuncture is considered a science in China, one with complex and varied techniques. In effect, Mayan acupuncture stagnated with the Spanish conquest and never approached the advanced state of modern Chinese practice.

PLASTERS AND POULTICES

In Mayan medicine, poultices and plasters were commonly used in the form of burning charcoal to warm and stimulate the body. Poultices could be made out of animal, vegetable, or mineral products, such as from herbs, fat, or clay.

"Moxibustion" developed alongside acupuncture in China. Heat is applied to the skin by burning mugwort, called *Zhen Jiu* (needle and fire). In Mexico, estafiate, a dry leaf, takes the place of *Zhen Jiu*.

For Mayan medicine, especially acupuncture, to have followed Chinese so precisely, the Mayans, I believe, must have copied Chinese drawings. It is not possible to pass forty-nine separate points for acupuncture by word of mouth. This means the Maya must have copied Chinese drawings during or after the Song dynasty, when they were first codified in China. Given this and the close similarity of the Maya and Chinese of the Shang, Qin, and Han dynasties, as described earlier, repeated voyages must have been made after those of the Shang dynasty, when the first "Chinese style" pyramids were built. The issue of repeated voyages will be explored further in later chapters. Genetics and advances in DNA science tell part of the story. So do the colossal structures left behind—thousands upon thousands of pyramids of the New World with characteristics that link their designs firmly to China.

CHAPTER 9

Pyramids in Mexico and Central America

Pyramids with artwork buried in them tell us a great deal. Olmec pyramids have Shang inscriptions and are aligned to the same star, Kochab, that the Chinese use. Town planning is the same for Olmec, Maya, and Han dynasty pyramids, with the same areas set aside for ceremonial and public use. Monte Albán is a half-scale copy of Emperor Qin's mausoleum, with similar satellite tombs and ceremonial tombs. The shapes and sizes are the same—Emperor Qin's and Cholula. Chinese and Mayan pyramids are set in the same location in relation to mountains and rivers. Tombs at Teotihuacán and Chichen Itza were found to contain Mongolian skeletons. Chinese jade is found at Tikal and the shroud at Jucutacato shows Asian merchants arriving in multi-masted ships.

Pyramids were built by every great ancient civilization. The construction and purpose usually were quite similar. There were three main functions: burial of a chief; the establishment of a religious center with rooms for priests and their ceremonies; and finally, a capacity for predicting celestial events—essential in all societies in order to establish the times for sowing and harvesting crops. Each society had its own emphasis. The principal use for the Egyptians, of course, was a monument over a burial chamber, and study of the heavens was secondary. On some Mayan pyramids, on the other hand, very elaborate astronomical observations were made, and these had first priority.

There are more than ten thousand pyramids in Mexico, more than any other country. Mexico also has the world's largest pyramid—the base of the Great Pyramid of Cholula is 1,300 feet on each side, almost twice the size of the Great Pyramid of Giza.

The oldest Mexican pyramid was built in the marshes around La Venta in about 1400 B.C.; the most recent is near Uxmal and was built around 1100 A.D., a spread of 2,500 years. We will focus on descriptions of pyramids from several eras: La Venta of 1400 B.C.; Monte Albán, c. 300 B.C., a transitional site between Olmec and early Maya; Cholula, south of Mexico City, the world's largest, started c. 200 B.C. but added to later; Teotihuacán, a politically important site north of Mexico City, c. 200 B.C. where the magnificent pyramids of the sun and moon awe visitors to this day; and finally Chichen Itza c. 900 A.D. on the Yucatán Peninsula. This chronological selection covers the principal phases of the development of civilizations in Central America.

LA VENTA

In 1862 a colossal stone Olmec head was found in the Mexican state of Veracruz. Sixty years later, after further substantial discoveries, specialists began to recognize a unique style of art and architecture, which they called Olmec, meaning "inhabitants of the rubber region."

This Olmec culture was the first to establish large urban centers and exclusive trade networks that covered a vast area from Central Mexico to what is now Honduras, as evidenced by ceramics, stonework, and beautifully carved jade. The Olmec were renowned for their majestic pyramids and for being the first people in the Americas to develop writing and a system of numbers based on dots and dashes. Their importance lies in their culture, which later peoples of Central America, notably the Zapotec and Maya, adopted and adapted.

At La Venta, then an island in the river, now part of a swampy area, the Olmec built their first capital in about 1400 B.C. The site was near the confluence of the Tonalá River and its tributary, the Chicozapote. Together the rivers and sea provided an abundance of fish and game, crustaceans, and wild birds. The Olmec were good engineers and developed an irrigation system in the surrounding countryside.

They planted the classic trio of maize, beans, and squash and developed a method of using lime to release the vitamins in corn, which they ate, as well as deer, crocodiles, turtles, and all manner of sea and freshwater fish.

Thousands of tons of stone were used to construct the buildings of the city of La Venta, overlaid on rammed-earth foundations. The main pyramid faced a ceremonial rectangular area, on each side of which were ceremonial buildings for the priests. The common people lived outside the main complex.

Some very fine art has been found at the site, which is described in greater detail later.

The Olmec were the founding civilization of the Americas.

MONTE ALBÁN

Monte Albán, located in Oaxaca, capital of the Mexican state by the same name, is about three hundred miles southwest of La Venta. This for me was a very enjoyable part of the trip to Mexico. We stayed at a hotel above colonial Oaxaca, and from there we could see the adjacent mountains on which Monte Albán was built. We dined on a balcony overlooking a splendid Victorian garden, richly planted in the style of the rain forest—a wonderful prelude to our expedition to Monte Albán itself.

The site is dominated by a great pyramid that overlooks a grand plaza, flanked by satellite pyramids containing burial tombs and the remains of palaces—the whole set against distant mountains. The air was like champagne. Monte Albán is a transitional site between Olmec and Maya, revealing both Olmec writing and figurines. Monte Albán was also a link between the north and south, where goods were traded from Teotihuacán in the north and from Honduras in the south.

Monte Albán boasts some very fine art—notably a wonderful pottery jaguar in the Olmec style, and paintings of a series of male figurines performing ritual dances. The figures of the dancers have round heads on short necks, slanting eyes, and broad foreheads. There were also Olmec inscriptions that are said to have the same characteristics of the Maya. The site is dated to 500 B.C. The view looking south over the complex to the southern pyramid is one of the greatest in the world.

CHOLULA: THE WORLD'S LARGEST PYRAMID

Cholula is a four-hour bus journey north from Monte Albán, through a wild mountain area. From Mexico City it is two hours south, across the altiplano. When the Spanish conquistadors found this colossal pyramid they pillaged the facing stones to build their own city at Pueblo. When the raw earth was exposed by this looting, first grass then trees grew over the mound, so it came to resemble a natural hill. The deception was completed when the Spanish built a chapel on top, among the trees. A range of tunnels has been dug into the interior, nearly eight miles of them, through which visitors trudge today. The base was originally 1,475 feet across, twice the size of the base of Cheops but almost precisely the size of the base of Emperor Qin's pyramid at Xian.

Cholula's claim to fame was its superb pottery, probably the world's finest, first produced when the site was inhabited about the same time as Monte Albán, around 1500 B.C. This sublime pottery was exported all over the Olmec and Mayan world (to be described in more detail later). Cholula people also developed eggshell-thin pottery, which was exported to China by Zheng He's fleets.

TEOTIHUACÁN

I first visited Teotihuacán, on the altiplano an hour north of Mexico City, in 1972, accompanied by Miguel, an old and very knowledgeable guide. On a beautiful summer's evening I watched the sun set from the Pyramid of the Moon and vowed to return to try to discover the site's secrets. Teotihuacán is much the same age as Cholula and Monte Albán, but the complex was built on a grander scale. Teotihuacán was a heavyweight political and military state at its apogee, around 600 A.D., with a population of 125,000, where Aztecs later came to venerate their ancestors. It was about ten times the size of London in the same era. Its culture was influenced by the Olmec and its architecture was copied in later Mayan sites, notably Tikal.

In the 1970s an American civil engineer, Hugh Harleston Jr., took about nine thousand measurements at Teotihuacán. He found that along the center line of the complex, markers were placed to correspond with the orbital distances of the inner planets around the sun—the asteroid belt, Jupiter, Saturn (Pyramid of the Sun), Uranus (Pyramid of the Moon); Neptune and Pluto were represented by two mounds farther north. He found the front wall of the Pyramid of the Sun is exactly perpendicular to the point on the horizon where the sun sets at the equinoxes. The rest of the buildings were laid out at right angles to the Pyramid of the Sun.

From the wealth of evidence, Harleston deduced a series of numbers that to him meant that the builders knew the precession of the Earth's axis over a period of twenty-six thousand years—a matter that will be referred to later when we consider the Dresden Codex of the Maya.

The presence of Chinese artifacts at Teotihuacán was discussed by James Churchward in 1926, who also noted the studies of anthropologist William Niven.

Churchward described a tomb he examined at the nearby Haluepantla

> which contain the finest artefacts I have ever seen in Mexico. I am inclined to think the room was thirty feet square, its walls were made of concrete and crushed down to within a foot of their bases. Below was a tomb. In the center, on a raised rectangular platform, also of concrete, lay the skull and some of the bones of a man who could not have been more than five feet in height. His arms were very long, reaching almost to the knees, and his skull was decidedly of a Mongolian type. Around his neck had been a string of green jade beads. Green jade is not a Mexican mineral.

Lying beside the body was a string of 597 pieces of shell. I say string, but the buckskin thong which had once borne them was long since rotted to dust, and the wampum, or money, lay as if it had fallen from a string. With this money lay the greatest find of all—the little Chinaman.[1]

CHICHEN ITZA

Chichen Itza is far to the south, in the center of the Yucatán Peninsula about eighty miles east of Mérida. While it is a very beautiful site, the pyramids are of the same era as Gothic cathedrals in Europe, to give you an idea of their relative youth. Other Mayan and Olmec pyramids are two thousand years older—built earlier than the temples of Greece and Rome. The brilliant mathematicians and astronomers of those early pyramids seem to have been forgotten. Chichen Itza symbolizes elegant decay and death.

The central pyramid at Chichen Itza, Kukulkan, was built by the Toltec in the late tenth century, when the Maya were collapsing. It is a superb, graceful pyramid of white stone. The setting is accentuated by a carpet of smooth lawn, around which are a series of elegant stone buildings, notably a large ball court, the largest such ancient site in the Americas.

Relevant to our discussion of astronomy is the *caracol*—meaning "shell" in Spanish—a round observatory with small windows aligned both to the sun's position at the equinoxes and to the position of Venus at various important times—notably when emerging from behind the sun, as will be discussed later.

COMMON CHARACTERISTICS OF OLMEC AND
MAYAN PYRAMIDS IN CENTRAL AMERICA

These visits and observations, combined with research, open us
to certain clear conclusions. First of all, the complexes looked the
same—stepped pyramids with flat tops surrounded by satellite
pyramids for burials of lesser chiefs. The central pyramid was
a burial mound and also aligned in such a way as to be used as
an astronomical platform. The principal pyramid had a burial
chamber at its base, reached by interior passageways that were
always painted in red cinnabar. The tomb held the body of the
king, surrounded by goods to accompany him into the next
life. In that respect, the Central American pyramids resembled
Egyptian, but their shape was totally different from the Egyptian
trapezoidal—these were much flatter, with more emphasis given
to the surrounding plazas and palaces. All were of rammed earth,
originally faced with stone, and were positioned with mountains
or hills as a backdrop. The whole complex was aligned on a north-
south axis.

I was greatly interested in the precise alignment of the pyramids because it seemed to me this might establish the type of
astronomy practiced there. As mentioned in Hugh Harleston's
study of Teotihuacán, was meridian passage of the sun studied?
To this end I planned to arrive at noon, when the sun should be at
its highest. By studying the shadows I assumed I could determine
when this moment had arrived. Then I could place a pole due
south and use my watch to establish the alignment by setting the
twelve o'clock hand to south.

Alas! I had forgotten we were in the tropics and that the sun
was virtually ahead at noon with almost no shadow. As navigators we used to be taught a method called "ex-mer" to account for
this, but I had forgotten how ex-mer worked, so I had to abandon
use of the sun! I waited for nightfall instead so that I could use
Polaris, the North Star, to point at due north.

Many Mexican archaeological sites are closed at sunset but sound and light shows came to our rescue, notably at Uxmal—a particularly beautiful demonstration a few minutes' walk from the Jungle Lodge where we were staying. Here I found the principal pyramid was aligned at about 15 degrees, which seemed to make no sense whatsoever since it appeared to have no relationship to the sun's position at equinoxes or solstices.

Almost all of the sites have Olmec or Mayan writing and dates (dots and dashes), which makes it possible to obtain an approximate building date for each—I say approximate since the majority of sites were built over a long period. At Tikal, for example, huge pyramids were built in the jungle over a one-thousand-year span. Many sites had later structures built on top of earlier ones. The great pyramid at Cholula was the final overlay of six previous smaller pyramids buried beneath (the smallest of course being the oldest).

In any case, I could get a reasonable approximation of the dates and could compile a table of age against alignment. This brought the fascinating disclosure that the oldest pyramid at La Venta pointed 4 degrees west of north—356 degrees—while the newest, Uxmal, was substantially east of north—15 degrees. (I disregarded Chichen Itza because it was built by the conquering Toltec and not by Maya.)

The era when the principal pyramid pointed due north—zero degrees—was when Moral-Reforma, an Olmec/Mayan crossover site in modern-day Tabasco state, with a double pyramid, was built, around 1000 B.C. In fact, there was a fairly even progression: the alignment gradually shifted eastward about 3.5 degrees every one thousand years. The next step was obvious—use software to establish Polaris's position at 1000 B.C. I found it was nowhere near the North Pole but the star Kochab was. I tracked Kochab's apparent shifting position and found the Olmec and Mayan pyramid alignment tracked Kochab from 1400 B.C. until 900 A.D. Why was this?

Alignment of Twelve Olmec and Maya Pyramids

	PYRAMID	ALIGNMENT (DEGREES)	WHERE ALIGNMENT WAS TAKEN FROM	AGE
1	La Venta—Olmec	356	Complex A	c. 1400 B.C.
2	Comalcalco—Olmec	356	Temple 1	
3	Teopantecuanitlan—Olmec	359	Ball Court	c. 1200 B.C.
4	Moral-Reforma—Olmec / Maya crossover site	001 / 002	Complex 5 Complex 1	c. 1000 B.C.
5	Monte Albán Transitional	002	South Platform	c. 500 B.C.–300 A.D.
6	Teotihuacán (own identity)	002	Pyramid of Sun and Moon	c. 300 B.C.–300 A.D.
7	Tikal (Maya)	002	Great Plaza and South and North Acropolis	400 A.D.–600 A.D.
8	Copan (Olmec?)	004	Pyramid 26	
9	Copan (Maya)	006	Pyramid 16	
10	Palenque (Maya)	009	Great Plaza	
11	Palenque (Toltec)	012	Temple of Inscriptions	c. 600 A.D.
12	Uxmal Maya (and Toltec?)	012–014	South Group	c. 1400 A.D.

Speed 16 degrees over c. 2,800 years or 6 degrees over first 2,000 years, then a sudden jump around 600–800 A.D.

ALIGNMENT OF PYRAMIDS

Why the Pole Star Changes—Kochab to Polaris—Precession of Earth—Celestial North

The Earth's rotation causes a slight bulge around the equator, so the Earth is not a perfect sphere but is slightly flattened—an oblate spheroid. The sun's mass is attracted to this bulge and gives the Earth a nudge, which makes it wobble like a top (called *precession*). This wobble means the Earth's axis does not point to the same celestial pole all the time, but the axis draws out a spherical circle in the heavens over a 26,000-year period, the radius of the circle being 23°30'—that is, every 13,000 years the Earth's axis changes from a position 23°30' west of the former celestial pole to one 23°30' east, a total of 47 degrees in 13,000 years or 3.6 degrees every 1,000 years.

In short, looking at the celestial pole one sees a different piece of sky over a 13,000-year cycle, which then repeats.

Assuming the pyramid builders were using Kochab as their marker for the north celestial pole, the change of alignment over 2,000 years from La Venta c. 1400 B.C. to Copan c. 600 A.D., a change of 8 degrees (from 356 to 004) is accounted for by the Earth's precession of 3.6 degrees every 1,000 years.

Then there is a big leap to Uxmal (014 degrees), far more than could be accounted for by the Earth's precession. It could be caused by the pyramid builders shifting to another star, not

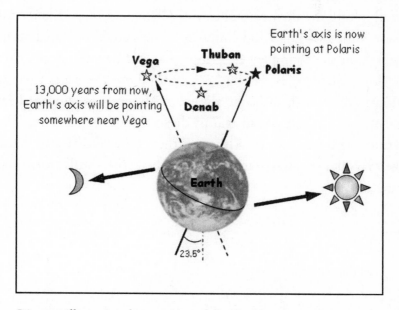

Diagram illustrating the precession of the Earth's axis.

Kochab, or by a "nudge" to the Earth's precession caused by a comet impact after about 600 A.D. There is considerable argument among astronomers about whether the Earth's axis does change orientation more than 3.6 degrees every thousand years. Consider the motion of a slowing, wobbly top. Sudden changes are perhaps due to a comet impact—the same effect as nudging a gyroscope.

I have no doubt Kochab was the guiding star for the alignment of these pyramids. Did the Olmec and Maya decide on this for themselves (which seems quite an obvious possibility if they knew where true north was) or did they get their inspiration from abroad? The first thing I needed to examine was the alignment of Emperor Qin's pyramid near Xian, which is guarded by the terra-cotta warriors. I had climbed this pyramid in 1990. It could be dated accurately since Chinese records show it was started in Qin's lifetime—210 B.C. Qin's pyramid was aligned at 1 degree, based on Kochab in 210 B.C.! What about other Chinese pyramids that could be accurately dated?[2]

I also learned that nine Chinese emperors built mausoleums similar to Qin's over their burial tombs beside the Wei River, overlooking the then-capital city of Chang An (now Xian).[3] Of these, Emperor Jing's and Empress Wang's could be dated accurately and the alignment determined at 002 degrees, once again tracking Kochab, as having been built about the same time as Monte Albán with the same alignment. In great excitement I set the plans for Monte Albán against those of Qin's mausoleum. The results were fascinating. Although they were of different sizes, their layout appeared to mirror each other, with similar form and function.

A FURTHER COMPARISON BETWEEN MONTE ALBÁN AND EMPEROR QIN'S TOMB

It is evident that the construction of mausoleums was of central importance to the emperors of ancient China. Their construction "consumed as much as one third of state revenue during the Han dynasty and involved tens of thousands of convicts and others sentenced to forced labor in lieu of fines," according to Professor Thomas Bartlett of La Trobe University, Melbourne, Australia, whom I had met when lecturing at La Trobe in 2006.[4]

> *Like the mausoleum of the First Emperor, Han Royal burial chambers were also covered by large above-ground mounds. These were centered at the center of funerary gardens which, in turn, were enclosed within rammed earth walls. The Emperor and Empress of each region were placed in separate burial chambers, with their own funerary garden within the same mausoleum. Buildings for holding ceremonies were constructed inside or near the funerary gardens ... many smaller burial mounds were erected nearby. These satellite burials belonged to members of the royal family and high officers, who were honored by becoming the emperor's attendants in the after-life.*[5]

Bartlett's descriptions can be applied quite closely to Monte Albán. Comparing Monte Albán and Bartlett's description of Qin's mausoleum, we find that both structures are flat-topped pyramids with the same angled slopes. They are set in similar surroundings with a backdrop of mountains and are made of rammed earth faced with stone. Both are sacred places with areas set aside for religious ceremonies in relatively similar positions. Each is dominated by the tomb pyramid and the tomb is reached by internal passages and stairways, painted in cinnabar red, leading to a burial chamber where the deceased was surrounded by objects of everyday life.

Satellite mounds and ceremonial halls were in the same position relative to the burial pyramid. The site was reserved for priests and dignitaries, out of bounds to working people. Both had areas for offerings to the gods. The sites in both cases were surrounded by rich farmland. And finally, both had similar alignment with Kochab.

By now I was thoroughly hooked, just as was the British scientist and historian Joseph Needham fifty years ago when he wrote of his visit to Central America: "This adventure, indeed, had some of the quality of the *déjà vu*.[6] And I was deeply impressed during my stay with the palpable similarities between many features of the high Central American civilizations and those of East and South East Asia."

Needham, a fellow of the Royal Society and a noted Sinologist, was "particularly struck by the similarity between the pyramids and enclosed courtyards of the Mesoamerican ceremonial centers and the sacred enclosures and steeped pyramidal platforms of Peking and often traditional Chinese capitals [viz Xian]. Like the Mesoamerican pyramids which were used for making sacrifices, the Chinese platforms were surrounded by areas designated for offerings to the gods. . . ."[7]

In short, as I stated earlier, Monte Albán appears to be a half-scale replica of Emperor Qin's tomb, built in the same era.

Emboldened, I decided to compare Olmec and Mayan astronomy with Chinese astronomy of the same era, meaning the Shang and Han eras, described in some detail by Needham, James Jacobs, and Ernst Förstemann.

As we mentioned earlier, the Spanish bishop of the Yucatán, Diego de Landa Calderón, burned every Mayan and Olmec book he could lay his hands on. Fortunately four escaped, notably the Dresden Codex. We also have inscriptions on the stelae themselves, the oldest of which is at San José Mogote in the Oxaca valley near Monte Albán, with signs dating from 600 B.C. Stelae twelve and thirteen at Monte Albán date to 500–400 B.C. and contain details of calendars. The two earliest Maya dates—using the same dot and dash as the Olmecs—are from 292 and 320 A.D.

The Dresden Codex, dating as early as 1000 A.D., apparently survived destruction because it had already been sent to Europe, where its thirty-nine double-sided sheets surfaced in 1739. The codex gives a detailed account of Mayan astronomy. The Maya, like the Olmec, observed and recorded the repetitive motions of the moon and planets to predict where they would be in the future. To allow for these predictions they developed their numbering system, based on twenty (compared with our base, ten), as described earlier. With these tools they could count and predict thousands of years into the future. The observations were made by priests to enable rulers to decide on propitious dates to launch wars and other important enterprises. The Dresden Codex includes ephemeris tables that predict eclipses, tables for the rise and transit of Venus, and a similar ephemeris table for Mars. The calendar was based upon the moon; months alternated between twenty-nine and thirty days.

A REVIEW OF CONTEMPORARY UNDERSTANDINGS OF PREHISTORIC ASTRONOMIC KNOWLEDGE[8]

The German scholar Ernst Förstemann identified Venus in the Dresden Codex with the number 584. This is the period of Venus's journey around the sun and the eclipse intervals when Venus could not be seen from Earth since it was behind the sun.

In 1917, Herbert Spinden concluded that the Paris Codex, one of the other surviving Mayan books, depicted a zodiac of thirteen constellations. In 1937, Alexander Pogo compared dates in the Dresden Codex with actual observations in the Mayan lands and concluded the tables predicted lunar not solar eclipses.

So by the 1930s it was generally accepted by astronomers that the civilizations of Mesoamerica had developed advanced astronomic knowledge thousands of years ago. Inscriptions at the Temple of the Sun at Palenque in Chiapas state enabled John Temple to show the Maya had a diary based upon the moon. Inscriptions on stelae at Copan record the vernal equinox and the winter solstice, while an autumnal equinox is recorded at Yaxchilan. The 26,000-year precession cycle described earlier is evidenced in various forms. Alonso Mendez and Edwin L. Barnhart have analyzed inscriptions at Palenque that they think equate to a solar year of 365.242203 days—fantastically accurate.

Ephemeris tables of the moon were also extremely accurate, according to John Justenson in 1989. Evidence of lunar dates are first recorded in 357 A.D. at Uaxactun. The eclipse cycle is evidenced at the Temple of the Sun at Palenque, dedicated in 692 A.D. The ratio of 81 moons in 2,392 days is equal to the ratio in the later Dresden Codex: The whole-number ratio is 29.530864 days from new moon to new moon—an error of less than ten seconds. Later astronomers claim the Maya were even more accurate—calculating the moon's lunation to within one second.

Anthony Aveni and others considered the Dresden Codex staggeringly accurate for Venus's orbit around the sun—an error of 0.08 days in more than 481 years!

There are important comparisons that can be made between Olmec and Mayan astronomy on the one hand and Shang and Han dynasty astronomy for the same era. According to Needham, Han dynasty astronomers also used a lunar cycle for their calendars—calendars of twenty-nine and thirty alternating days, the same system used by the Olmec and Maya. Han astronomers had also worked out the period of Venus's orbit around the sun as 584 days and meridian passage of the sun as 780 days (true figures 583.9 and 799.9). They had gone further in establishing Jupiter's orbit as 398 days and Saturn's as 378.

Needham also compared other interesting mathematical formulas in the Han and Maya calculations, using all the while two constants, referred to by the Han as *chi-mu,* representing a planetary cycle; and day, month, and year cycles, *thung-mu.*

> *With the Han value for the lengths of lunation, the smallest number of lunations which would give a round number of days was eighty-one (i.e., 2392 days) and when this was combined with the lunar eclipse cycle of one hundred and thirty-five months, the former multiplied by five and the latter by three, both give four hundred and five lunations of 11906 days. This is the shortest period of whole days in which the eclipses cycle could be completed and is identical with the Tzolkin of the Mayas.*

In short, the astronomy of the Olmec and the Maya coincides with that of the Shang and Han dynasties of China. The pyramids are also so similar that one must have copied the other.

Did the Chinese copy the Maya? This could be argued but it is not supported by DNA evidence. No indigenous American DNA has yet been found in Chinese people. There is, however, as Dr. Tony Frudakis stated in his speech at the Library of Congress Zheng He Symposium in May 2005, "substantial and statistically significant East Asian admixture in the DNA of Indigenous American peoples of twenty, thirty and sometimes forty percent."[9]

Moreover, as far as I know, there is no evidence of indigenous American peoples in or near Chinese tomb pyramids.

There is, however, copious evidence of Mongolian Chinese people at Olmec and Mayan tomb pyramids in the form of Shang dynasty writing at La Venta and other Olmec sites; a buried Mongolian general at the Pyramid of the Sun, Teotihuacán; East Asian admixture in the genes of Campeche Maya (Uxmal); Chinese faces and figurines at Monte Albán; graffiti showing Chinese faces at Tikal; Pacal's death mask at Palenque; and Chinese ceramics in cenotes at Chichen Itza and adjacent Maya ports.

So I say that the Olmec and Mayan pyramids were built using Chinese expertise—from Chinese people who were present at the building of thousands of pyramids in Mexico, Guatemala, Honduras, and Belize and who remained over many centuries to assist in developing astronomy. There was a very large number of Chinese in Mexico, Honduras, and Guatemala from 1400 B.C. to 1000 A.D.

CHAPTER 10

Pyramid Builders
of South America

The next logical step after our examination of pyramids and the pyramid builders of Mexico and Central America was to move along down the line to seek further similarities with ancient explorers in South America.

Aside from the pyramids themselves, there are smaller signs closer to the ground from which we can track proof of commerce and transportation of people and their ideas. For example, spondulix shells (*spondulix* means a form of money) thousands of years old, originating on the coast of Ecuador, have been found in graves at Tikal—evidence of trade between Ecuador and Guatemala. Small copper axes originating in South America and identified as currency have been found in graves at Copan in modern Honduras, not far from the Guatemalan border. We received photographs of giant Olmec heads found at Monte Alto, near La Democracia, on the Pacific slope south of Guatemala City, as well as other photos of a large lion that appeared similar to Chinese works, found at El Baúl, also near La Democracia.

All in all it seemed there had been trade between Ecuador and Tikal, and furthermore (as discussed in earlier chapters) between Tikal and Teotihuacán, north of Mexico City. I wondered if the Ecuadorean people who were trading with Tikal were pyramid builders similar to those in the north. Was there "a pyramid belt" across Central and South America?

In search of answers, we flew to South America to find out the age and type of pyramids in South America.

Whatever contact there was between South America's Andean coast and Central America, one has to note the extraordinary geography of South America, from northern Peru down to southern Chile. The Andes straddle the equator, and as they continue south they widen. Thus the coastal plain that is a hundred miles wide in Ecuador gets narrower and narrower until in Chile it is sometimes only twenty miles wide. A grassland plateau emerges between the peaks where the Andes massif broadens, some 11,500 feet high. Innumerable small rivers run westward from this plateau down to the Pacific Ocean, like the legs of a centipede. East of the Andes, a wide, hot, low plain stretches to the Atlantic. As moist winds spread westward, they deluge the Brazilian rain forest, then dump the residue on the Andes peaks, where, due to the mountains' height, it falls as snow. Between September and April the winds freshen and snow reaches the high slopes of the western Andes. With summer this snow melts, sending water cascading down the centipede-like rivers into the Pacific, through a bone-dry strip of desert along the coast.

The dry desert coast is a result of the Pacific's cold Humboldt Current, which flows northward from the Antarctic up to the Chilean and Peruvian coasts. The combination of this cold current and a persistent high-pressure system in the central Pacific prevents rainfall—indeed, there was no word for rain in either the Quechua or Aymara languages of Chile and Peru. In winter, however, the coast is covered by a fine mist that burns off in the morning sun. An old Chinese name for this fine mist was Peru ("pei-ru").

As the Humboldt Current rises to the ocean surface it brings millions of tons of plankton from its depths. Small fish feed on the plankton, attracting larger fish, which in turn attract sea lions. The rich water yields three-quarters of a ton of fish per acre, almost a thousand times the world average.

Birds gorge themselves on the fish: Millions nest ashore, providing an endless supply of guano fertilizer. So the ancient peoples living along the Pacific coast of southern Ecuador, Peru, and northern Chile had an endless bounty of fish, crustaceans, birds, and sea lions for food. Their rural valleys were full of water for a quarter of the year and they had plenty of good fertilizer. So it is not surprising that this stretch of coast has produced rich human civilizations since the dawn of time. The land has as much to offer as the Nile, Euphrates, Ganges, or the rivers of China or of Central America.

These rich civilizations produced art of great beauty and trade goods of considerable value. They would have been considered valued trading partners for the sophisticated Chinese.

Marcella and I first traveled to the Andean coast in 1997 and crossed the Andes by bus at Tambo Quemado, Bolivia. Then we descended to the Pacific near Arica, and headed southward into Chile. In 2003 we visited the glaciers of southern Chile. In 2006 we traveled south from Lima to Paracas. So we have traveled the whole Pacific coast of South America, from Ecuador to the Strait of Magellan, over the course of three journeys.

Our plan on our most recent trip was to head south and stop at five great archaeological sites on the way down through Peru to Chile. We planned to stop for a couple of days at the pyramids of Túcume, near Chiclayo, then at the pyramids of the sun and moon near Trujillo, at the huge ruined city of Chan Chan, at the pyramids of Sechín near Casma, then Paramonga, and finally the great pyramid of Pachacamac, south of Lima.

TÚCUME

The local people living in the narrow coastal plain of northern Peru call the dozens of pyramids that surround La Reya Mountain "Purgatorio"—Purgatory. Here the famous site of Túcume encompasses twenty-six major pyramids and platforms in a site of 540 acres.

This group of pyramids is in the fertile Lambayeque Valley, the largest valley on Peru's northern Pacific coast. Father Cabello de Balboa, a Spanish priest and writer who moved to Peru in the mid-1500s, said that Túcume was founded by Cala, a grandson of the legendary Naymlap, who founded the Lambayeque royal dynasty in around 1000 A.D. Cala is said to have gone to Túcume to "start new families and settlements, bringing many people with him." It would seem this was around 1000–1100 A.D., when the old regional center at Batán Grande to the south of the Chancay River was burned and abandoned.

NAYMLAP AND CALA

Folk legend says that Naymlap arrived in a fleet of balsa-wood ships, along with an entourage of courtiers, servants, and women.[1] He established quarters close to shore and built a temple called either Chota or Chotuna. Naymlap and his people prayed to an idol made of green stone he had brought with him. It was known as the god Yampallec, apparently the origin of the valley's name, Lambayeque.

Naymlap's name and image appear in ceremonial artifacts over time, including knives and funeral masks. Naymlap's name appears to come from the Muchik language, meaning "water bird." Figures of a plumed figure are often found on artifacts in the region. Local legend said he had at least three children, one of whom was Cala, the traditional founder of Túcume.

Evidence of Naymlap's and Cala's work is seen all around the Lambayeque valley. A large irrigation canal, the Taymi, brings water from the Chancay River (Ciudad Chancay means "City of Chinese Silk" in Spanish). There are numerous smaller tributaries leading off the Taymi Canal, resulting in very fertile land around the pyramids.

Huaca 1 is a stepped pyramid with a long, narrow access ramp. The pyramid boasts two huge plazas, the biggest of which is 689 by 259 feet. On top of Huaca 1 are a series of rooms at different levels with access ramps and stairways—probably living quarters of the Lambayeque elite.

Huaca Larga, or the long pyramid, is the longest adobe structure known.

Huaca Balsas nearby is little more that a derelict pyramid today, heavily damaged by El Niño floods and by looting. However, it has a beautiful frieze known as the "Mound of the Rafts," which shows a bird-man and a mystical bird leading a boat with crew ashore.

Much of the complex was built of baked mud bricks—millions of them in the tenth century A.D., before the site was conquered by the Chimu in 1375 and absorbed into the Inca Empire in 1470. Spanish conquistadors led by Pizarro arrived in the region in 1532. There are twenty-six large adobe pyramids located at the site, which covers about 540 acres. Eroded by centuries of flooding, the monuments are a shadow of their former glory. It is very difficult to reach any conclusions, save that the site and pyramids are enormous—a colossal endeavor.

The area around Túcume is delightful, featuring sugarcane and Peru plum trees. Museums display some of the riches extracted from the tombs, but many of the items excavated in graves at Túcume are now displayed in Lima, six hundred miles to the south.

From the tomb excavations we know that the Moche people who lived at Túcume grew corn, beans, chili peppers, potatoes, and squash and dined on ducks, llamas, guinea pigs, and fish. To this day cattle are brought down from the mountains in winter to graze on grass that grows in the mist created by the cold Humboldt Current. The most surprising aspect of the tombs when excavated in 2001 was the size of the bodies—between five foot, nine inches and six foot tall, nearly a foot taller than the average Moche—a dominant elite, perhaps from Naymlap's family? Some of the mummies had suffered from Asian viruses and diseases that must have been carried by sea, as discussed earlier.

From Túcume, we traveled about 150 miles south along the Pacific to visit the Moche pyramids, the Huaca del Sol and Huaca de la Luna, near Trujillo. We arrived in time to see a cold, misty dawn, no surprise. As at Túcume, the mist is produced by the Humboldt Current, and it burns off usually around three hours after sunrise.

One saw immediately that the Huaca del Sol has been badly damaged over time. The conquistadors actually redirected the flow of the Moche River to wash away part of the pyramid so they could reach the tombs below. Even so, the pyramid remains the largest man-made structure in pre-Columbian South America, reaching nearly 155 feet, as large as the Cholula pyramid. In 1990, nearly 65,000 square feet of remarkable mural paintings were found at the Huaca de la Luna (Pyramid of the Moon), several hundred yards away. The yellow, white, red, and black paint is in good condition and vividly depicts the feline deities similar to those of the jaguar we have seen all over Central America.

The pyramids are in such bad shape other than these friezes that it is difficult to make much sense of the site. However, we do know that in 1638, Father Antonio de la Calancha wrote he had found a huaca in Trujillo thirty-six years earlier that featured armed horsemen carrying swords and lances.[2] A reproduction shown on the next page features the carved swords of soldiers who could be Japanese, Mongolian, or, some say, Korean.

Reproduction of Oriental horsemen as described by Father Antonio de la Calancha.

Whatever those figures might be, the fertile plain that we visited, comprising the rich provinces of La Libertad and Ancash, includes one hundred villages and small towns that bear Chinese names and were there when the Spanish arrived.[3] The names not only appear to be Chinese—they have coherent meanings in Chinese. Chawán, in the district of La Pampa, in the province of Pallasca, means in Chinese "land prepared for sowing." Chankán (Chau cán), in the district of Cahvamayo, means "to harden metals." Was there a mine there before the Spanish came? Cha-Man (Chamán) means "covered in sand"; Chang-Ten (Chantén) is "crop lands" or "best quality"; Chaolán (Chaulán) means "prepare for combustion." Chu Chan, a hill in the district of Huancaverica, is Chinese for "dawn." Chulín (Chu-Lin) means "wood or forest." "Hong" (Hon or Jon) is Chinese for "red"—meaning red clay earth? Hupá (Jupa), cultivated lands in Huasta district, signifies a legume plant. Ko-Lan (Colán), a very old town at the bottom of a ravine, is Chinese for "difficult passage"—very apt considering the topography of the place. Lay-Chy (Laychí) is a sweet Chinese fruit. Lahán (Laján) means "clamor."

Lin-Chi (Linché) in Chinese means "snake." The village is

on the big, steep, rocky valley of the district of Chincha Baja. Mong-Tan (Montán) is on the summit of a mountain range from where the torrent of Montán flows. Mongtán in Chinese means "big stream." Pay-Han (Pay Ján) in the district of Trujillo means "damaging drought" in Chinese. Chan Chan (Chan Chán) was an area occupied by the Chinese where there are enormous ruins. Chan Chán was the old name for Canton in China—where there still exists a village called Chan Chán. Hong Kong (Joncon) on the River Moche means "red hole" or "red country."[4]

In summary, in northern Peru's Ancash and Libertad provinces there are ninety-five villages or towns that have names that are Chinese and have no significance or meaning in Quechua, Aymara, or any of the eight Peruvian dialects, nor do they mean

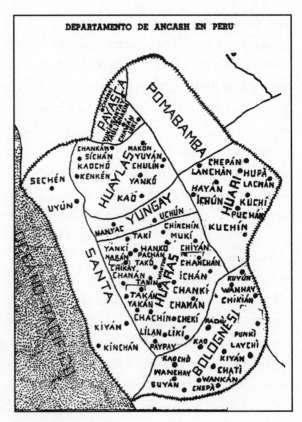

Map of the Ancash province in Peru, which contains a plethora of villages and small towns with Chinese names.

anything in Spanish. There are also 130 geographical names in Peru that correspond to the similar names in China.

The remarkable connection with China goes beyond names. The people in the Eten and Monsefu villages until one hundred years ago were said to have understood Chinese but not each other's dialects.

On the map below, the dots show Peruvian names that correspond with geographical names in China. They stretch from the borders of Ecuador in the north to Ka province in the south—more than a thousand miles—stopping where the full effect of the north-flowing Humboldt Current begins to be felt.

We have also seen that the Inca people of Ecuador have signif-

The dots on this map show Peruvian names that correspond with geographical names in China.

icant East Asian DNA as do people of the coast south from Ecuador. Juanita, the Virgin of the Sun, whose body (dated 1420 A.D.) is now at Arequipa University, also has Chinese genes—from Taiwan. It seems to me that enormous numbers of Chinese came and settled in Peru before the Spanish Conquest.

When we first visited South America forty years ago, the great city of Chan Chan, the largest pre-Columbian city in the Americas, was hardly known other than to archaeologists. Its awesome size and complexity have come to light only after years of intensive excavations. Three aspects are immediately striking. First is the colossal scale of the place. It covers 7.7 square miles, with a central 2.3-square-mile urban core dominated by a series of huge enclosures—a city more than twice the size of medieval London, meaning of the same era.

The second vivid image is the regularity of the enclosed area—rectangles within rectangles on a north-south axis with streets east-west and north-south providing access to the rectangles. The third powerful impression is the dominance of the twenty-five-foot walls both surrounding the city and within. It is a totally different urban plan from anything we have seen in North, Central, or South America. The plan could be a replica of medieval Canton (Chan Chán to the Chinese). Could the Peruvian Chan Chan (Canton) have been built by the builders of the Chinese Canton (Chan Chán)?

The similarities between Chinese and ancient Peruvian coastal cities is the subject of a study by Jorge E. Hardy.[5] Hardy gathered aerial photos and maps comparing the Peruvian Chan Chan and Chinese cities of the same period. He wrote: "We find an interesting similarity in urban plans and even in the elements utilized in their design between cities of Peru's northern coast and Chinese cities of the same epoch."

Hardy focused on a number of characteristics, including the notable wall around the Peruvian city, which was intended to separate Chan Chan from outsiders. He said that the building of an imposing wall around the periphery of a city was just as important to a small city as Chan Chán in China. "In both cases," he wrote, "the wall symbolized the abrupt physical and cultural separation of city and country."

Focusing on the layout of cities, Hardy said that both the Peruvian and Chinese cities of Chan Chan were similarly composed of straight rather than curved lines and that streets always met "at the right angles yet never forming a checkerboard arrangement." He described compact housing in both cases, which left room for open space in the city, "an uncluttered urban layout." He found that in the cases of both the Chinese and the South American ancient city, no single building dominated the landscape because of its size or importance as a structure. "Chan Chan huacas or temple mounds were only rarely built inside the citadels," Hardy said. "The blind walls of the dwellings, forming continuous plains interrupted only by occasional doorways, were the principal visual and directing feature of the streets of Chan Chan as well as those of Chinese cities."

Hardy's fascinating comparisons included an analysis of land tenure—in Chinese cities and in Peru's Chan Chan, land could not be privately traded. The lords of Chan Chan controlled land and water. Hardy compares the irrigation schemes of the Chinese with those at Chan Chan and the fact that the unskilled population lived outside the cities.

According to local legend, the Peruvian city of Chan Chan was founded by Taycanamu, who arrived in ships with dragon-headed prows—a royal fleet. After establishing a settlement he left his son Si-um in command and then disappeared over the western horizon from whence he had arrived. By 1450 the Chan Chan empire was at its height, stretching to Rio Chancay in the south, covering roughly 15,000 square miles. Chan Chan was at the center of a chain of local capitals absorbed into the Inca Empire between 1460 and 1480 under Topac Yupanqui.

Between Chan Chan and the interior, up to the foothills of the mountains, is the Pampa Esperanza irrigation system—a mass of canals originally with locks and sluices to collect and distribute rainwater from the centipede rivers. This fertile land is where the villages still now have Chinese names. China in the fourteenth and fifteenth centuries had extensive experience building locks, dams, and irrigation systems (please refer to *1434*, chapters 17, 18, and 22 for further information on this subject).

Here is a summary of the evidence, then: the legend of Taycanamu, the layout of Chan Chan, the irrigation schemes, Chinese names of villages, the presence of South American plants that were found in China before Columbus.

The obvious inference is that Taycanamu was one of Zheng He's admirals. This Chinese admiral founded the "American" Chan Chan based on Chan Chán (Canton) in China and started irrigation schemes that enabled crops to be grown for the inhabitants of Chan Chan and for export. Sweet potatoes in particular were shipped from the Americas across the Pacific to Asia and Oceania. Naymlap was, in my view, either a Song dynasty admiral or an officer of Kublai Khan's fleet.

This would explain the suddenly acquired metallurgical skills of the artisans of Chan Chan. It was built to serve as a trading city. There are nine large rectangular compounds within the city, each surrounded by high walls. Each of these is divided into three distinct sectors: The northern sector, which served as the main entrance to that particular compound, had a series of courtyards and storage and administrative areas. The central sector, which contained the king's residence, had a large burial platform in the southern sector. A large shallow walk-in well or sunken garden (the water table was higher in those days) showed Chan Chan probably contained many gardens, again as a Chinese city would have done.

Chan Chan's status as a trading city dealing in high quality and high added-value manufactured food is supported by archaeological evidence. In his book *Lost Cities*, Paul G. Bahn

The frozen Bering Strait and one of the Diomede Islands, located in the middle of the strait. Many historians believe that the first "Americans" arrived by traipsing across barren, icy tundra from Asia some fifteen thousand years ago. However, recently uncovered evidence shows that ancient man made abundant use of ocean currents and winds to sail to the Americas as far back as forty thousand years ago.

Images from along the Silk Route. Sad though it is to relate, the story of the Silk Route as a continuous conduit from China to the West, which supposedly facilitated fabulous Chinese ceramics and silk reaching Persia and Venice, is a myth. The Silk Road was a vibrant commercial highway, but the land route ended at Jiayuguan. Goods bound for the West must have gone by ship, not over land.

279

ZEA MAYS.— Linn.— Blanco.
VAR. COMMUNIS. Kunth.

Depicted here *(counterclockwise from top)* are zea mays, the great American crop otherwise known as corn; tobacco; and the infectious hookworm—items all understood to have traveled between continents after the arrival of European colonists in America and the proliferation of the slave trade. However, recent evidence indicates that these organisms must have been transported by sea centuries before the age of Columbus. For example, the discovery of hookworms in Brazilian remains dating to 7,200 years ago as well as in Amazon Indian populations allows for no alternative, as the parasitic worm could never have survived a slow, generations-long migration across the cold, harsh conditions of the Bering Strait.

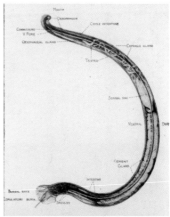

The stepped pyramids of China *(top)* are remarkably similar in shape to those found in Meso-america *(right)*.

Faces with Asiatic features can be seen clearly in Olmec art.

These pre-Columbian Peruvian ceramics display Asian features in the faces of their subjects.

Juanita, the Inca Ice Maiden *(bottom right)*, whose DNA was found to be Taiwanese.

Mesoamerican artwork displays numerous similarities with pieces found in ancient Asian civilizations. Parallels abound in both form and function between the works on the left (originating in China) and those on the right, each of which is highly suggestive of a direct artistic lineage from Eastern settlers to early American civilization.

The Aztec Calendar Stone (also known as the Sun Stone), discovered in 1790, is an enormously sophisticated artifact proving ancient Americans had time to develop advanced understandings of astronomy, geometry, and mathematics. While the Aztecs employed two systems of date (a 260-day religious calendar—*tonalpohualli*, as depicted on the stone—as well as a 365-day agricultural calendar—*xiuhpohualli*), other Mesoamerican civilizations, like the Olmec and the Mayans, developed very similar systems. Our research has uncovered startling links between the Olmec and Mayan calendars and those of the Shang and Han dynasties; overlaps in their practice of astronomy abound, as they both employed the same use of a lunar cycle–based month, as well as calendars of twenty nine and thirty alternating days.

"Nova Cataia," a Chinese settlement sheltered away for ages on Cape Breton Island, in Nova Scotia, Canada. The northernmost ancient Chinese oceangoing outpost we have yet discovered, Nova Cataia appears to have been the North American capital city for the Chinese. Depicted here is a cut stone (a piece of the expansive walls that would have protected the site) and the remains of stone terraces on this huge, tragically underexcavated and underexamined American settlement.

One of the Palos Verdes stone anchors, discovered in the 1970s by divers southwest of Los Angeles. After extensive research on these mysterious artifacts by both the University of California and the University of San Diego, we can now conclude that these anchors are Chinese in origin and have been lying at the bottom of the sea for centuries (as evidenced by manganese deposits built up on the surface of the stone). Though many have suggested that the anchors may have come from fishing vessels, the huge concentration that has been unearthed is much more indicative of a wrecked fleet, which further supports the theory that ancient Chinese civilizations traveled to the Americas in great numbers.

Cave art at Pedra Furada, Brazil, provides reliable and widely accepted carbon dating that extends human habitation back to roughly 40,000 B.C.

analyzes the nature of commerce and enterprise in Chan Chan. The diversity of production was so immense, archaeologists have concluded that "thousands of crafts people and specialized traders lived in areas surrounding the citadels (the rectangular inner compounds) providing the elite with imported and manufactured goods that included finely woven textiles, wooden and stone carvings, metalwork and pottery. Raw materials, such as stone, metal, wood, art work and even partially manufactured goods were brought to Chan Chan from the edges of the kingdom and beyond, mostly by caravan."

The beast of burden in those caravans was the llama, and scientists said the llama caravans must have been huge, with traders carrying exotic goods produced by skilled craftsmen from one capital to another, traversing the Andean peaks and valleys. "At least two separate areas within Chan Chan have been identified as caravanserais, centers of trade where the llama packers lived and traded. The traders enjoyed the privilege of living inside the city—an indication of their importance to the Chimor," Bahn writes.

Cities south of Trujillo down to Lima, such as Chancay, appear on Diogo Ribeiro's master chart of the world, published in 1529. This remarkable map was published before the first European expedition under Francisco Pizarro reached as far south as Trujillo, Chan Chan, or Chancay. Nevertheless, it named them "Cities of Chinese Silk." To have done so the cities must obviously have existed before the arrival of Pizzaro and must also have been trading in silk—which at that time could only have been imported from China. The imprint of this embroidered silk has been found by archaeologists at Chan Chan.

The full extent of the length and depth of Chinese trade on the Pacific coast of Peru is evident in exhibits at the Rafael Larco Herrera Archaeological Museum, in Lima. Rooms are filled with shelves containing 4,500 exhibits from graves starting in the Cupisnique period (1000 B.C.) through the Moches (400–800 A.D.)

to the more recent Nasca, Chimu, and Chanca periods. Claudio Huarache, the curator, showed me distinctive paintings of Chinese merchants from Moche, Chanca, and Nasca graves along the whole coast of Peru, from north to south and spanning the past two thousand years. A ceramic figurine of one of these merchants appears in the first color insert of this book. Evidence from the graves is corroborated by the Chinese customs and games that are still present in Peruvian and Chilean society.

SIMILAR CUSTOMS——CHILE AND CHINA

Some of the customs identified and compared between Chinese and South American cultures are quite distinctive. In both China and Chile, for example, people observe the same practice of covering chicken heads; they make similar types of lassos; and the Chinese and Peruvian method for treating smallpox is the same: they cover pockmarks with milk. As we've seen, Peruvian and Chilean cultures repeat similar legends about giants who come from the sea on fleets of ships. According to the Peruvian historian Maria Rostworowski de Diez Canseco, the Chinese lord based at Tambo Colorado in southern Peru was said to have possessed one hundred thousand ships. Peruvian use of *quipu* strings—a system used for accounting—is the same as in China.

Cristóbal de Molina says certain Chilean tribes have Asian names—Aruacans from Arual in Burma, Promancians from Prome, on the Burmese border; Poy-Yus from Po Yeon in Cochin China; Cunches from Cunchi in Sichuan; Pi Cunchi from North Cunchi ("Pi" is north in Chinese). In Peru the method of sacrificing sheep is the same as in China, as are methods for recording time by the meridian passage of the sun. Similarly, the determination of time by the moon's phases by adding one month every twelve years is the same in China and South America. To this day an oasis near Ica in the south of Peru is named "Huaca China," which is translated as "The Chinese Pyramid," a name given by the local Peruvian people in the Santa valley who claim that the site was once the burial place of Chinese.

THE COASTLINE OF SOUTH AMERICA

It seems to me the whole Pacific coastline west of the Andes, from Rio Esmeraldas in Ecuador as far south as Chilean Patagonia, was a vast series of Chinese settlements built up by repeated voyages over thousands of years, culminating in Zheng He's voyages. These later voyages are reflected in Zheng He's 1418 map and corroborated by the wrecked Chinese junks found by the first Spanish to round Cape Horn and sail northwards up the Chilean coast.

With all of the emphasis on Zheng He's map, we must recognize earlier Chinese explorations that paved the way for the voyage of 1421. The role of Marco Polo, sailing under Kublai Khan, has gained importance in our understanding of China's excursions to the New World.

PART III

China's Explorations to the North

CHAPTER 11

Kublai Khan's Lost Fleets

MARCO POLO'S ACCOUNT OF THE MONGOL FLEET

Marco Polo traveled from Venice with his father and uncle in 1271, when he was seventeen years old. He remained away for the next seventeen years and chronicled his life and adventures. In the third book of his travels,[1] he describes a fleet commissioned by Kublai Khan in search of riches on an island he had heard of:

> *Kublai the Great Khan, who now reigneth, having heard much of the immense wealth that was on this island [Japan], formed a plan to get it. For this purpose he sent two of his barons with a great navy, and a great force of horse and foot. . . . They sailed until they reached the island aforesaid, and there they landed, and occupied the open country and the villages, but did not succeed in getting possession of any city or castle. And so a disaster befell them, as I shall now relate.*

. . . And it came to pass that there arose a north wind, which blew with great fury, and carried the great damage along the coasts of that island, for its harbors were few. It blew so hard that the Great Khan's fleet could not stand against it. And when the Chiefs saw that, they came to the conclusion that if the ships remained where they were, the whole navy would perish. So they all got on board and made sail to leave the country. But when they had gone about four miles they came to a small island, on which they were driven ashore in spite of all they could do, and a great part of the fleet was wrecked and a great multitude of the force perished.[2]

A number of historians have rejected Marco Polo's account, saying that he made it up. However, a discovery in the late twentieth century showed that Marco Polo's story was in fact true—he only underestimated the scale of the invasion fleet.

In the 1970s Japanese trawlers operating in the sea off Imari Bay in southwestern Kyushu dredged up pottery and artifacts buried in sludge. In 1981, Professor Torao Mozai of Tokyo University began a search with sonar equipment. His team found a treasure trove—spearheads, warrior helmets, stone balls for catapults, a cavalry officer's sword, stone mills for grinding gunpowder, and anchors. A new museum was opened on Takeshima Island to exhibit the treasures. Local fishermen donated their own discoveries: a bronze statue of Buddha, and bronze seals of authority.

In 1991 the Kyushu Okinawa Society for Underwater Archaeology continued Mozai's work. They found an anchor twenty-four feet long and weighing a ton—clearly used for a huge ship. Its stocks were of Chinese granite, its flukes of red oak. Thick anchor ropes leading into deeper water led to the discovery of the first wreck of Kublai Khan's fleet. Within the wreck are more than seven hundred artifacts—day-to-day pots and pans and, most fascinating of all, exploding shells filled with shrapnel. Marco Polo's account has been corroborated.

KUBLAI KHAN

In the 1260s Kublai Khan's troops had rolled into China and Khan was enthroned as Chinese emperor and great khan of all the Mongols. He and his brother Hulegu controlled the world from the Pacific to the Mediterranean. In 1268 Kublai decided to take on Japan. The Japanese military rulers, the Bakufu, ignored his envoys' demands. Kublai therefore built a huge fleet of nine hundred ships and prepared to invade Japan from Korea—only the narrow Tsushima Strait, about one hundred miles of sea, stood in his way.

In October 1274, 23,000 Mongol Chinese and Korean soldiers joined 7,000 sailors and the fleet set sail. They overran the island garrison of Tsushima and then landed beside Hakata Bay. The Japanese fought bravely, falling back on the fortified capital of Kyushu. There on October 20 the wind shifted. Kublai's ships began to drag their anchors—nearly three hundred ships, a third of the fleet, were lost and half the army drowned. The survivors returned to Korea at the end of November—the Japanese were saved by the divine wind, the Kamikaze.

However, Kublai Khan was not the type of emperor to be put off by losing a few hundred ships. His envoys returned the next year to Kamakura, where the Japanese executed them—a dreadful slight on the great khan. This time Kublai ordered that a fleet of 3,500 junks be built in China and appointed 100,000 Chinese warriors for the next invasion of Japan.

Three separate fleets sailed for Japan in 1281, rendezvousing on Takeshima Bay. On July 30 another terrible storm struck. "A green dragon had raised its head from the waves . . . sulphurous flames filled the firmament." Thousands of ships sank, drowning a great part of the huge army. "A person could walk across from one point of land to another on a mass of wreckage." For a second time the divine wind, the Kamikaze, had saved Japan.

Kublai Khan decided on a third invasion but five years later, in 1286, he abruptly canceled it. He had a huge fleet at the ready but with nowhere to go.

FROM ASIA TO THE AMERICAS

After examining the Kangnido map at Kyoto, I decided to gather more evidence. This would take me across the Pacific to the Salish Sea (formerly called the Strait of Juan de Fuca), on the coastal boundary between the northwestern United States and Canada.

I set up a meeting with the eminent anthropologist, Dr. Gunnar Thompson, who I consider to be the leading expert on pre-Columbian voyages from Asia to the Americas. He has spent thirty years of his life on this quest and amassed a huge volume of evidence, publishing many very readable books in the process. *Nu Sun* tells the story of Asian voyages to America from 500 B.C. to 900 A.D. *The Friar's Map of Ancient America 1360* AD describes Nicholas of Lynn and the Franciscan Map of America; *American Discovery* is a summary of voyages over millennia, describing how the Americas became "a meeting ground of races and a congress of ethnic diversity—the first United Nations." If anyone knew of the travels of Kublai Khan's fleets, Thompson would.

In 2011, Thompson published a new book, *Marco Polo's Daughters,*[3] which was highly relevant to my search and described three maps at the Library of Congress, in Washington, D.C. The maps detail Marco Polo's voyage in Kublai Khan's ships to North America. The maps and descriptions were bequeathed by Marco to his daughters Bellela and Moretta.

Bellela tells the following story. Sometime around 1277 (or

1287, after Kublai Khan had abandoned his assault on Japan), Kublai's wife dispatched a Mongol fleet to convey a gift to the queen of Sakhalin Island—in short, diplomacy, not war, was now Kublai's foreign policy. Marco's ship was caught in a typhoon and was driven north to the Kamchatka Peninsula, known as the "Peninsula of Stags." There Marco met a Syrian fur trader named Biaxo Sirdumap, who told him that to the east lay a distant land from where the furs were obtained. Bellela's description accompanies a somewhat crude but easily recognizable map showing Southeast Asia, China, Siberia, the Bering Strait, Alaska, the Arctic Sea, and the northwest coast of North America. Thompson's request to have the Library of Congress map authenticated apparently has not been fulfilled.

The direct link with Marco Polo (apart from his daughters' notes) is a note on one of the three documents, the Pantect Map, with this inscription:

Map of India and Tartary by Marco Polo, of the numerous islands which he had explored, so that the Great Khan, to honor him, had entrusted him with authority over a province of his realm. No one had sailed more eastwards . . . a sundry desert three thousand miles from the realm [China]. But Marco Polo sailed with ten ships and went so far by sea that he reached a chain of islands and as far as a large peninsular. Caves on both sides were found there and people wear trousers and skirts of seal skin and deer skin. Done at Venice. c. AD 1329. Moretta Polo.[4]

The "Map with Ship" in the Rossi Collection clearly shows East Asia, the Aleutians, the entrance to the Northwest Passage, Alaska, and the West Coast from British Columbia to Mexico. It was drawn in about 1297 and is held in the Library of Congress. If the map is dated circa 1297, then Marco Polo, in Kublai

Khan's fleet, had "discovered America," and not Christopher Columbus—another applecart turned over.

The first European explorers who reached Siberia and Alaska by sea were Vitus Bering, the Danish-born Russian naval explorer, arriving in 1728, and whose name of course was given to the surrounding sea and the strait; and Captain James Cook, British Royal Navy explorer, on his third and final Pacific voyage in 1778. Therefore, if there were any European maps published prior to 1728 that showed the same area as Marco Polo's map, and if such a map was linked with Marco Polo's map, it would be evidence that Polo's map was genuine.

Thompson pointed to evidence that starts with the pioneering mapmaker, Gerardus Mercator, whose world map of 1569 shows Siberia, the Bering Strait, Alaska, and the Arctic Sea and was published more than two hundred years before Captain Cook charted Alaska. As a result, we can compare the two maps side by side, which shows their striking similarity. Thompson also provided the link between Mercator and Marco Polo.

Mercator wrote to his close friend John Dee, the English astronomer-mathematician-occultist, that he had obtained a copy of "a Marco Polo Map."

Mercator's 1569 world map also shows Hudson Bay, which Mercator describes as "Mare est dulcum." Yet Henry Hudson did not "discover" the bay until 1610, forty-one years after it appeared on Mercator's map. Did Marco Polo get to Hudson Bay?

I think he did. My reason, with help from Thompson, is Marco Polo's extraordinary description of Polaris, which he says was "behind him" whilst appearing to have a southerly bearing. How could Polaris, the North Star, be behind someone?

If Polo had been in the Beaufort Sea, skirting to the south of the permanent pack ice in, say, the McClure Strait at about 75 degrees north and 122 degrees west, as he believed, steering north by his magnetic compass, his true course would have been southeast. This is because the Magnetic North Pole, which is composed of molten iron, wanders about underneath the Earth's crust. Today it is leaving Canadian territory for Siberia. In 1569, when Mercator issued his chart, the reading would have been farther south, at the southern part of Melville Island, approximately 75 degrees north, 110 degrees west.

During Marco Polo's travels in the late thirteenth century, Polaris's apparent position would have been about 4 degrees offset from today's true north, at about 86 degrees north, due to the Earth's precession. So to Marco Polo, steering southeast but thinking he was traveling north, Polaris would have appeared behind his left shoulder. This is such an extraordinary phenomenon that Marco Polo must surely have been speaking the truth—he was approaching Hudson Bay.

Mercator's map of 1569 also shows the route eastward from Hudson Bay to the Atlantic—notably Baffin Island, the Davis Strait, Greenland, and the Labrador Sea. The first accepted European explorer to have reached those parts, Martin Frobisher, sailed there in 1576, though he did not enter Hudson Bay. So someone else appears to have provided the information to Mercator. Perhaps it was Kublai Khan's fleet continuing their voyage. Once in the Labrador Sea, the cold Labrador Current would have carried them southeast to the Grand Banks. There the Gulf Stream would have taken over and taken them northeast, in an arc across the North Atlantic. Had it been a calm summer it is entirely possible they would have reached the Azores.

It seems Professor Bruges-Armas and his team who carried out the DNA study of the Azores people were correct. They postulated that the Mongolians came to the Azores. Kublai Khan's fleet also reached the deep Antarctic, on a separate voyage penetrating far into the Weddell Sea, as his charts show. We can see from Zheng He's charts of the Antarctic that he built on Kublai Khan's, and discovered even more Antarctic islands and circumnavigated the entire continent. Kublai Khan's charts, warships, armaments, and experience provided an invaluable foundation for Zheng He's voyages.

We can, I think, be quite confident that Kublai Khan's fleets reached the Azores—from the Kangnido map (based on Chu Ssu-Pen's map of 1320), the description of the islands on that map, and the Mongolian DNA. Where else would Kublai Khan have visited after the Azores? The Kangnido shows the Mongolians knew of the Mediterranean and that it could be entered by the Straits of Gibraltar.

We can be sure Kublai Khan's ships reached Spain. A thirteenth-century account describes King James of Aragon receiving an emissary from the "Great Khan" in 1267.[5] An excerpt from chapter 457:

And, when we were come from Montpelier we went to Perpignan and arrived in this same day a message from the King of the Tartars. And we say that about this we were very honored because in that day had come a letter of the highest king of the world with a lot of love.

This information is confirmed in several documents and chronicles. Jerónimo Zurita, in his *Anales de Aragon,* wrote:

In the history of King (James I) it seems that several times he received embassies of the Tartars; and in the year 1260 he has wanted to pass with his navy to that part against the people of the Tartars, when I conjecture, because the wars that were within this nation and his king [Kublai Khan's invasion of China against the Song dynasty] had been requested for the great Khan.[6]

Certainly by this time sea trade between China and Mediterranean countries was commonplace. Ibn Battuta (1325–54) describes trade between Morocco and China. He sailed in huge Chinese ships manned by one thousand men, capable of staying at sea for months on end. In 1330–34, China's Wang Dayuan sailed along the same route but in the opposite direction of Ibn Battuta, from Quanzhon in China to Morocco and back again. He also traveled to northern Australia from China and chronicled his journeys in *Dao Yi Zhi* ("Descriptions of Barbarians and the Islands"). In this book Wang Dayuan describes an eruption of Mount Etna that did in fact occur.

Marco Polo's account of voyages in Kublai Khan's ships to North America also correlates with the map in the Doge's Palace in Venice that includes details of the Pacific coast from Alaska down to Mexico. Roundels on the map state it was drawn from information provided by Marco Polo and Nicolo da Conti (see second color insert in this book).

In summary, the evidence on these maps for Kublai Khan's voyage to Pacific America, on the Kangnido map for his voyages to the Atlantic, Africa, and the Antarctic, and the accounts of King James I of Aragon show Kublai Khan's fleets sailed the world and provided the world maps that Zheng He later greatly improved upon.

CHAPTER 12

The 1418 Chinese Map of the World

I have been studying the story of the great Chinese admiral and explorer Zheng He since a visit to Beijing in 1990. In 1418, Zheng He had produced a world map with features instantly recognizable then as they are today. Three years later, on New Year's Day, 1421, Zheng He helped bring foreign leaders to the inauguration of the Forbidden City, demonstrating his worldwide reach. My own research has taken me to every continent.

There has been a constant accumulation of evidence about Zheng He's role as an explorer, often accompanied by controversy about the 1418 map and the 1763 copy that we have available to us. However, nothing has shaken my clear view of the map's authenticity.

Just before publication of my first book, I reviewed Zuane Pizzigano's 1424 chart, which was uncovered in 1953 and is held at the James Ford Bell Library in Minneapolis. After analysis, the

museum curator, Emeritus Professor Carol Urness, agreed with
me that the islands shown on the Pizzigano chart were Puerto
Rico and Guadalupe. Hence somebody must have been in the
Caribbean seventy years before Columbus, to have so accurately
drawn the islands.

In October 2001, I visited the Portuguese archive, the Torre
do Tombo in Lisbon, established in the fourteenth century, to
research the possibility of a secret Portuguese voyage to the New
World. I was confident of finding evidence of the secret voyages
carried out by Prince Henry the Navigator's caravels, but to my
astonishment found that the Portuguese in 1424, when the map
was published, had known nothing of the islands in the Caribbean. However, seven years later, Henry sent caravels to find
them. In other words, the great navigator obviously knew they
were there. How?

Research also shows the Portuguese claim that Don Pedro,
Prince Henry's older brother, had visited Venice in 1428 and
brought back a map of the whole world. To the east, it showed
the way to China, and to the west, South America, with what we
now call the Strait of Magellan, called in those days the Dragon's
Tail. In short, the Portuguese were claiming that they had maps
of the whole world in 1428, before the first European voyages
of exploration started. Logs and records of the famous explorers
Columbus, Magellan, da Gama, Cabral, and Dias all showed they
had extensive charts of the world before they set sail.

I quickly found that the Portuguese claim was true. The Map
Library of the British Library houses copies of maps of different parts of the world, showing the world before Europeans
reached those parts. Australia, for example, appears on maps of
the Dieppe School more than two hundred years before Captain
Cook reached there; South America and the Pacific appear on
the Piri Reis and Waldseemüller maps, published before Magellan
set sail. So, although I could not at that time say that there was a
map of the whole world, I could show that the whole world was

charted before European voyages of exploration started, and that the leading European explorers had maps. Nobody could explain this.

The next major milestone came from Gunnar Thompson, who in 2004 was a visiting professor at the University of Hawaii. He was studying a map published by Albertin di Virga between 1410 and 1419. (The final figure in the date of the map is obliterated.) Nobody has ever doubted the authenticity of this map. I reviewed the map with him in April 2004 in the United States and was convinced that Di Virga's map was genuine. (You can view the map in the second color insert of this book.)

The map shows the whole of the Eastern Hemisphere—just as the Portuguese claimed—from the northwest Atlantic, right through to northern Australia. The shape of Africa is shown long before European voyages of exploration started; Indian Ocean islands appear eighty years before Da Gama entered that ocean; Japan is depicted more than a century before Europeans reached there. The north coast of Siberia is accurately drawn with its rivers one hundred and fifty years before the Russians reached them. The northern coast of Australia is in its correct position relative to Asia and Africa more than three hundred years before Captain Cook charted it.

Di Virga's map was discovered in a secondhand book shop in 1911 in the Bosnian town of Srebrenica, then part of the Austro-Hungarian Empire. The collector who purchased the map, Albert Figdor, took it to the Austrian State University in Vienna, where it was examined by the leading cartographer, Professor Franz von Wieser. Von Wieser authenticated the map the following year in his thesis *Die Weltkarte des Albertin di Virga* (The World Map of Albertin di Virga). The map was then photographed; authenticated photos were acquired for the collections of the Egyptian prince Yousuf Kamal and the Bibliothèque Nationale, Paris. In 1932, Figdor decided to auction the map, but it was stolen and the original has never reappeared. The map was brought to public attention by Leo Bagrow in his *History of Cartography* in 1959 and again in 1992 in *Cartographica*, then, finally in 1996 by Thompson, the first modern scholar to appreciate its immense significance.

The Di Virga map is detailed and accurate. The rivers Ob and Lena in Siberia, the Niger, Volta, and Orange rivers in Africa, the islands of São Tomé and Principe in the Gulf of Guinea, the Japanese islands are all shown with their correct shape and position. The position of Spain is accurate relative to Australia, of Siberia to South Africa, and West Africa to Japan. The map must have been a copy of a non-European map, because in 1419 (the map's latest possible date), European voyages of exploration had not started and the Portuguese had not yet traveled along the Atlantic coast to describe the contour of the shape of West Africa down to the "bulge." The only people who could possibly have produced the original map were the Chinese. To reach and map that area required a massive fleet and such a fleet must have been coordinated to sail the world at the same time.

It was evident that the Di Virga map would bolster my thesis on Chinese explorations and that one day the original Chinese map of the Eastern Hemisphere from which Di Virga had copied his map would be found. I based several talks about Chinese explorations I gave in 2004 and 2005 in Southeast Asia and China on the Di Virga map and outlined my arguments as to how, one day, the original Chinese map would be found.

The Portuguese claim that in 1428 they had a map of the Eastern Hemisphere that showed the way to the Indies was demonstrably true. But what of their additional claim, that in 1428 they also had a map showing the Western Hemisphere and what we now call the Strait of Magellan?

I turn next to the map published by the German cartographer Martin Waldseemüller in April 1507, whose credentials are impeccable and have not been challenged.[1] I reviewed the map, which was acquired by the Library of Congress in 2003, in the summer of 2004. The significance of the map is clear. It shows the Pacific, the Andes, and South America before Magellan had set sail in 1519. It therefore is evident that someone had been in the Pacific before Magellan and had mapped twenty-three thousand miles of the American coastline. The immediate problem I saw was that the map did not make sense: North and South America looked nothing like the continents as they are. They resembled an elongated snake. Waldseemüller had used the most extraordinary methods of projecting his map. It was projected from a globe onto a flat piece of paper in a heart shape. The consequences of this were that a degree of longitude near the equator was some ten times what it was near the poles and, conversely, a degree of latitude near the poles was some ten times what it was near the equator. Even more curiously, longitude and latitude scales varied from one part of the map to the other and South Africa poked out the bottom for no apparent reason at all. (You can view a photograph of the map in the second color insert.)

For several months I wrestled with how to make sense of this—how could I convert what Waldseemüller had drawn into a map that we would all understand? Then one lovely summer's day, as I was working at dawn in our garden gazebo, a heron arrived in the New River for his breakfast and perched just a few feet away. I watched the heron, admired its patience as it craned its neck over the river that runs at the back of our garden. Suddenly its neck pounced and then swelled. It dawned on me that if I reversed Waldseemüller's process and put back onto a globe what he had on a flat piece of paper and then photographed the globe, I would have a map in the form we would understand today.

So I immediately went to our basement office and photocopied Waldseemüller's map into black-and-white. Then I went down the photocopy of the Atlantic coast of South America and marked points every six hundred miles—a, b, c, d, and so on—and wrote down on a separate piece of paper the latitudes and longitudes of each point. I repeated the process for the Pacific coast of South

America and then of North America, finishing with the Atlantic coast of North America. I then transposed these points onto a globe and connected points a, b, and c. Suddenly there sprang out of the globe what Waldseemüller had originally copied from. An extraordinary likeness of North and South America to what we would recognize today, with its correct landmass, shape, and position relative to Africa. Before Magellan set sail, Waldseemüller had drawn a wonderful map of the Americas from a globe. I was certain that one day we would find the Chinese map of the Western Hemisphere that Waldseemüller had used.

With that knowledge I informed the Library of Congress, the owners of the map, and arranged to give a number of talks about my findings. The library invited me and supporters of the *1421* theory to speak at a symposium they were arranging in May 2005. I am most grateful to the Library of Congress for their courage.

The advance text of my talk, together with the supporting maps, was posted on our website in early 2005. The critics knew what was coming.

A group led by the National University of Singapore protested my appearance at the Library of Congress. The director of the library's Asian Division, Dr. Hwa-Wei Lee (now retired), succinctly replied in an email to the critics: "It is none of your business to tell the Library of Congress whom we should or should not invite to participate in our international symposium on Zheng He."[2]

After the Library of Congress's symposium in May I traveled to Asia and gave a number of talks in Singapore, Hong Kong, and mainland China in which I set out my reasons for believing that one day a Chinese map would be found whose Eastern Hemisphere is the same as Di Virga's and the Western Hemisphere the same as Waldseemüller's.

Again the fact that my journeys were promoted in advance, with details placed on our website, led to a barrage of abuse directed at anyone who invited me to give a talk. The invective was concentrated on the organizers of an exhibition in Singapore that was to be mounted from June to September 2005, titled "1421: The Year China Sailed the World." Our intention was to place the sequence of maps ending with Di Virga and Waldseemüller in this exhibition and also copies of even earlier Chinese maps of the Americas.

We highlighted Gunnar Thompson's findings concerning Kublai Khan's maps of the Americas, found at the Library of Congress, and Charlotte Harris Rees's collection of even older Chinese maps of the Americas, which she had inherited from her father, Dr. Hendon Harris. All of these were to be exhibited in Singapore. Despite protests—even a letter to the prime minister of Singapore—the exhibition attracted huge publicity in Southeast Asia and mainland China.

Harris Rees, in her book *Secret Maps of the Ancient World,* tells of the enormous fleets available to Chinese rulers since the time of Emperor Qin (210 B.C.), who sent a fleet to search for immortality. Tai Peng Wang has similarly researched the size of fleets during the Song dynasty, which ruled in China from 960 to 1279, as Thompson has done with those of Kublai Khan, who established the Yuan dynasty after that. The combination of these experts' views tells us that thousands of ships had been available to Chinese emperors for the past two millennia with which to sail to and from the Americas.

Chinese knowledge of the Americas is shown in ancient maps, not least the Shan Hai Jing, which Harris Rees describes so well.[3] In the millennia before Christ, Chinese maps show thin strips of land at the western and eastern edges of the world, with China in the center. (You can view a copy of one of the Harris maps in the second color insert of this book.)

The early Chinese explorers thus knew the latitude and positions of the Americas but they had no method of determining longitude, so they could only hazard a guess at their widths. This was corrected by Kublai Khan, who instructed Guo Shoujing to

devise a method of determining longitude so the true size of the
khan's empire could be known.

My prediction that a map would be found that showed the
entire world, Western as well as Eastern Hemisphere, came true
quicker than I imagined. A prominent Chinese attorney and art
and antique map collector, Liu Gang, contacted our office to in-
form me that he thought he had an actual 1763 copy of Admiral
Zheng He's 1418 map (see second color insert).

Liu Gang, a founding partner of the major Beijing law firm,
Commerce and Law, had come across the map at a small secondhand book shop in Shanghai in 2001. At the time, he hadn't heard
about the 1421 theory, and the claims that Zheng He had traveled
to America. Without context, Liu instead was simply impressed
with the map because it was so beautifully drawn and obviously
very old. His own judgment, based on years of collecting, was
that the map was genuine. He purchased it for five hundred dol-
lars as a curiosity, then filed it away with his collection of other
early Ming maps. He did take it out from time to time to examine
it, and showed it to an appraiser at Christie's who agreed that it
was very old and not a newer fake.

Four years later, in September 2005, Liu happened to spot ver-
sions of *1421* in English and Chinese at a bookstore in the Beijing airport. He bought a copy and opened it to the map tracing
Zheng He's voyages. Liu Gang instantly realized that the map
in his archive might be the most valuable map in the world and
certainly the first map of the entire globe.

He only contacted me after reaching out to six Chinese cartographers, enclosing photos of the 1418 map. When none responded
or even acknowledged his letters, he contacted my office on October 14 and after an email exchange sent us a copy of the map.

The problem was that I didn't see his message immediately,
because it was placed in a stack with other overnight mail. When
I finally did see it, I dismissed the copy and paid no attention,
assuming wrongly that it was a montage of Di Virga's map of

the Eastern Hemisphere and Waldseemüller's map of the Western Hemisphere. It was some while before my cowriter, Ian Hudson, brought the map to my attention and pointed out that it had come from Liu Gang.

Even then I was suspicious. The map still seemed to be a combination of Di Virga's and Waldseemüller's maps. If it were genuine, it was a substantiation of my explanation in *1421*, though it also meant that Zheng He had a whole world map even three years earlier than I had thought. Marcella and I discussed the possibility that I was being set up by a forger. Nevertheless, the details in both hemispheres were almost identical to Di Virga and Waldseemüller. If it had been forged, it would have been the work of an exceptionally skilled operator who was not only able to write in medieval Chinese but also intimately acquainted with the other two mapmakers.

After two days of debate, Marcella and I decided the scenarios for the map being a forgery were unlikely. Liu himself was a prominent person and his reputation as an attorney and as an art collector would have been ruined if he were caught knowingly passing a forgery. But if someone else had been involved, how might that have happened? Liu had bought the map four years before I had reconstructed Waldseemüller's. No one else would have had the raw material to do it. The same was the case with the Di Virga map. In 1419, the latest date for that map, European voyages of exploration had not started. How can you forge something that hasn't happened and that no one knows about?

Finally I traveled to Beijing to meet with Liu Gang. We decided to have the map authenticated and dated either at Cambridge University in England or Waikato University in New Zealand, both well known for their accurate dating of maps.

We also agreed that we would announce the discovery of the map three weeks after certification of the dating was completed— on January 16, 2006, in Beijing, and the following day at the National Maritime Museum in London.

Unfortunately, though, we hadn't accounted for Christmas, when the Waikato dating department would be closed, and so we wouldn't be able to meet the January 16 deadline. Despite the risk—both Liu's and my reputation would be shattered if the map were found faulty or fake—Liu and I decided to announce the map anyway. He agreed with my analysis that there was no way that a modern forger would have known about the existence of the other maps. In agreeing to announce the map, he showed a huge amount of faith in my judgment.

The news was covered in newspapers, radio, and television around the world. At the news conference, Liu made it clear that this was a stellar discovery with "the potential of the information in the map to change history."

Despite the care of our analysis, we met criticism and complaints once more, amazingly, in fact, even before some of our critics had even seen the map at our news conference. We subsequently learned that the premature statements that the map was a fake were coordinated by people at the National University of Singapore as a spoiling exercise.

Some criticism was expected, but the complaints were based on foolish reasoning. First, one critic charged that the Chinese in Zheng He's era did not know the world was round. This incredible assertion did not need answering—one might as well contend that the Ford Motor Company had never made automobiles. Second, some critics called it a forgery by claiming that a number of place-names on the map did not coincide with the names for those same places during the Ming dynasty. The most glaring foolishness came from the National University of Singapore, where some claimed that simplified Chinese characters used on the 1418 map did not come into use in China until Mao Zedong introduced them in 1949. This was easily proved to be incorrect—some simplified Chinese characters had been in use for a thousand years.

Every word that the critics alleged was not in use in the Ming was analyzed by our team, which included experts in Ming calligraphy as well as in Persian, Arabic, and in the languages of minority peoples within China that were in use during the Ming dynasty. We found that the critics were correct in stating that a number of the words on the map were not in use in the Ming, but they were in use by the Hui peoples of Yunnan and by Hui Chinese in particular. So we could show that the cartographer came from Yunnan and was a member of the Huihui, or Hui, people. This, in our opinion, only reinforced the authenticity of the map.

Nevertheless, we continue to weigh all criticism seriously; each challenge has been analyzed and we remain on solid ground. For example, we determined that the original cartographer was not only a Huihui, probably with a Persian background, but also lived and worked in Quanzhou (some names are slang used in Quanzhou).

Every criticism known to us has been placed on our website.[4] So, to the best of my knowledge and belief, the critics have failed across the board to show any inconsistency. By rejecting the map before they had seen it, some academics have, I think, brought their universities into disrepute, not least of them the National University of Singapore.

THE SUBSTANCE OF LIU GANG'S MAP

Liu Gang's map provides remarkable information about Zheng He's voyages. A full rendering of every place-name and the nomenclature of mountains, rivers, bays, inlets, and islands would take a book in itself. I have selected two examples—what is shown on the 1418 map in South America and the position of Australia. Later on we will consider the rivers shown on the North Atlantic coast of North America, as well as Europe. A full summary of what the 1418 map shows is provided on our website.[5]

The 1418 map shows South America with one apparently unknown river on the southwest coast, together with inscriptions that say in Chinese "Here the people practiced the religion of Paracas" and "Here the people practice human sacrifice."

I was not familiar with the reference to the Paracas religion, nor with the river of the same name shown on the map in southern Peru. Marcella and I decided to travel to the region in May 2006 to have a look. It was quite easy to narrow the search to that stretch of coast. South American civilizations there are as old as any on the planet. The Caral-Supe civilization is 4,000 years old. For comparision: Chinese civilization is some 3,900 years old; India, 4,600; Egypt, 5,300; Mesopotamia, 5,700; Minoan, 5,000.

The greatest civilizations on this stretch of coast, starting with the Caral, followed by Chavin, were based between the Lambayeque River in the north of Peru and the Pisco River in the south. South of the Pisco River, the coast narrows considerably and north of Lambayeque the Humboldt Current and fish supplies peter out. So this stretch of Peruvian coast was home to the richest civilizations of them all and would have been where the great trading cities existed when Zheng He's fleets roamed the oceans. We knew this was where we should begin our search.

Peru is awash with evidence of Chinese visitors for the past two thousand years. A list of the principal evidence is found on our website.[6] We've already discussed the villages with Chinese names in Peru's Ancash province. The Inca people have East Asian admixture in their blood to such an extent that their DNA profile could almost be called Chinese.[7]

It is relatively easy to narrow where Zheng He's fleets would have visited. Peru appears on the Chinese world maps long before the 1418 map was published. Zheng He's nautical chart also shows Peru. Peru also appears on Diogo Ribeiro's master chart of the world in 1529. Ribeiro's map, which was published before the first Europeans, that is, Pizarro's expedition, reached Peru, describes Peru as "province and cities of Chinese silk." Assuming that the latitudes on Ribeiro's map are correct, which they appear to be, it would seem that "the cities of Chinese silk" he describes were between Chan Chan, to the north of Lima, then coming south, Chancay, Pachacamac in the southern suburbs of modern Lima, then Paracas, four hundred miles south of Lima. Records tell us that Chancay suddenly started to mass produce pottery in the 1420s, some of which they called "china," so my first thought was that Chancay was the port that Zheng He visited. In medieval Castilian the name means "city of Chinese silk." So he probably did trade there, but unfortunately, on our journey we found that the place had been so badly looted it is impossible to be sure. So we needed other clues.

PARACAS

Soon after viewing Liu Gang's map of 1418, I researched Jesuit and Franciscan records to determine when the religion was first mentioned in European annals. To my surprise, there were no accounts of the name. To investigate further, we then drove south to the Paracas Peninsula, where today there is a national reserve protected by the Peruvian government. Within this reserve is the Julio C. Tello Museum, where we learned the answer to the riddle. The Paracas people buried their dead in very rich funerary bundles made of a fabric made from local cotton and vicuña wool, colored with the most beautiful natural dyes. The fabric was first seen on the Lima market in the late nineteenth century and examined by Max Uhle, a German archaeologist, who named it "early Inca culture."

In 1925 the Peruvian archaeologist Julio Tello visited the Paracas Peninsula and excavated areas that he called "Cerro Colorado" and "Wari Kayan." These were two cemeteries characterized by Tello as "cavernas" and "necropolis" styles. Tello realized that what he had found was not Inca culture at all but a new culture, which he called "Paracas." So Europeans did not know of this culture until 1925, yet it appeared with that name on Liu Gang's 1418 map. The name has been used by the local people for centuries and, in my view, would only have been placed on the 1418 map by somebody who had been there.

To the north of Paracas Peninsula is the Pisco River, to the south the Eka River. The Pisco and Eka rivers and their tributaries are the same shape as the river shown on Liu Gang's 1418 map. When we visited in May 2006 both were dry, although they had been running with water because their banks were lush and fertile. We traveled up both rivers. At one time the Pisco would have been at least ten miles wide, as one can see from the erosion of the cliff banks twenty miles upriver, near the ancient Incan outpost of Tambo Colorado. At Tambo Colorado the river forks, just as shown on the 1418 map, so it seemed to us that the Pisco River was the most likely candidate for that shown on the 1418 map. We decided to learn what the first Spanish found when they reached the Pisco, a century after Zheng He's voyages.

The most complete account of what the Spanish found is that of María Rostworowski de Diez Canseco in her book *History of the Inca Realm*. After explaining that the name Chincha is the equivalent of Chinchay (meaning "Chinese silk," in medieval Catalan), she describes the Inca "Topac Yupanqi's peaceful conquest of the Chinchas and how they were absorbed into the Inca hierarchy, and of the courtesy first extended by Topac Yupanqui to the Chincha leader and then by Huana Capac and Atahualpa." Rostworowski describes how when the the lord of Chincha met Pizarro, the lord was being conveyed along in a carriage without wheels in the same procession as the emperor Atahualpa. In short, the Chincha lord was of similar status to the Inca chief. Atahualpa explained that the Chincha lord once had one hundred thousand ships. Bartolome Ruiz, one of the first Spaniards to visit the place, described catching a Chincha raft at sea laden with goods of great value. Pizarro's coat of arms includes a Chinese junk, as one can see in Seville's General Archive of the Indies.

Rostworowski describes a number of similarities between Chincha and Chinese peoples. Alone among ancient Peruvian people, the Chincha were expert at astro-navigation using the star, Cundri. They were very skilled merchants, traveling as far north as Ecuador and using a type of copper money as international currency. They were expert smiths of silver and gold.

She also describes the legends of the people farther north who referred to foreigners arriving before the Spanish expedition. They came by sea in fleets of rafts. The foreigners settled among them. She describes Chincha as being a rich and prosperous province of Incas, speaking their own language, Runa Simi, rather than Quechua of the Incas. She concludes, "Why did Chincha become seafarers and how did they learn skills of navigation? Our present knowledge does not permit a satisfactory answer—perhaps they came into contact with navigators from different places who taught them maritime skills."[8]

TAMBO COLORADO: A CHINCHA CAPITAL

In *Prehispanic Cultures of Peru*,[9] author Justo Caceres Macedo emphasizes the importance of Chincha merchants. He describes an origin story in which the Chincha valley was conquered by outside invaders who were devoted to an oracle, Chinchacama. The Chinchas, Macedo says, formed alliances, grew in number, and traveled "to the land of the Collas and the shores of Lake Titicaca at the time the Incas were found in Cusco." Spanish explorers arriving in the sixteenth century found a vibrant, prospering Chincha society, "the most prosperous and prestigious in the Andes." He described commerce and trade as being extensive, moving beyond the Chincha valley, north on the Pacific coast to Ecuador, and south to Valdivia in Chile. According to Macedo, there were as many as six thousand Chincha merchants conducting such trade in the century before Spaniards arrived.

Chincha was conquered by the Incas during Topac Yupanqui's reign and annexed to the empire in 1476 A.D. When the Incas peacefully conquered the Chincha, they took over the site at Tambo Colorado and added new buildings to it.

RITUAL SACRIFICE

The 1418 map says the peoples of South America practiced ritual sacrifice. This is correct. About ten years ago, the volcano of Sabancaya erupted, splattering hot ash on the nearby volcano of Ampato, melting the snow. Further eruptions threw out of the melted earth the Virgin of the Sun, buried about 1440 after the ritual sacrifice. She was named Juanita. Her perfectly preserved frozen body can be seen in a deep freeze at Arequipa University. Her body was taken to Tokyo University for DNA tests and carbon dating. She died in about 1440 and hence was conceived in about 1425. Her DNA has substantial Chinese (Taiwanese) admixture. (You can view a photograph of her in the first color insert of this book.)

I believe that the river shown on the 1418 map is the Pisco. The people did practice ritual sacrifice and they did practice the Paracas religion. Some of Zheng He's sailors had love affairs with the local people and one of the offspring of these was the young Virgin of the Sun, Juanita. The Chincha were descendants of Zheng He's fleets.

AUSTRALIA

It appears on the 1418 map that Australia is in the wrong position. A number of critics have asked how this could be when Zheng He's fleets were so adept at astro-navigation and had mastered the principles of latitude and longitude. The reason is that in 1418

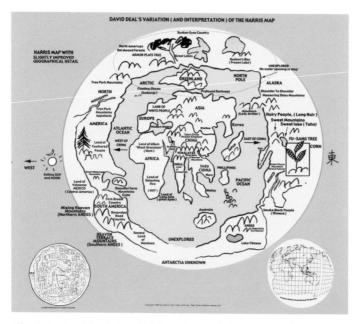

The "Hendon Harris World Map 5," one of the earliest Chinese maps of the Americas (c. 2200 B.C.), and David Alan Deal's modern-day interpretation of the "Harris World Map."

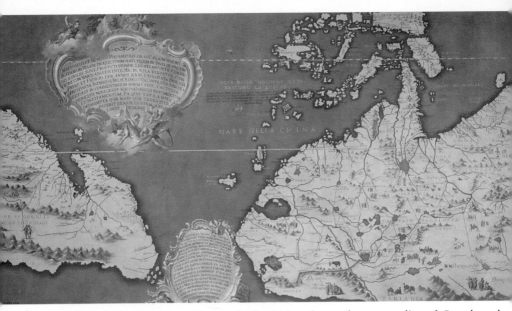

This map in the Doge's Palace, Venice, clearly depicts the northwest coastline of Canada and North and Central America set "upside down" (with the north at the bottom), as was the practice of Chinese cartographers. The map has roundels stating it was composed from information brought from China by Marco Polo and Nicolo da Conti.

Marco Polo's map—"The Map with Ship" from the Rossi Collection depicts a similar coastline to the Doge's palace map.

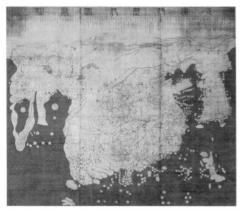

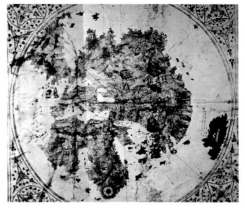

The "Kangnido" world map of 1402 by Ch'uan Chin and Li Hui shows the Azores in the Atlantic before the Portuguese discovered these islands in 1439.

Di Virga's map (latest date 1419) delineates the Eastern Hemisphere of the world with remarkable accuracy, before European voyages of exploration had started.

Left hemisphere of Shanhai Yudi Quantu, c. 1607.

The Liu Gang map, found in a small secondhand bookshop in Shanghai in 2001, proves that the Chinese in the era of Zheng He not only had a sophisticated understanding of Earth's geography but had indeed made exploratory voyages to the American continents.

"Universalis Cosmographiae," the Waldseemüller map of 1507, shows the Pacific coast of the Americas before Balboa or Magellan set sail. Compare the shape of the Americas with the Shanghai Yudi Quantu.

The right hemisphere of the Shanghai Yudi Quantu, c. 1607.

Waldseemüller's 1506 "Green Globe."

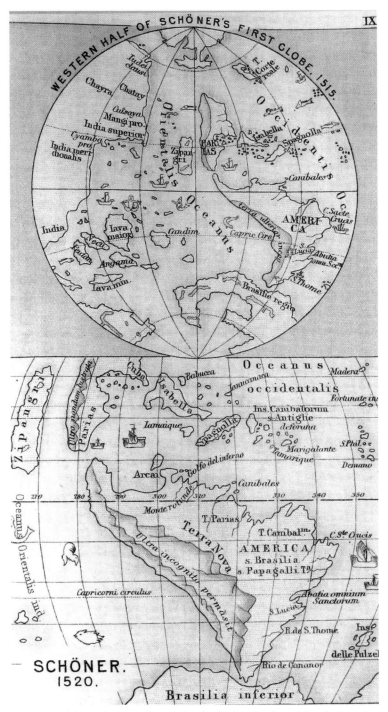

Schöner's globes of 1515 and 1520 clearly depict North and South America. They show the Strait of Magellan, supposedly first "discovered" after the strait had been drawn on these globes.

the Chinese had not worked out a method of projecting what is on a globe onto a flat piece of paper. The two hemispheres of the 1418 map are in fact a globe cut in half, with each half of the globe then drawn out as it looks to the observer on a flat piece of paper. Thus Australia is left dangling in the middle, between the two hemispheres, in the middle of the Pacific. The maker of the 1418 map solved the problem by superimposing the two hemispheres. In effect, this cuts out the Pacific.

If the two hemispheres are pulled apart, Australia is left dangling in the middle, in the correct position relative to Southeast Asia, China, and South America. We plan to use computer graphics programs in the future to place the two hemispheres of the 1418 map back on the globe, as they originally were. Unfortunately, such programs are extremely expensive.

Other places shown on the 1418 map will be described later. Let us now start with the visit of Zheng He's fleet to North Carolina.

CHAPTER 13

North Carolina and the Virginias

THE 1418 MAP LEADS US TO NORTH AMERICA

Further research into Zheng He's 1418 map takes us beyond the
original thesis I presented in *1421*. We have now been able to
broaden our search. Thus after 2006 I began to focus increasingly
on the role of rivers in exploration and settlement.

The areas of the 1418 map with rivers around them appear to
be described in the most detail. Rivers are the lifeblood of inland
civilization, providing much-needed nutrients and moisture for
agriculture as well as transport corridors and abundant fish for
food. Hence the great deal of importance that is afforded them in
maps of the world.

By looking at Liu Gang's map closely we can concentrate on
various points around the world that are of specific importance
and interest. One such area is the Northeastern Seaboard of North
America, which the 1418 map shows in great detail, with mountains and river systems delineated. Inscriptions on Liu Gang's

map note that "there are more than one thousand tribes and kings here. . . . Most of the people here have learned equitation and toxophily . . . anthropophagi . . . the land of this area is rich in gold and silver, and the people here use gold as currency. . . ."

The map shows two river systems on the Atlantic coast of North America. The northernmost one, opposite Greenland, is clearly the St. Lawrence River. What, however, is the southernmost river system on the North American continent, as depicted on this remarkable map? Although there is a wealth of evidence to suggest that the Chinese had navigated far up the waters of the Mississippi, this great river for some reason does not seem to appear on Liu Gang's map. The river system that we can see empties into the Atlantic on the northern tip of a promontory—in the same position and with the same shape as Cape Hatteras, part of the Outer Banks of North Carolina. Leading inland from Albemarle Sound, behind the Outer Banks, is the Roanoke River, forking just to the southwest then to the northwest, as shown on the 1418 map. The 1418 map shows this river branching into three arms—the northwest arm is in the same position as the New River (which becomes the Scioto River, located in what is now Ohio), the southwest arm is initially the New River and then the Tennessee, and the southeast arm is the Cape Fear River. This is corroborated by the mountains shown on the 1418 map; counterclockwise, to the north are the Blue Ridge Mountains, then the Cumberland Plateau to the west, to the southwest the Appalachians, and in the south the Piedmont. The only mistake the cartographer has made is to show the branches of the river joining near what is now Roanoke, Virginia, when in fact they all rise in the Appalachians, to the west of Roanoke.

The area around the Roanoke River system is replete with evidence of the Chinese fleet's visit. However, we were not the first to come to the conclusion that on crossing the Atlantic via the equatorial current, the fleets would sail through the Caribbean and then northward up the coastline of South Carolina, North Carolina, and Virginia.

I described earlier how Jerry Warsing used evidence about Machado-Joseph disease to analyze the presence of Chinese mariners in North America decades before the arrival of Columbus. In about 2000, Warsing came to the conclusion that a huge fleet under the command of Zheng He had met a storm off the Cape of Good Hope, which swept them north and then northwest before dumping them on the coast of Virginia, around what is now Southport.

Warsing's research, as I noted, began when he was contacted by a leader of a local Indian people, the Melungeons, to research into why the Melungeons of West Virginia have such a high incidence of Machado-Joseph disease.

Warsing's research, confirmed by scientific studies, showed that the disease was prevalent in Yunnan province, China, before the Portuguese got there; it also occurred among the aborigines of Australia (in Arnhem Land) and in Yemen. Thus the Portuguese could not have spread the disease to China—it must have been the other way around. This line of evidence led Warsing to Zheng He's voyages. By 2002 Jerry had come to the conclusion that a huge Chinese fleet had spread the disease around the world in the 1430s. He was considering writing a book about the subject in January 2003 when he heard me on the radio, being interviewed on *The Diane Rehm Show* on National Public Radio. He contacted me and invited me to Virginia.

The basis for Warsing's argument was that sailors aboard Zheng He's fleets were suffering from the disease and passed it on to people they met while ashore in foreign lands. With limited funds, he was able to carry out a little DNA research and found that some Mingo people had a high admixture of East Asian genes. Although the samples were too small to be statistically significant, Warsing considered the possibility that there might be some truth in the Mingo claim that they were not Indian people, but the descendants of shipwrecked sailors.

Concurrently, our research into the DNA of Native American peoples turned up some fascinating data. A pattern was developing—in every country that Machado-Joseph disease has been found, there is corroborative evidence of "Chinese DNA" among the native peoples. Gabriel Novick's report has shown that a significant quantity of coastal-dwelling Native American peoples have high levels of East Asian admixture that seemingly did not result from migration routes over the Bering Strait, but from sea voyages. In addition to DNA evidence, in all of the places where Machado-Joseph disease was found we had other corroborative evidence of the Chinese fleet having visited there.

Warsing's research into the Melungeons, coupled with ours and that of so many distinguished geneticists, produced quite a story. Further investigations led Warsing to the eventual conclusion that a fleet of some two hundred ships under the command of Zheng He had been wrecked in about 1432 on the coast between modern Southport, North Carolina, and Norfolk, Virginia. Confronted with the marshy inhospitable coast, they marched inland up the Cape Fear and Roanoke rivers and settled in the western foothills of the Appalachian Mountains between Salem and Asheville, North Carolina. Some of them also settled en route in West Virginia, where they left a proliferation of stone buildings—two-story stone houses, barns, and mills—as well as weirs, fish ponds, reservoirs, and the like. Warsing believed that they had also left a selection of Chinese plants, pallowaddy and rice, along the way. He believes their survivors are among the tribes of the Ming Ho (Mingo), Wyo Ming, Lyco Ming, Shawnee (name corrupted from Oceanye Ho), and Melungeons.

There were several ways of verifying Warsing's and our research. In my view, one of the key elements in piecing together the story of the Chinese visit to North Carolina and Virginia is the accounts of European explorers. If, as so many of them do, they describe meeting Chinese people on their travels in the New World, then surely this is the proof needed. The full results of our research are published on our website, but in short, in almost every place where we claim the Chinese settled, the first Europeans came across Chinese settlements. To us, this was incredible. How had historians managed to ignore Coronado's accounts of finding Chinese junks with gilded sterns? How could they explain away Columbus's secret records of his meeting with Chinese miners in "bird" ships, or the accounts of so many other historians who noted a Chinese presence in the Americas on their arrival there?

Warsing had come across similarly tantalizing accounts. He details the Oceanye Ho, whose name was later corrupted to Shawnee, a group defeated by a colonial army in 1794 at the Battle of Fallen Timbers, in Ohio. On their capture they vehemently protested that they were not "American Indians" but foreigners.

The Shawnee were also described in detail by Captain John Smith, the colonial leader in Virginia famed for his dalliance with Pocahontas, in the diary he kept while held a prisoner by Powhatan.

James Mooney (1861–1921), an early America anthropologist, lived among the Cherokee for a time and collected oral history accounts of Native Americans. In one account, Mooney tells of a visit to the Cherokee by very tall people from the west:

James Wafford, of the western Cherokee, who was born in Georgia in 1806, says that his grandmother, who must have been born about the middle of the last century, told him that she had heard from the old people that long before her time a party of giants had once come to visit the Cherokee. They were nearly twice as tall as common men, and had their eyes set slanting in their heads, so that the Cherokee called them Tsunil' Kalu', "the slant-eyed people," because they looked like the giant hunter

*Tsul' Kalu. They said that these giants lived far away in
the direction in which the sun goes down. The Cherokee received them as friends, and they stayed some time,
and then returned to their home in the west. . . .*[1]

This account tallies extraordinarily closely with the travelogue that a reader of our website referred us to by George William Featherstonhaugh. In his travelogue,[2] Featherstonhaugh
discusses the topography and geology of the area as well as the
flora, fauna, and the customs of the local native peoples, and their
treatment by the settlers.

In particular, he described a visit to what he could see was an
ancient mining site.

*Numerous heaps of the ore were lying about, with mica
slate containing garnets. . . . Several smaller excavations
had been made not far from this long one, and the rock
at each place was in the same state, bearing evidence of
having lain a very long period of time exposed to the
action of the atmosphere.*

A local man who accompanied him to the site said that old
Cherokee chiefs had told him they knew nothing about such
mining activity, and "that the Indians had never attempted any
thing of the kind, nor had any white men made them in the memory of the oldest amongst them."

But the man also told Featherstonhaugh that the Indians
spoke about the excavations in traditional stories, and that there
were strangers

*who came into the country they did not know where
from, with yellow countenances and of short stature.
That they behaved very civilly, and after staying awhile
and traveling about the country, they went away and*

returned with eight or ten more, and resumed their dig-
gings. After remaining some time, they again left the
district and returned a second time with about sixty of
their companions, bringing presents with them of cloth,
silk, yellow money, and other things, and began to es-
tablish themselves in the country by building huts, and
digging amongst the rocks.

The Cherokees, perceiving they always returned
with increased numbers, held a council, and deeming it
unsafe to have so many strangers in their country, sur-
prised and massacred them all. . . .

This is merely scratching the surface. We have collected countless legends of Native Americans describing how their "ancestors
came by sea from the east," how Chinese naval landing parties
were wiped out by Native American war parties, and huge ships
that sailed up rivers to explore these beautiful lands.

To sum up this part of our discussion, it's clear that a civilized
and sophisticated group of Chinese were living in the New World
by the time the Europeans arrived there. For further backup to
our studies, Ian was in charge of further investigations along the
Eastern Seaboard of the United States, this time ranging southward from Virginia to the Outer Banks of North Carolina.

CHAPTER 14

The Eastern Seaboard

The Outer Banks are a string of coastal islands that form a protective barrier along North Carolina, separating the Atlantic Ocean from the inland waterways of Albemarle and Pamlico Sounds. We had seen these on the 1418 map and this is where our research was centered.

Near the coast of southeastern Virginia and northeastern North Carolina lies the Great Dismal Swamp, behind which lies the sprawling Atlantic coast and miles of sandy white beaches. The Outer Banks are of particular historical interest in that pioneering aviators the Wright brothers, Orville and Wilbur, experimented with their crafts on the sand dunes, and this is where their first manned flight took place at Kill Devil Hills, just outside the town of Kitty Hawk.

As one drives south the peninsula becomes increasingly narrow, jutting out farther into the Atlantic until it comes back on itself, stopping at Hatteras Bight. There stands the 210-foot Cape Hatteras Lighthouse, the largest brick lighthouse in the United

States, which has guided and warned mariners about the treacherous shoals since 1802. Just offshore two sea currents collide—the Labrador Current, which brings cold water south, and the Gulf Stream, which carries warm waters north. Sandbars extend fourteen miles offshore, creating dangerous and narrow but navigable waters, and impassable shoals. Hundreds of ships have grounded or been torn apart in the turbulent waters over time, their hulks still resting in the sand. Not surprisingly, these waters have acquired a chilling nickname: the Graveyard of the Atlantic.

After arriving at the Outer Banks, Ian drove to the farthest point of Highway 12, which runs along the spine of the barrier islands, and then took a ferry to Ocracoke Island. People were preparing for Fourth of July celebrations and there was a weekend buzz in the charming tourist town center.

Ocracoke, part of Cape Hatteras National Seashore, is a long, narrow island with miles of sandy beaches. It was known to be a favorite anchorage for Edward Teach, otherwise known as the pirate Blackbeard, in the eighteenth century. It is also home to great biodiversity, not least the famed Ocracoke ponies. Legend has it that they were brought to Ocracoke and to the other outlying islands of Assateague and Chincoteague from European shipwrecks, but we had heard rumors of their Mongolian heritage.

Since *1421* was first published we have been inundated with information about horses and their presence in the New World. Horses were once believed to have been extinct in the Americas for more than ten thousand years, until they were supposedly reintroduced by Columbus and those who followed him. But early Europeans described horses being present and already in common use by many of the Native American peoples they encountered. This is noted on the 1418 map, where it is stated "most of the people here have learned equitation and toxophily."

The evidence is extensive. In the journal *Ancient American*, James P. Scherz interviewed a Menominee Indian named Pamita. When asked, "Did you get the little horses from the Vikings?"

she responded, "No, from the Chinese. . . . People from across the seas came to visit and we went there to visit. . . ."

In his book *The Horse in America,* Robert West Howard describes Native Americans in South Carolina and Georgia mounted on Chickasaw horses when European explorers first encountered them. These were small, hardy horses, different from European horses, but similar to the Tajikistan blood ponies used by the Chinese cavalry.

Howard mentions that in the early years of the colonies, wild ponies (small, like Chinese ponies) only 13 to 13½ hands high and 600 to 700 pounds roamed the foothills of the Blue Ridge Mountains. In 1670, tobacco planters near Williamsburg, Virginia, complained about the bands of wild horses. It is thought that these wild bands were ancestors of those now on Chincoteague Island.

We are also interested in the wild ponies found on Assateague Island, close to the Great Dismal Swamp. A wrecked Chinese junk was discovered in the swamp in the mid-eighteenth century, as we will later describe. There are many opinions as to the history and origins of the Assateague ponies, but none are conclusive. We think it more than possible that they are remnants of the great Chinese fleet, which had boats big enough to carry large quantities of horses for successful breeding.

James Bowles's findings on this matter are both concise and logical.

> *The fact is that the Columbian and pre-Columbian caravels from Europe were far too small for horses. Horses can weigh 1000 lbs apiece and more, and they eat, drink, and go constantly. . . . As for breeding stock, no one in their right mind would stable a stallion near a mare on a small ship. And no one capable of tying their own shoes would allow their breeding stock to escape them once the ship landed [as we're told happened]. Horses*

are far too expensive, and good breeding stock is far too
valuable, to allow that to happen. On the other hand,
both the Chinese junks and the pre-Columbian Arab
rigs were each of a style large enough for horses. . . .[1]

It is not a surprise that Chinese ships would have come to
these waters and that some met with disaster. Seafarers to this
part of the coast, renowned for its savage hurricane season and
treacherous shoals, would have been relieved to enter the relative calm of Albemarle and Pamlico Sounds. Here they could rest
in the lee-side shelter provided by the Outer Banks and plan at
what point to proceed to the mainland. Ancient mariners would
have found abundant food and water along the North Carolina
coastline.

As with their previous voyages, we are certain that the Chinese fleet would have left behind a cornucopia of flora and fauna.
The Virginias and North Carolina were no exception to this rule.

Along with the ubiquitous Chinese chickens encountered
all along the American coast by the Europeans who arrived in
the fifteenth century, there was a trove of other fauna that really
should not have been there. We have read European accounts of
unusual parrot species on the coast; Jerry Warsing's research includes information about interesting varieties of monkeys.

With regard to birds, we know that the turkey—a type of large
Central American pheasant—had reached the New World before
Columbus set sail. We have read records of turkey being eaten at
the feast celebrating the marriage of Philip II, Duke of Burgundy,
to King John of Portugal's daughter in the fourteenth century.
Turkeys are not known as long-distance flyers and must surely
have traveled there with human assistance.

ANOMALOUS DISTRIBUTION OF PLANTS

Various strangely anomalous plants and trees of Chinese origin were found in Virginia and North Carolina before they could have been propagated by the first settlers.

The legend of the Cherokee rose, *Rosa laevigata*, is a poignant story:

> *When the Trail of Tears started in 1838, the mothers of the Cherokee were grieving and crying so much, they were unable to help their children survive the journey. The elders prayed for a sign that would lift the mother's spirits to give them strength. The next day a beautiful rose began to grow where each of the mother's tears fell. The rose is white for their tears; a gold center represents the gold taken from Cherokee lands, and seven leaves on each stem for the seven Cherokee clans. The wild Cherokee Rose grows along the route of the Trail of Tears into eastern Oklahoma today....[2]*

However, there is evidence suggesting that the rose, which is native to Taiwan and southern China, appeared in the Americas before the Europeans came and expelled the Cherokee from their lands.

The incidence of rice paddies in the local environs was of interest. As was the wealth of mulberry trees, honeywort root, Yellow Delicious apples, and not least the empress tree, *Paulownia tomentosa*. The empress is plentiful, grows wild in the Virginias, and is considered an invasive nuisance in America. Empress wood, however, is highly valued in the Orient.

Giovanni da Verrazano, the Florentine explorer, reported finding orange and almond orchards growing in the Carolinas. Both Asian plants are the kind of produce that Zheng He developed for maritime supply.

Like Featherstonhaugh's account of the Chinese mining party massacred by the Cherokee, there are similar stories that reflect on the sophisticated technology that the Chinese brought with them.

Jerry Warsing has come across numerous unidentified stone buildings, although indigenous groups were not known to have built in stone. The first European settlers to arrive found the buildings already constructed when they arrived there. Warsing also has seen curiously anomalous stone structures at Walnut Gap Trail, near Asheville, North Carolina; walls in Fayette County, North Carolina; structures in Fort Branch, Pineville, Glenfork Junction, and Orton Rice Plantation, in Brunswick County, all in North Carolina; and another near Berkeley Springs, West Virginia. The writings of the colonist William Strachey seem to corroborate Jerry's research.

A SURVEY OF VIRGINIA

Our 2008 U.S. tour included a meeting with Charlotte Harris Rees in Virginia. She has been carrying on the work of her late father, Dr. Hendon M. Harris Jr. (1916–81), an American missionary based in Taiwan in the mid-twentieth century. Dr. Harris collected seven map books, which included unusual round world maps, and located twenty-three similar maps in international museums or collections. He was convinced that these maps were descendants of a long-lost "mother map" that originally accompanied the *Shan Hai Jing* ("Classic of the Mountains and Seas"), the world's oldest geography text, written in 2200 B.C. The *Shan Hai Jing* described exotic far-ranging expeditions, including to Fu Sang—a beautiful land to the east of China that we believe to be North and Central America.

After initially questioning the accuracy of her father's work, Charlotte decided to take his map collection to several experts for study. Meanwhile, in 2006 she edited and published a new version of her father's book, *The Asiatic Fathers of America*.[3] The maps have now been reviewed by such specialists as Dr. Cyclone Covey, emeritus professor at Wake Forest University, an author and longtime scholar of ancient American history. Dr. Covey is also well-versed in the *Shan Hai Jing*.

As Harris Rees's website, asiaticfathers.com, elaborates, "By the time of his death [in 1981,] Harris was aware of 23 other similar maps of this style (in addition to his seven) in prestigious museums and collections around the world. He correctly surmised that there were probably a few more. In effect, the true meaning of these maps has been hidden for years—right in plain sight.

"The Harris maps were printed from wood block. Most are on mulberry-bark paper and are written in classical Chinese. Although varying in ages they have only minimal differences. The oldest of the Harris maps are believed to be from the Ming dynasty [the 14th to 17th century]."[4] Harris believed that the maps descended from much earlier maps.

Charlotte's abridged version of her father's book won rare praise from a distinguished scholar, Dr. Hwa-Wei Lee, mentioned earlier, the former chief of the Asian Division at the Library of Congress. Hwa-Wei Lee reviewed *The Asiatic Fathers of America* and concluded:

This scholarly and yet easy to read book is a major contribution to the early history of the Americas and the relations to China and other parts of Asia. There is much evidence that Chinese were in America hundreds if not thousands of years before Columbus. Based on the rare Asian maps collection of her late father, Dr. Hendon M. Harris, the author has painstakingly researched, including using the resources of the Library of Congress, to present her findings that Chinese had indeed travelled by sea to the Americas since 2000 B.C. . . .

Harris Rees's research on these maps and the subject of early Chinese exploration of the Americas is spelled out in her books *Secret Maps of the Ancient World* (2008, 2009), *Chinese Sailed to America Before Columbus* (2011), and *Did Ancient Chinese Explore America? My Journey Through the Rocky Mountains to Find Answers* (2013).

A BURIED MING MEDALLION

One of the most fascinating discoveries about Chinese presence in the Americas involves hard evidence—a material find that supports the information we have gleaned from Zheng He's map. In 1994 an American antiquities collector, Robertson Shinnick, had begun using a metal detector to search for old coins and other items of interest and eventually focused on an old, isolated churchyard atop a hill near Asheville, North Carolina. After months, he came across what he first described as a curious three-inch diameter disc with a strange inscription.

Shinnick's find had been entirely a matter of intuition and luck, because he had no particular indication that he might uncover such an antiquity in that area. He had won the opportunity to search in the churchyard after being interested in doing so for some time. Though the area had seen modern development, including a church, Shinnick knew the history of the place. Records showed that a white settler, Samuel Davidson, had built a cabin there in 1784 but was killed by Cherokee who considered him a trespasser on their land. Shinnick's blog *Digger's Diary* describes the locale as having "many old tombstones in the cemetery and according to the sign out front, the original church had been established only a short time after" Davidson was killed. "The long-vanished original church was probably a log structure, as were most antebellum buildings in the region."

Shinnick conducted a number of surveys at the churchyard,

the first in the winter of 1994 during a driving blizzard. His early finds were U.S. coins from the late nineteenth and early twentieth centuries, but he continued searching the site through the spring and into the summer. Then finally in August, he dug out the medallion, "a curious bronze or brass disc, which had a plain back and a small cartouche on the front with Chinese characters. It was about four inches deep. I was mystified as to its identity. Obviously it was fairly old and had almost certainly been in the ground at least 50–100 years (after all, it was deeper than the 1894 half dollar that was found a few feet away, though that doesn't prove anything)."

Shinnick understood from the beginning that the site easily qualified as having been occupied by Native Americans for a long time before Europeans might have been there. Its attractive characteristics were obvious, including a promontory that offered a good view of the surrounding area. "Twice while digging in other churchyards in the area," he wrote, "I accidentally unearthed stone projectile points, one of them from the Paleolithic era." It made perfect sense. "What is good real estate today has usually been considered good real estate for centuries, if not millennia." Frequently, plantations had been built on Native American sites. For example, on the coast of Georgia he found fragments of pre-Columbian pottery, sometimes mixed with artifacts from the colonial period. "I often hunt these sites when they are being cleared for modern construction, which will add yet another layer to the archaeological strata. . . ."[5]

Nevertheless, in the case of the medallion, Shinnick did not at first think it had much value, even if it was obviously beautifully made. He put it aside as an interesting curio and thought little about it for more than a decade. Eventually, though, in 2006, he decided to search for information about the object using the World Wide Web, which of course was not widely available when he found the disc twelve years earlier.

The disc could have vanished into obscurity again had it not come to the attention of Dr. Siu-Leung Lee through a third party. Dr. Lee, a researcher living in Columbus, Ohio, was immediately intrigued by the Chinese inscription on the medallion, found to read in translation: "Authorized and awarded by Xuan De of Great Ming." A simple search showed that the Xuan De era (1426–1435) came in the reign of Xuan Zong, "the fifth emperor of the Ming Dynasty."

Without any idea of the authenticity yet of the medallion, Dr. Lee offered to buy the medallion from Shinnick. Shinnick agreed and sold it to Lee for what he described as a modest sum, "slightly higher than the very low value I had in my head, and I was satisfied."[6]

Shinnick closed his report on his role of the affair by saying that if verified, the find was evidence and an answer to "a potentially large historical riddle. . . . I personally can attest to one thing—the medal was truly dug out of the ground, by me personally, as I have described. Beyond that, the rest remains an enigma."[7]

Dr. Lee was a chemist, but had studied Chinese history and calligraphy for some time and hosted an online bulletin board, asiawind.com, which helped him gather information on Chinese antiquities, calligraphy, and culture. He started at the beginning by visiting the location where Shinnick had dug. He thought that the place where the medal was unearthed would be of vital importance—a place that was, sad to say, the site of countless battles and huge loss of life between the local peoples and the first European settlers. Hundreds of Cherokee Indians were massacred in many bloody battles. In 1776, right after the American Declaration of Independence was written, the United States government offered land grants to the soldiers in lieu of monetary payment. The Cherokee homeland was given to the soldiers, resulting in yet more conflict and massacre. The Cherokee people were later driven more than a thousand miles away to Oklahoma in 1838–39 in the historical event known as the Trail of Tears, during which thousands of Cherokee Indians died. During the colonial era, 90–95 percent of the Cherokee perished.

How could such a medallion end up on a rural hilltop in former Cherokee lands in North Carolina? Dr. Lee's analysis was astute and logical. He said, for example, that it was unlikely that a latter-day Chinese immigrant left it there in the nineteenth century. Chinese émigrés, of course, came to the United States starting after the 1850s, but most went as indentured laborers to mine gold or work on the railroads on the West Coast. They did not venture to the American South; convicts and slaves built the railways in that part of the country. Few Chinese came through Asheville. Even if a Chinese laborer at some point in history had ventured to the area, it was unlikely he would be carrying such a medallion; it was plain and not ornate and therefore did not have obvious monetary value. Neither was it likely that European missionaries might carry such an object with them.

In any case, Dr. Lee said, the medallion showed little wear or corrosion. On further analysis, it was found to be made of brass, which again would match with Chinese manufacture. It was during the Xuan De era that China began to blend copper and zinc to make the alloy, using it on precious vessels in which to burn incense.

The mere presence of a Xuan De Chinese medallion thousands of miles from China does not of course imply that it was transported there by the Chinese. Dr. Lee has, however, managed to piece together a set of corroborative concepts that seem to provide a far more convincing story. Slowly, Dr. Lee's early skepticism about early Chinese voyages to America was eroding. The medallion was apparent evidence of the presence of Chinese explorers, possibly Zheng He's team in the Ming dynasty, in the areas controlled by Native Americans before Columbus came to the New World.

While Dr. Lee did not make a categorical statement about the authenticity and dating of the medallion, his cautious approach did not stop the usual critics from declaring the find was a fake.

Dr. Lee's analysis was that the medallion fit into the way in which the Ming emperors conducted affairs. It was customary that emperors send gifts to other nations to announce their victories and successes. He said that such a medallion "represented the highest authority of the emperor and was only delivered by a diplomat like Zheng He or his deputy." After Zhu Zhanji died, China isolated herself from the rest of the world for another 150 years.

As Dr. Lee began to research the Cherokee in more depth, he found fascinating cultural similarities between the Native Americans and the Chinese. The Cherokee people have two original flags, one with a white background and a depiction of the famous constellation known as the Big Dipper in red, which they call the peace flag. They also have a war flag, with the same design but reversed in color.

As we have seen in previous chapters, the observation of the stars had been routine practice in China for thousands of years. The Big Dipper, part of the larger constellation Ursa Major, was regarded as the most important constellation by the Chinese, as far back as the first dragon motif in Henan, probably 6,500 years ago. The cup of the Dipper is typically used as an aid to trace an imaginary line to Polaris, the North Star. The constellation is featured on several flags in ceremonial parades from the Song to the Qing dynasty. The Ming emperors were especially fond of the Big Dipper in association with their Daoist beliefs. Zheng He used Polaris and the Big Dipper to calculate latitude.

Moreover, the Cherokee were not known to have a written language until one was developed in the early 1800s, never mind a need for recording their celestial observations. They had no knowledge of other constellations on record. So it is quite strange that they did not write, yet placed so much reverence on a star constellation that seemingly was of no interest to them.

Extending Dr. Lee's inquiry, it is still reasonable to ask why the medal had been found so far inland. Who could have brought it there and why? He had his theories and suspicions. But proof was wanting. The medallion was unique and unlike any other that has been found. He hoped that one day another would surface elsewhere in the world, and the strange brass medallion would be placed in its proper time and setting.

This leads to another story. The neighboring coastal tribe in the area, the Catawba, has a long tradition of making ceramics. Some of their pottery designs are very similar to the bronze censers made in the Xuan De era. They also make tripod pottery identical to Chinese ceramics, and are the only North American peoples to do so.

The Catawba and Cherokee were rivals but also traded with each other. Could the Catawba tribe have been the first to have made contact with Zheng He's fleets?

The Europeans, especially the English, had been trying to reproduce Chinese porcelain for ages, but without success. In 1712–22, a Jesuit missionary learned the secrets of Jingdezhen—China's world-famous porcelain capital—and wrote two long letters home about the process used there. However, European potters still could not produce true porcelain, for lack of china clay. The first production of white clay in North America was by the English-born potter Andrew Duché, who worked in Savannah, Georgia, around 1730. Several decades later, Josiah Wedgwood, the famed founder of the porcelain industry in England, dispatched Thomas Griffiths to America to look for china clay. Griffiths succeed in a nefarious manner: He kidnapped the wife of a Cherokee chief, and then forced the chief to lead him to a white clay pit. The Wedgwood company began to ship tons of the white clay to London. Even so, throughout the remainder of the eighteenth century, English porcelain simply could not compete successfully with Chinese imports.

All the while, however, pottery in North Carolina was being

produced in a style reminiscent of Ming pottery, produced both by Native Americans and European settlers. It had taken China close to ten thousand years to perfect the production of fine china, a skill not so quickly and easily learned, not even by the technologically adept Europeans of the time. How could the Cherokee and Catawba Indians master this technology so well?

Along with the prowess of Cherokee craftsmen, one must note that in the Cherokee language the word for china clay (*kaolin*) is *unaker*. In a Chinese southern dialect the word is strikingly similar: *uk-nake*. Is this a coincidence? The name *uk-nake* was used throughout the Ming dynasty. The word was then replaced by other terms, such as *kaolin* for china clay. A Jingdezhen porcelain expert told Dr. Lee that Zheng He, on his voyages, quite conceivably could have brought clay bricks (*petuntse* or *baidunzi*), and some of the porcelain workers could have been on board to look for new sources of raw materials. The knowledge of finding and preparing the proper clay material was very likely passed down by these Chinese potters.

THE GREAT DISMAL SWAMP

One final note from this portion of the North American tour was a stop at the Great Dismal Swamp, a visit to our "holy grail"—a wrecked Chinese junk that was first uncovered 250 years ago.

With so many Chinese arriving in the Americas, there was likely to be evidence of ships that had been wrecked there. The first great challenge the fleet would have come across would have been the tempestuous winds that batter the North and Central American coastline in the late summer and early fall. For as long as the region has been inhabited, hurricanes have caused untold damage and misery to coastal settlers, as well as the fishermen and merchants who ply its shores. With such a magnitude of hurricanes there were bound to be shipwrecks, and this was one of the first things that caught our attention in the area.

The Great Dismal Swamp appears to hold just such a mighty piece of evidence. The swamp was drained on commission by some friends of George Washington in 1769. In the course of their work, they came across a huge old Chinese junk. It was the stuff of rumor and legend; the fact was that no one could explain how an ancient Chinese sailing ship ended up in the muck on the Atlantic coast between North Carolina and Virginia.

The Great Dismal Swamp is an enigma—a huge expanse of forested wetlands formed more than one million years ago, where, despite its gloomy name, wildlife of all shapes and sizes thrives.

George Washington enters the story because he invested money before the American Revolution in projects to reclaim unusable land. He and others visited the swamp in 1763 and founded the Great Dismal Swamp Company. A portion of the area is now a U.S. national wildlife refuge. One of the canals built by the reclamation projects is named for Washington. In the course of dredging and draining, workers in the swamp company uncovered the hull of a boat in remarkably good shape. It was not a surprise that the wood was still intact and had not rotted. What was surprising was that the hull that emerged was that of a Chinese junk, and not a European caravel.

The waters of the swamp were already well known at the time for their preservative qualities; locals drank the water saying that its properties promoted long life. The amber-colored water contains acids derived from the bark of assorted trees that grow there—notably cypress and juniper. These acids prevent the growth of bacteria. The waters in the swamp are rich in minerals and low in oxidants, and thus the wood of the wreck was preserved in the swamp for many years.

At first, the discovery seemed astounding. But there was an explanation. The waters off the coast, as we have noted, are prone to forceful hurricanes, which sometimes can send storm surges far inland. Any ship caught in the rising seas and raging winds would naturally seek safe harbor in Pamlico or Albemarle Sound.

This was not at all a surprise to us, either. We believed that the junk sank in the swamp long before it was drained by Washington, since it was sighted as an old wreck before this initial drainage. We have corroborative evidence from the accounts of the first European explorers, including Pedro Menéndez de Avilés, who founded St. Augustine, Florida, in 1565, and others who had described the wrecks of Chinese junks, or groups of Chinese encountered both to the north and the south of the swamp. Furthermore, Francisco Vásquez de Coronado, another Spanish explorer of the same period, reported seeing junks with gilded sterns near an estuary of the Mississippi River.

Ever since the dredging work by George Washington's recovery company, reports of the Chinese junk in the Great Dismal Swamp have surfaced occasionally. However, evidence has remained elusive, among other reasons because the area was used during World War II as a practice site for air force bombing runs. Although a great deal of work throughout the years had gone into making the various canals in the swamp navigable, including their widening and the addition of several stone locks, as far as we know the wreck was not seen again until 1939. The U.S. Army Corps of Engineers had purchased George Washington's company for strategic reasons and built a canal linking the Great Dismal Swamp and Norfolk with Albemarle Sound, where the Roanoke enters the sea.

The Corps of Engineers kept detailed records of its work at the swamp. To date we have found the Annual Report of Chief of Engineers, U.S. Army for 1928, 1933, and 1943. These summarize the dredging and canal clearance, not least budgets and expenditure. The bulk of the expedition was in 1929 and 1932, and in the southern Elizabeth River rather than in the Great Dismal Swamp canal itself. While clearing the waterway they found the Chinese junk, which was obstructing the canal. They had to cut part of its hull to leave a navigable channel. The engineers' records do not say which waterway was being cleared nor do they give the position of the junk.

The next steps will be to locate the records of 1929 and 1932, the Corps of Engineers "Inland Waterway" wreck charts, and to search the Norfolk Maritime Museum's records and the U.S. Army Corps of Engineers Museum's records.

This fascinating story was also recounted in *Coronet* magazine in January 1945:

> *When the government took over the Swamp and dredged some of the ditches, strange looking hulks of ships were found sunk in their marshes. One, a large Chinese craft, had to be cut through. Sunk in her quagmires are the skeletons of other ships that now belong to the ages—all bearing silent testimony that Old Dismal's rule stretches far down the corridors of time. . . .*

The wreck was discovered yet again, on a third occasion, in 1943, when a fighter bomber took off from Norfolk Naval Base but developed engine trouble and crash-landed into the swamp. The U.S. Navy searched for the crash site and in doing so came across the junk. This information came to us from a family member of the navigator of the bomber.

Narrowing down the search to where we believe the search party for the missing bomber would have been, we can see that the runway from the Norfolk Naval Base is aligned 100/280 degrees. We therefore searched the Great Dismal Swamp along a 280-degree line from the runway, especially where it crossed channels. We found twenty-one wrecks but none appeared to be Chinese, even though some were very old. Besides exploring the area, we have also sought advice from local residents, historians, and farmers. To date nothing has materialized, but we are always hoping for the elusive phone call.

The 1418 map leaves no doubt that the river shown is the Roanoke and therefore that a junk sailed up river from Albemarle Sound. Traveling inland up the Roanoke, we reach the Chowan River, and then the Nottoway. A friend of the *1421* website, Richard Perkins, was brought up 120 miles up this river near the town of Jarratt. He recalls:

> *The place where I was raised was the uppermost navigable limits of the Nottoway River. . . . There has always been a story told around here that when the first white settlers (explorers came through the area) they met "white" people who were unknown to the English settlement in Jamestown and that these people were living in an established settlement in stone houses. . . . I do remember seeing the foundation walls. . . . Also I know of several locals who were in possession of blue and white porcelain fragments which were found in this area as well as one person who many years ago found a strange sword buried in the field for hiding. I have seen this sword once . . . it was dark colored but not rusted as one would have expected. . . .*

Chinese junks could have sailed up the Nottoway past the western edge of the Great Dismal Swamp, where one was wrecked in a location that is bearing 280 degrees from Norfolk Naval Base. The plane that crashed was airborne for around seven minutes before engine trouble forced it down. So we should be looking in the Nottoway River near Winton for both the junk and the crashed bomber.

It seemed that the Nottoway was drawing us closer to our goal. We had read several accounts of Europeans arriving in the area to find Chinese settlements already there. The real clincher was provided in October 2004 by a reader of our website, Alec Loker. Loker referred us to the records of the seventeenth-century

English explorer Lieutenant Marmaduke Parkinson, one of the first Europeans to explore North Carolina. The records of the Virginia Company of London describe his journey. He traveled north from Jamestown, toward the Potomac River. The records describe Parkinson and others visiting one of Chief Powhatan's houses, where they saw a "China boxe." On being asked how the box came into his possession, Powhatan "made answer that it was sent him from a King that dwelt in the West over the great hills [the Appalachians] some ten days journey whose country is near a great sea, he having the boxe, from a people as he said that came hither in ships, that were clothes, crooked swords and somewhat like our men and were called Acamack-China. . . ."

Powhatan's brother then offered to take Parkinson's group from their current location, Henrico, near the modern city of Richmond, Virginia, to visit this [Chinese] king, 150 miles west to the ridge of hills running south and north [the Appalachians]. "The discovery whenst will bring forth a most rich trade to Cathay, China, Japan and those other of the East Indies to the inestimable benefit of this kingdom. . . ."

The possibility of this mysterious settlement warrants more study, of course.

The main hurdle to tracking down present-day leads is modern development. More often than not, where once an old stone foundation stood, there now stands a school or shopping mall. Concrete evidence has often been lost to time. Sometimes, however, we can find remarkable evidence that has withstood development and discovery. This was the case of the settlement of Nova Cataia, sheltered away for ages on Cape Breton Island, part of the Canadian province of Nova Scotia.

CHAPTER 15

Nova Cataia:
The Island of Seven Cities

Important leads and angles in our research often have come to us thanks to dissemination and broad international interest in our books. We also benefit from leads provided by visitors to our website, along with meetings with like-minded researchers at the many conferences we have attended around the world. One such opportunity led to the examination of the northernmost ancient Chinese oceangoing outpost we have seen, a site remote enough that it has resisted discovery, analysis, and modern development. We have named it Nova Cataia, obviously a Chinese settlement of immense importance to our understanding of the discovery of the Americas.

The information came to us in December 2004 from Paul Chiasson, a distinguished Canadian architect. Chiasson spent his childhood on Cape Breton Island, on the far eastern coast of North America, to the north of the Nova Scotia peninsula. As a child he often explored the abundant wilderness of the island, and grew to learn about its inhabitants' history and folklore.

The local Native American tribe, the Mi'kmaq, established a cultured and civilized community. The first Europeans that encountered the Mi'kmaq reported that tribal members knew how to write on bark paper. In fact, the Mi'kmaq were the only indigenous people of North America who could write, and they also were well versed in the arts of astronomy and astro-navigation.

Mi'kmaq tradition has it that they were educated by a great god who had sailed across the ocean in huge ships with trees on their decks. The great lord was called Kluscap. Then, before the first wave of European explorers arrived, the visitors sailed away home, as quickly as they had arrived. In their wake they left remnants of their civilization—a stone city up on a steep escarpment overlooking the Atlantic Ocean.

Chiasson always recalled this as nothing more than a local fable, but about fifteen years ago he decided to explore it fully. He followed a well-built road lined by the remains of what appear to be stone walls that twisted up onto the side of a mountain from the desolate shore. At the summit, surrounded by the Atlantic on three sides, Chiasson came across the ruins of a deserted city.

Over the course of several years he researched the site, both up on the cold windy hills, and in libraries back at his home in Toronto. In 2004 he had collated sufficient information to give him the confidence to publish his research and announce it, alongside members of the *1421* team, at the Library of Congress's International Zheng He Symposium. His book, *The Island of Seven Cities,* was published in May 2006.

One of the first indicators of the site being Chinese were the ruins of a two-mile-long wall that surrounds the city. It originally had a stone base and was about fifteen feet wide and the same height—two-thirds of the corresponding dimensions of the Great Wall of China, and the same size as the Great Wall of Vietnam, which was built by Zheng He. Construction methods employed here included a rammed-earth base, also the same as those of the Great Wall of China.

The town could be accessed via a gate facing north—easily identifiable when Chiasson conducted an aerial inspection and took photos of the site. The ruins consist of a series of stone platforms, each situated in a commanding position, as the town slopes down to a river on its northern side. It is clearly a Chinese ruin; it is quite different in layout from Roman, Arabic, or European towns. It is about twice the size of Machu Picchu and a third the size of Roman London. Radiating from stone roads were outlying villages, again laid out by the rules of Chinese town planning. The roads are lined by stone walls with a total length of more than five miles.

Chiasson's first question was to figure out why the Chinese should settle on an incredibly remote and seemingly barren land off Nova Scotia. "Nova Cataia," as we shall call the site, happens to sit at the northern edge of the huge Emery seam of the Sydney, Nova Scotia, coalfield, the "Newcastle" of America. Coal was a prerequisite for driving China's industrial efforts and a highly prized commodity. Furthermore, the settlement was at the center of some of the richest mineral mines in the world. Prospectors would have hit the jackpot, with an abundance of gold, iron, zinc, lead, copper, cobalt, potassium, sodium, zircon, and topaz. Gold mines were found around the Bras d'Or Lake (the site controls entrance to the lake and its name means "arm of gold"). Gold is also found up and down the local coast. The site is ideally placed to exploit sea salt, gypsum, lead, zinc, antimony, manganese, and iron from the Kemptville seams in Yarmouth in the south and from the Clyborn valley goldfields in the north. All of these were within easy sailing distance from the settlement.

Cedric Bell, our compatriot, discovered ore, smelters, carbonized fuel, ore crushers, and a harbor with docks that had been built centuries before at the foot of the Chinese town, which today is called St. Peter's. As far as we are aware, Cedric Bell was the first to discover this harbor (in 2005). Bell, who has worked with us for some time, is a chartered engineer and member of the Institute of Marine Engineering, Science, and Technology.

According to Joseph Needham's seminal work, *Science and Civilization in China*, the Chinese have been crushing, separating, and smelting ores since the Han dynasty (220 B.C.). Nova Scotia's mining history includes the production of gypsum, anhydrite, salt, aggregate, barite, coal, gold, copper, lead, zinc, tin, antimony, and manganese. The East Kemptville Tin Mine has thirty-six minerals, including apatite (phosphorus), beryl (beryllium and emeralds), biotite (mica), bismuthinite (treating ulcers), lead, tin, antimony, fluorite (pottery glazes), galena (silver), pyrite (iron), dolomite (marble), copper, and quartz.[1]

For a relatively industrialized country such as China in the mid-fifteenth century, the wealth of the land would have been seen as a veritable treasure trove. From the abundant ores they could have made cast and wrought iron, steel, bronze, pewter, mortar, and a variety of glazes, paints, and medicines. The position of the settlement was ideal for a people who came to exploit the natural resources.

Below the ruined city lies one of the finest harbors in North America, around which a variety of trees grow—especially hardwood and pine required for ship repairs. The harbor is enclosed by a deep narrow channel that can be protected by cannon mounted on the headland on which the settlement stands. Similarly, the settlement is situated above another narrow channel to the east. This channel leads to a large inland lake rich in fish. Later this lake became a French center for collecting gypsum, coal, and furs.

The plateau in which the Bras d'Or sits is in effect a huge sponge. Rivers flow from the plateau to the sea, providing fresh water and the means to use locks to raise barges from sea to plateau (as in the Panama Canal); there is power for turbines to crush ore and fire smelters, water for paddy fields, and separate streams to carry sewage and effluent to the sea.

The surrounding sea, not least the Grand Banks, is the richest fishing ground in the world, where the cold winds of the Labrador Current meet the warm Gulf Stream. Walruses and whales, rich in fat and vitamins, congregate off the peninsula. All manner of crustaceans are abundant. Back on land, moose and elk and fat partridges are there for the taking. Wild berries are everywhere.

How would the settlers have arrived there in the first place?

A junk passing the Cape of Good Hope in South Africa would be carried by wind and tide to Nova Scotia via West Africa, the Caribbean, and North America's Eastern Seaboard. From there the Gulf Stream would carry the junk to Europe and back in a circle to the Cape Verde Islands, thence to South America and home to China via the trade winds in the Pacific Ocean. Cape Breton Island is in a pivotal position, and for that reason it became the focal point for early European exploration of North America.

EARLY EUROPEAN ACCOUNTS OF THE CITY

One of Chiasson's first lines of inquiry was whether the city was documented in European records of the time. He found several descriptions, but then all activity seemed to suddenly stop, around 1558. Nicolo Zeno (c. 1499) tells the story of a group of fishermen who sailed to Labrador then south along the eastern coast of Canada. On reaching Nova Scotia he discovered "a fair and populous city," where the king sent for interpreters to translate books in his library. Zeno says that the people of that city "in the past had commerce with our people" (that is, with Venice).[2]

Later, Miguel and Gaspar Corte Real (1501) brought back slaves from Nova Scotia to Portugal. We are told that one of the slaves wore "Venetian silver ear rings," and another possessed a gilt sword. John Cabot (1497) reported on his return that he had found "the land of the Great Khan." João Álvares Fagundes describes St. Ann's Bay, which the site overlooks: "in a beautiful bay [were] many people and goods of much value." Jean Alfonse, Jacques Cartier's navigator (1535–36), sailed from Quebec down the St. Lawrence and across the Gulf of St. Lawrence to Cape Breton Island, which he described as "a large island once populated by people." Alfonse further describes it as "Tartarie."[3]

Accounts by Venetian, Spanish, Genoese, French, Portuguese, and English explorers describe Cape Breton Island, Nova Scotia, as having a fair and populous city (which they never saw) with a good library, where the principal harbor sold goods of great value. Yet the site has never appeared on any maps at any time and remained, until Paul Chiasson's discovery, unknown. When the first European arrived they found no one but Mi'kmaqs. The Chinese had gone.

Accounts from 1558 and onward make no further mention of the settlement, although the headland on which it stands is depicted on maps without any sign of habitation or human activity. So it appears that sometime between 1536 (when it was last mentioned) and 1558 the settlement ceased to exist. Mi'kmaq legends say Kluscap prophesied the coming of the Europeans and sailed away with his family to his home on "the other side of the North Pole." Today the bay is deserted—the city abandoned.

LAYOUT OF THE CITY

Chiasson's experience as an architect was to prove vital in examining the layout of the site and the provenance of those who designed it. The site did not appear to be of European origin— the layout seemed to be entirely different to contemporary European cities. There was a significant lack of streets, village green, guildhall, or church. Also, most early European settlements in North America were built on the coast or beside rivers—never on mountain plateaus. Nor did it seem to be an Arab site. Arab cities radiate outward from a central mosque, formed almost like a spiderweb.

Chiasson's research led him to contend that the layout of the ruined city was Chinese, with a wall of "standard" Chinese construction. Typical layout was based around a series of courtyards, with houses coming off them. The foundations were of classic Chinese construction, facing south, with rooms leading off a central courtyard. Roads linking the city and outlying villages are dual carriageways of typical Chinese measurements, built in stone.

The villages are built on level high ground, with uninterrupted views over St. Ann's Bay. The villages command access to streams that flow north, south, and west down from the plateau of Cape Breton. In short, they are in a fine defensive position where one could observe ships entering and leaving St. Ann's Harbor and, possibly, bombard them. It seems arguable, therefore, that the villages are in fact a garrison with barrack blocks and stables. An army besieging the city would need to command the plateau on which the villages stand; it would have to land its troops from St. Ann's Bay, but that means being vulnerable to bombardment by troops on the plateau. So whoever commanded the plateau commanded the settlement.

By controlling the six fine harbors in the immediate vicinity of the site with an interlocking defensive system, the Chinese would have gained not only a protected anchorage where ships could be repaired and careened but also fresh water from nine local streams, an array of wood of different types, geese and seals, and the bounty the Bras d'Or Lake provided, not least coal, gypsum and copper mines, furs, freshwater oysters, and fish.

In May 2005 after talks at the Library of Congress's Zheng He Symposium, I went to Canada, accompanied by Paul Chiasson and Cedric and Patricia Bell, and visited Nova Cataia to see it all in person. Cedric and his wife spent fifteen days at the site. That gave Cedric enough time to conduct a survey with great intuition and at an astonishing speed, using magnetic anomaly analysis. (This method is described in more detail on our website.)

Cedric's research at Nova Cataia showed that Chiasson's historic discovery so far has only uncovered a small part of the Chinese base. It is vastly bigger in both scale and scope and probably would have required the work of tens of thousands of men to build it. This can be vividly illustrated by the roads that lead up to the site from both sides—from St. Ann's and from the Bras d'Or Channel. There must be more than ten miles of well-paved dual carriageway stone roads, protected along their length by stone walls, some of enormous cut stones. Cedric Bell's research detected the remains of stone gatehouses built into the walls about every hundred yards. From St. Ann's Bay around the north coast to St. Andrews Channel at New Campbellton, stone walls protect the site, punctuated now and then by gatehouses and canals. The scale of the whole endeavor is mind-blowing.

The scope of the site is as ambitious as its scale. From the ore crushers with water-powered turbines, as well as the grave sites and storehouses that Cedric Bell has located, it is obvious the Chinese came to mine and refine metal, not least gold—hence the obsession with protected stone-walled roads. They brilliantly exploited the character of the site, not only to provide food and water but also to use water power for a host of activities. An endless supply of fresh water on the plateau was channeled through aqueducts to wells to provide drinking water on the plateau as well as in the harbors below. The streams were damned by a series of locks to bring supplies up from the harbors to the plateau— coal and fish up, refined metal down—much as the Panama Canal uses variation to hoist cruise ships and tankers from Pacific sea level across the mountains to the Caribbean.

Other streams were used to provide washing facilities and toilets for the religious city and the many barracks found within the twenty square miles of the whole settlement.

WHY THE SITE HAS REMAINED HIDDEN

Due to the steepness of the escarpment on the east and west side of the site, the site can only be seen from the north, that is, from the sea. Here the Chinese were most ingenious in aligning the long axis of the site with the Ciboux Islands, which are about five miles away from the site and appear to be an extension of it. Mariners would be foolhardy to attempt to approach the site between the Ciboux Islands and the northern extremity of the cape on which the site is situated. In practice they would approach St. Ann's Harbor from seaward of the Ciboux Islands. Nearer the islands, the site is obscured by them; farther away it is too distant to make out detail. This, in our opinion, accounts for the Portuguese describing the site merely as "many fires burning" or "cape of smoke"—they could not discern what *caused* the fire and smoke. It also explains the source of the smoke. It also explains why St. Ann's Bay is described thus—"in a beautiful bay [were] many people and goods of much value"—without any description of how the people and goods got there before the Europeans arrived. As Chiasson repeatedly points out, no European ever saw the city, which has not appeared on any European map to this day.

Besides conducting a thorough survey of the area, Cedric also found what he believes to be concrete evidence of Chinese occupation of the site in the form of carved stone animal heads. Cedric has found these in other sites around the world and is sure that they are indicative of a Chinese presence. We have been requested not to show photos of the heads or give their precise location, because Cedric is worried about possible looting.

At the northern edge of the site, Cedric detected round Buddhist-like graves. The discovery is based on the magnetic anomaly survey—we have not disturbed the graves. The ideal Chinese location for graves is where there is a backdrop of distinctive mountains, and the graves face the sea or a river.

The graves are within seventy feet of a position predicted by a Buddhist priest to whom we were introduced in Hong Kong, after he had studied a topographical map of the site. We understand that the particular sect of Buddhists who we believed died there left nail clippings and pieces of clothing in the graves, but not the actual bodies.

THE MI'KMAQ

Mi'kmaq legend gives hints at the arrival of unknown beings. A version of the legend describes the dream of a woman long ago, when only Indians lived on the land.

> *"A small island came floating in towards the land, with tall trees on it, and living beings. . . . The next day an event occurred that explained all. Getting up in the morning, what should they see but a singular little island, as they supposed, which had drifted near to the land and become stationary there. There were trees on it, and branches to the trees, on which a number of bears . . . were crawling about . . . what was their surprise to find these supposed bears were men." Josiah Jeremy to Silas Rand in* Legends of the Mi'kmaq.

To me, this describes men manning the rigging and sails of a huge junk, hove to offshore. The Museum of Natural History in Halifax exhibits Mi'kmaq rock carvings, in particular one of a large ship with junk rigging and a high, square bow—in short, a junk. Mi'kmaq rock art also depicts men wearing long robes—not a European mariner's dress but clothes that the Chinese admirals wore.

Chiasson has studied Mi'kmaq history and culture in detail. The first Jesuit priest found that the Mi'kmaq had a written language, the only Native American people on the continent to be able to read and write, so we can assume foreign visitors had taught them. These foreign visitors were led by a venerable chief named Kluscap, who, according to the Mi'kmaq, lived on the promontory that Paul Chiasson discovered. Kluscap also taught them a civil way of life, including how to live in peace under good governance, and practical skills such as how to fish with nets and how to navigate by the stars.

Kluscap and his followers left at some point, legend also says, to return to "their homes at the far side of the north pole." They traveled once more on great ships "with trees" on their decks.

Chiasson's book describes the indigenous local people, the Mi'kmaq, as having a written language, and exhibits copies of this language modified by the Jesuits. Mi'kmaq history says the language was taught them by visitors who settled long before Europeans arrived on the site; that is, it was taught to them by the Chinese. Chiasson believes the Mi'kmaq were already Christians when the first Europeans arrived. They acquired Christianity from the Chinese.

COMPARISON BETWEEN THE MI'KMAQ PEOPLE OF NOVA SCOTIA AND THE YI PEOPLE OF YUNNAN

Yunnan province in China has twenty-six minority peoples, of which the Yi are far and away the most numerous. Kunming hosts a Yi village for tourists. The Yunnan Museum for Minority Nationalities is replete with artifacts, clothes, domestic utensils, and implements of the Yi people. We have found a number of striking similarities with the Mi'kmaq.

Mi'kmaqs and Yis delight in woven clothes featuring bold colors, notably red and blue. Both peoples wear long dresses and embroidered shoes—so similar are their dresses that if two mannequins were clothed side by side, one in Mi'kmaq and the other in Yi clothes, an observer could not tell the difference. Both Yi and Mi'kmaq girls are entitled to wear conical black hats on reaching puberty—as far as we are aware, they are the only Chinese people and the only Native American people to follow this unusual custom.

The similarities go further than hats, dresses, sashes, and shoes, extending to braided satchels, decorated baskets (colored with black ash), earrings, and necklaces. Both people make use of medicinal herbs and had sophisticated methods of catching and breeding fish—in stone fish ponds, and at sea using harpoons and nets, methods the Mi'kmaq say they were taught by the visitors who settled among them.

Both cultures play dice, love gambling and drinking, and played a basic form of hockey. Both have an extraordinary fairy story of a "Rabbit in the Moon." Mi'kmaq and Yis have similar methods of burying their dead and honoring their ancestors. Each one of these customs and ways of life could be a coincidence, but taken together, coincidence seems highly improbable.

After reviewing the breadth and detail of information, it is clear that Paul Chiasson's discovery is by far the largest settlement yet found. Nova Cataia appears to have been the capital city for Chinese settlement in North America. We really hope more of a concerted effort will be made to investigate the site in the future, and much look forward to reading the latest fruits of Chiasson's research.

CHAPTER 16

The Pacific Coast of North America

In *1421*, we discussed important evidence about Chinese explorations of the coasts of North, Central, and South America, including the discovery of a junk in the Sacramento River, and legends, artifacts, and linguistic similarities in Mexico, Guatemala, and Peru. But new information and discoveries continue to surface and Nova Cataia is but one of them. There are still two others to discuss now: one off the Pacific coast of the United States, the other in Florida.

The amount of new material since publication in 2002 has done much to strengthen our understanding of the role of China in Pacific exploration, all the way from Alaska down through Central and South America. Although the Chinese journey across the northern Pacific was assisted greatly by the Black Current, it was still a long and arduous voyage.

The Aleutian Islands are a cluster of volcanic islands that arc around the curvature of the Earth, on the fault line between the North American and Pacific plates. They would have been an obvious port of call on the sea route to the Americas. There are hundreds of the islands and they would have been very hard to miss.

As with several coastal communities dotting the rim of the Pacific, the indigenous people of the Aleutians have Chinese DNA, as evidenced by the studies of Gabriel Novick and his colleagues. There is in fact an astonishingly close similarity between the Alaskan (Aleut) and Chinese DNA—their genes are closer to each other than North American Indian DNA is to Aleut.

The DNA of the native people of Vancouver Island tells a similar story. We were made aware of the pioneering work of Professor Mariana Fernandez-Cobo in the *American Journal of Physical Anthropology* in 2002. Fernandez-Cobo studied the DNA of the Salish people, who populated areas of the Pacific Northwest and the northwestern United States, inland as far as Montana.

Fernandez-Cobo and her colleagues analyzed urine of the Salish, the Navajo, the Guarani of the Amazon, and people of mainland Japan. The DNA of all four—the entire sequence, CAGTTAGA—is identical. The odds of this happening are 65,536 to one. In our view, the Salish, Navajo, and Guarani DNA can only have come from the Japanese sailors who accompanied the Chinese fleets.

There are a series of maps supporting the theory that the area had been comprehensively mapped before the arrival of the first European explorers. The Queen Charlotte and Vancouver islands all appear on the Waldseemüller map of 1507, and also on the Zatta map, drawn before Europeans reached British Columbia.

Furthermore the Zatta map of 1776 actually goes as far as to describe Vancouver Island as "Colonia dei Chinesi"—a de facto Chinese colony. Antonio Zatta was a Venetian explorer and cartographer who traveled with one of the first Russian exploratory missions to the area. His chart was published before George Vancouver or James Cook sighted the islands in the eighteenth century. Zatta's explanation for "Colonia dei Chinesi" was that the information came from Russian explorers: "La parte del Nord-Ouest Dell'America e descritta secondo le recenti scoperti de Russi. . . ." (The area of Northwest America is described by the recent Russian discoveries. . . .)

Delving into Zatta's research, it appears the recent discoveries were by Aleksei I. Chirikov, a colleague of Vitus Bering. As far as we know, the accounts of Chirikov's discoveries have not been translated into English. However, we have been told that Chirikov mentions Chinese maps and giving local people in the Aleutians Chinese presents, in which they showed no interest.

We are particularly interested in finding other records of Russian explorers who reached the Pacific coast of North America before other European explorers did so. We have also seen two maps drawn by the sixteenth-century Flemish cartographer Abraham

A map drawn by Antonio Zatta in 1776 describes Vancouver Island as "Colonia dei Chinesi"—a de facto Chinese colony.

Ortelius (c. 1569), one from Hebei University, Baoding, and one from the Mariner's Museum in Newport News, Virginia. Both of these were published before the first Russians reached the Bering Strait.

On his second map, Ortelius shows the Bering Strait, although he lived two centuries before Bering and Captain Cook reached Alaska. Furthermore, Ortelius's rendering of China is drawn with great accuracy, including hundreds of names and features.

There are numerous accounts in which the peoples along the coast, from Alaska and down all the way to southern Chile, describe pre-Columbian contact with visitors from across the Pacific Ocean. Critics have derided these stories as optimistic legends, but when taken together—hundreds of accounts we have received over the years—they are impossible to ignore. History is said to be written by the victors. However, many of these peoples simply did not have written languages and have relied on song and dance to re-create their stories, passing down their valuable history to future generations. These folkloric tales tell of visitors arriving, some by mistake, in shipwrecks blown in from the ocean, and people looking for land for mining, logging, and agriculture.

Recently, a reader brought to our attention a very interesting article with accompanying illustrated plate, from the Smithsonian Institution in 1892.[1] This article, "Chinese Relics in Alaska," by Lieutenant T. Dix Bolles of the U.S. Navy, describes a wooden mask that was donated to the institution in the 1880s. It was taken from a grave located near Chilcat Village, on the border of Alaska and Canada's Yukon Territory. The mask includes two large bronze Chinese temple coins that were used to portray the eyes. The age of the mask was estimated by discussions with the local Chilcats, who indicated that the grave was that of a medicine man who had died two hundred years earlier. This would date the mask to the late 1600s, therefore preceding Bering and his fellow European explorers. Bolles wrote:

I am free to confess that I see no other possible conclu-
sion to draw than that these coins were obtained two
hundred years ago, and the natural surmise is that they
came from a junk driven on the coast, Chinese most
likely. . . . To those who doubt the advent of junks on the
West Coast at this early date, these facts will probably
not be satisfactory, but it will be necessary for them to
break down by direct evidence such a strong plea. . . .[2]

Other instances of Oriental artifacts appearing on the Pacific coast include hundreds of pieces of ceramics unearthed in the narrow valley between Washington State's Vancouver Lake and the Columbia River. These artifacts include figurines, pipes, pendants, small sculpted heads, and decorated bowls. The Institute for Archaeological Studies, based in nearby Portland, Oregon, concluded that they were Asian in form, but it didn't take the matter further.

An article in the *Daily Colonist* of Victoria, British Columbia, on August 31, 1933, describes a Buddhist relic found in the northern part of the province, which was eventually in the possession of John Forsythe. The Chinese talisman dating back to 200 B.C. was found in an Oriental jar with other early Buddhist relics, entwined in the roots of an uprooted tree several centuries old.

The native tribes in the area appear to have similar cultural traits to their Oriental counterparts across the Pacific. For example, we can see striking parallels between totem poles in Seattle, British Columbia, and up the coast to Alaska, when compared with a Chinese mythical symbol—Tao-tie (To-tin), one of a Dragon's nine sons. To-tin (or To-tim) pronounced in the more ancient Cantonese dialect is almost exactly the same as totem. Pronounced "Tao-tie" in modern Chinese (Mandarin), the association would have been less obvious. In North America, totem has evolved to a multi-animal symbol, including bears, birds, and people. The cultural connection between the Totim on Shang dynasty utensils and the totem poles of North America is strikingly similar.

Professor Siu-Leung Lee, the prominent calligrapher and ethnologist, also refers to a birdman display of the Haida nation at the University of British Columbia's Museum of Anthropology, in Vancouver. Haida Native American legends say that all people are derived from this birdman. The bird is a tribal symbol of the people in eastern China six thousand to seven thousand years ago, Lee says.

SHIPWRECKS

The culmination of our research would be to find a shipwreck in the Americas that can be dated to pre-Columbian times.

In our book *1434*, we provide a detailed account of the enormous tsunami that resulted from a comet impact in the Pacific Ocean.[3] Researchers at Columbia University's Lamont-Doherty Earth Observatory, in Palisades, New York, focused in on the comet, estimated to have impacted Earth some time between 1430 and 1455. The resulting tsunami was more than 700 feet high when it touched islands such as Stewart Island in New Zealand, 400 feet at the Australian coast, and would have been devastating along the North and South American coasts. Besides the group of forty or so shells of wrecked junks that Dave Cotner has located on the Oregon coast (described in *1434*), which slammed onto the shore, rumors abound of plenty of other Chinese wrecks scattered along the dramatic coastline.

One of the more significant, though still highly controversial, finds in the Pacific took place more than four decades ago. In September 2007 Ian met with Bob Meistrell, cofounder with his twin brother, Bill, of the Body Glove wet-suit company, in Redondo Beach, California, near Los Angeles. In the 1970s, Bob, an experienced diver, came across a swath of round, stone rings, some of which were more than three feet in diameter off Palos Verdes, southwest of Los Angeles. Further research was to show that these were in fact Chinese stone anchors. Since then he has been trying to solve the mystery of the Palos Verdes anchors. Bob and his team eventually managed to salvage a few of the anchors but many of them remain on the sea floor. (You can see a photograph of one of the anchors in the first color insert of this book.)

The area of the find is now overgrown with kelp and diving the site is not recommended, not least due to the great white sharks that patrol the area, known chillingly as "the Red Triangle." On land, the recovered anchors were investigated by four separate authorities, who were unable to come to an agreement on their origin. Some say that they were mined from local Californian rock by Chinese fishermen in the nineteenth century. However, we and many others think the manganese deposits that had built up on the anchors indicate they were under the sea for centuries. Such a significant quantity of anchors also points to a wrecked fleet, as opposed to sporadic wrecks of fishing boats.

A U.S. Navy ship also came across the stone anchors in 1973. The report from that mission also said the anchors appeared to be quite old and obviously man-made. Specialists said that the anchors appeared to be of a style used on ships in the Bronze Age, between 1500 and 1100 B.C.[4] Once more, any mention of such anchors coming from a previously unaccepted source brought rejection from the scientific community.

Two scientists in California, Carl William Clewlow, an archaeologist at the University of California, and James Moriarty, an anthropologist at the University of San Diego, confirmed in a news release that the stones were in fact Chinese anchors and might have been as much as one thousand years old. Chinese historian Fang Zhong Po published an article in the magazine *China Reconstructs* that described the anchors as "perforated stones . . . made from a rock commonly found in southern China." The anchor was secured with a rope tied through the hole. He said the practice of making anchors had existed in China for thousands of years.

There were additional reports about the stone anchors, some round, some rectangular, also with holes in the middle.

A second site was reported, this one by a research vessel, the *Pioneer*, which retrieved a round stone with a hole in it off Mendocino Point, California, five hundred miles north of Palos Verdes. Again, the stone was covered with a thin layer of manganese. Professor Moriarty said that that kind of stone was not found locally and had originated in China. Scientists calculated it had been on the ocean floor for between two thousand and three thousand years.

New reports published in 1984 said that thirty-five more anchors had been recovered from Californian waters around Palos Verdes, some weighing as much as three hundred pounds. They were judged to be as much as three thousand years old.

Eugene D. Wheeler, in his book *Shipwrecks, Smugglers, and Maritime Mysteries*, states that Chumash Indians had drawn pictures of Chinese junks in caves. The Chumash live along the coast of south-central California and in the mountains north of what is now Los Angeles. Wheeler said the find brought theories that Chinese seamen could have entered the Santa Barbara Channel before the arrival of the Spanish explorers. We are eager to see these drawings and to date them where possible.

Dissenters continue to say that none of the evidence is absolute proof of Chinese presence. Some said that the same type of stone could be found in Monterey, California, on the coast about sixty miles south of San Francisco. Others said that the stone anchor could have been made by Chinese immigrants to California during the California gold rush of the 1850s. According to this argument, those who didn't find gold went back to fishing, their traditional occupation. These latter-day Chinese fishermen used their traditional skills, making anchors from local stone, according to the theory, with large stones used to anchor ships and smaller ones tied into fishing nets.

Argentine cartographer and historian Paul Gallez said there was indeed a problem knowing whether an anchor stone was one hundred years old or one thousand years old. The presence of a manganese coating didn't predetermine absolutely the age of the stone. "Yet again," wrote Gallez, who died in 2007, "the experts seem determined to defend a pre-established theory rather than to seek a scientific truth, for fear that this might endanger the ideas they have been expounding for years. Resistance to change is one of the main brakes to scientific progress."[5]

It had become increasingly difficult against all the evidence and analysis to say that these anchors did not indicate Chinese visits to the North American Pacific coast.

Beyond anchors, paintings, and legends that mention foreign arrivals, in California there is a huge selection of foreign plants and animals found along the coastline. Not least are Chinese roses and hibiscus (*Rosa sinensis*), which were found by first European explorers; Monterey pines, indigenous to China, are found along the coast; and the Torrey pine, which grows in the San Diego area, as well as on Santa Rosa Island, off the coast of California, and in China. One reader told us how it is commonly known that the China rose we call "Old Blush" has been grown for centuries in California. It has been supposed that it was brought to the Spanish missions by Chinese traders. However, there is another Chinese rose, Chi Long Han Zhu (White Pearl in Red Dragon's Mouth), which was only imported from China in the last few years of the twentieth century. Chi Long Han Zhu is now obtainable from several sources in the United States. It was not known in the United States prior to its twentieth-century importation from China. However, the knowledgeable horticulturist Fred Boutin has found what appears to be Chi Long Han Zhu growing as a feral plant in the Sierra Foothills of California.

Another case of transplant is the peach, *Prunus persica*. The peach originated in China, where it has been cultivated since the early days of their ancient civilization. The peach is generally believed to have been brought to America via the Spanish conquest. However, Nancy Yaw Davis, in her book *The Zuni Enigma*, contends that the Spanish invaders, on coming into contact with the Zuni people of the American Southwest, found that peaches had been long cultivated there. This hypothesis is supported by archaeological excavations discovering peach pits that were believed to predate the arrival of the Europeans to America.

Asian-type wild horses were still running wild on the deserts between Redmond and Prineville, Oregon, in the 1930s and 1940s. They were said to be Mongolian horses. According to Dr. Judi West, they were small, short-bodied, with big heads, and were smaller than wild ponies or any of the other small wild horses that ran in the area.

Ray White, a horse breeder and veterinary surgeon, contends strongly that the American horse never was completely extinct, as commonly believed; he feels that the Appaloosa of the Pacific Northwest was of Asian extraction. The Appaloosa, used almost exclusively by the Nez Percé Indians, was, in White's opinion, more of an Asian breed than Spanish, as are most mustangs.

The Appaloosa was a recognizable breed by the time Lewis and Clark passed through the area. The Nez Percé were the only Native Americans who were breeding horses. They understood breeding the best stallions to the best mares and practiced gelding inferior stallions. All other Native Americans caught their horses wild or stole them from one another. The Nez Percé horses were highly prized by their neighbors. They were known for their speed, endurance, and surefootedness. They were short-legged, stocky, and had large heads and thick necks. Their spotted rumps are the defining characteristic today. All these characteristics were common with the "heavenly horse" from China.

THE ZUNI ENIGMA

The Zuni is a most unusual Native American Indian tribe, located about 700 miles east of the Pacific Coast in the state of New Mexico in the American Southwest. The extensive literature published on this tribe since the 1870s includes detailed migration stories about a search for the middle, the exact center, of the world. Dr. Nancy Yaw Davis reports her findings in her book *The Zuni Enigma: A Native American People's Possible Japanese Connection.* [6]

Yaw Davis proposes the Zuni tribe is unique in language, culture, and biology partly because of a relatively late thirteenth century A.D. migration from the Pacific coast by Japanese Buddhist pilgrims in search for the middle of the world: At Zuni they found it. Zuni DNA was included in an important study by Novick et al and indicates some surprising similarities with Japanese. Earlier studies on histocompatibility (HLA) revealed that the highly specific blood feature in Zuni, B*3501 subtype, is identical to Japanese.[7] The Zuni do not speak Japanese, but some words are identical and other linguistic parallels between the Zuni and Japanese are quite startling. Here are just a few: English meaning to be inside: Zuni = *uchi*, Japanese = *uchi*; English, meaning leaf: Zuni = *ha*, Japanese = *ha*; English, meaning yes: Zuni = *hai*, Japanese = *hai*; English, meaning to wake up; Zuni = *okwi*, Japanese = *oki(ru)*. Religious terminology include: English, priest; Zuni = *Shiwanni*, Japanese = *shinkwan, shawanni*; (Sanskrit, *shiwani*); English, middle; Zuni = *wannaka*; Japanese = *mannaka*; English, deity; Zuni = *Bitsitsi*; Japanese = *Butsu*.

The Japanese ceremony known as Namahage and the Zuni ceremony called Uwanaga are both intended to scare children to behave well and obey their parents. Masked monsters, considered to be from the land of the dead, appear carrying knives and other weapons and threaten to kill and then eat the bad children. The masks of both ceremonies have horns and large bulging eyes with long hair and beards. In both ceremonies the monster has assistants who help frighten the children and collect the gifts of the parents to supplicate the monster. In Japan and the Zuni areas, the masked monsters traditionally appear after the New Year's ceremony, in mid-January. Both ceremonies are associated with purification and with protecting fruit trees, especially peach trees.

The Zuni tribe can be linked to the Japanese on a biological basis by looking at their teeth. The prevalence of an extra cusp on the upper first molar, called the cusp of Carabelli, shows this. The percentage of Native Americans likely to have such a cusp is 60.2 percent. The Pima Indians who live near the Zuni are 53.3 percent likely, while the Zuni drop to a 36 percent likelihood, which is similar to the Japanese at 31–35 percent.

Davis summarizes her work:

> [E]vidence suggesting Asian admixture is found in Zuni biology, lexicon, religion, social organization, and oral traditions of migration. Possible cultural and language links of Zuni to California, the social disruption at the end of the Heian period of the 12th century in Japan, the size of Japanese ships at the time of proposed migration, the cluster of significant changes in the late 13th century in Zuni, all lend further credibility to a relatively late prehistoric contact. . . . [8]

Another example of linguistic admixture can be found in the accounts of Thomas Edwin Farish, a historian from Arizona in the early twentieth century. Farish wrote that the language of the Tartars was a dialect linked to the Apache nation. Farish recounted a nineteenth-century anecdote about W. B. Horton, the superintendent of schools in Tucson, Arizona. Horton had been appointed to run a trading post on the land of the Apache nation. At one point he went on a buying trip to San Francisco and brought back a Chinese immigrant as a cook. Horton, said Farish, one night heard the voices of the cook and some Apaches.

> *Wondering what they were doing there at that hour of the night, he opened the door and found his cook conversing with an Apache. He asked his cook where he had acquired the Indian language. The cook said: "He speak all same me. I Tartar Chinese; he speak same me, little different, not much."*

Farish reported he had heard of that before, that Chinese Tartar could speak with the Indians.

> *From these facts it would seem that the Apache is of Tartar origin. From the fact that the Apache language was practically the same as that of the Tartar Chinese, color is given to the theory . . . that Western America was "originally peopled by the Chinese, or, at least, that the greater part of the new world civilization may be attributed to these people. . . ."*[9]

These provide a snapshot of some of the many streams of evidence for transcultural diffusionism, which have been uncovered over the years on the Pacific coast of the Americas. The evidence mounts, showing that pre-Columbian contact between Asia and the Americas has been consistent and significant. The "established" version of history negates this evidence as optimistic fallacy. However, as far as we can see, the torrent of evidence continues, and we are sure that the floodgates will burst someday soon.

In the meantime, we will turn to east central Florida, where despite encroaching development, another remarkable major discovery has occurred. Much more work is to be done.

CHAPTER 17

Stone Age Sailors: The "Windover Bog" People of Florida

In 1982, a backhoe operator outside Titusville, Florida, discovered bones as he dug into the rich soil at the bottom of a pond at Windover Farm, which was being prepared for a housing subdivision. That discovery led to the start of the Windsor Archaeological Research Project. Eventually, this would provide some scattered impressions about the lives and customs of a lost civilization that, still unidentified, was perhaps of European origin, people who came to the New World more than seven thousand years ago.

After the first discovery of the bones, further investigation revealed a graveyard with the remains of about 168 individuals, along with their implements and artifacts. The cemetery rests in the peat layer beneath the pond, close to Interstate 95 in Brevard

County, Florida, within a few miles of Cape Canaveral and about sixty miles from Disney World.[1]

The developers of the site, EKS Corporation, called in archaeologists and funded a project to study and conduct radiocarbon testing, which produced the result that the human remains were more than seven thousand years old.

As more skeletal remains emerged from the bog, scientists described the area as one of the most significant ancient cemeteries ever found. The characteristics of the bog layer had left the remains in a remarkable state of preservation.

One striking and poignant find about the remains was a child determined to be about three years old, wrapped in fabric that was made from native fibrous plants, and with toys in her arms, an object resembling a mortar and pestle, and a turtle shell.

The degree of preservation, in fact, was so remarkable that scientists found brain tissue, first in a woman judged to be forty-five years old, and later, in 1991, in recovered skulls; in some cases the brains were complete and intact. The brain matter had decreased in mass to about a third of its original size, but the characteristics of the brains were easily recognizable—each hemisphere and other details were evident. The discovery of brain matter that old, and the opportunity to analyze brain chemistry and DNA, was unique.

Glen H. Doran, chairman of the anthropology department of Florida State University, was one of the first scientists to study the find. Doran described such details as extremely worn teeth and the absence of ceramic artifacts, which indicated that the grave site was likely more than three thousand years old. Their ancestors, however, appear to have arrived in North America as many as seven thousand years earlier than that.

There also were indications that the recovered skulls had shapes that were not consistent with the heads of peoples usually categorized as Native Americans. Doran and other anthropologists were able to catalog the characteristics of the 168 people in the cemetery. They established profiles of who the people were, how they lived, and how long they lived. They determined that 67 of the individuals were younger than seventeen; they had an average life expectancy of 27–30, but if they lived that long they might live for about twenty more years. Some lived into their sixties and two of the individuals found lived to be about 75. The researchers also were able to determine that among 83 adults, 40 were men, and 43 were women.

Dr. Joseph Lorenz, a geneticist then at the Coriell Institute for Medical Research, studied the DNA of the bones of five individuals among the Windover bog people. He expected to find typical DNA markers for Native Americans, but instead found they appeared to be European.[2] Further examination of the brain material also indicated the bog people were of European origin.

CORROBORATION: THE X2 HAPLOTYPE

In *The Lost Empire of Atlantis*, I discussed how genetic markers were providing key information about ancient migrations. Among other issues, I focused on the spread of haplogroup X2.[3] I noted that there is considerable debate and questioning in analyzing DNA to determine when mutations took place for sub haplogroups.

A research team led by Maere Reidla, a geneticist at the University of Tartu in Estonia, identified the X2 haplogroup in 2003 and described its incidence among Europeans and North Americans, but not among populations of Asia or the East. Saara Finnilä has listed the percentages of X2 found in Europe and America. Michael Brown and Douglas Wallace, Emory University researchers, searched for this marker X, found at low frequencies in the remains of ancient Americans.[4]

But I noted that from the high percentages that could be determined, the X2 haplogroup appears to have originated in the

Near East and particularly eastern Anatolia. That would include the Minoan civilization, established in Crete and the Aegean Sea area. Nevertheless, there is no certainty about when members of the European haplogroup X2 arrived in the New World. The possible dates have a broad separation—either in approximately 7400–7200 B.C. or 3000–1800 B.C.

Those wide-ranging dates indicate one of two possibilities: that the X2 population in North America could have been caused by Y-DNA mutation from European X2 ancestors around 1800 B.C. or from a migration almost six thousand years earlier.

The dating of the bog people of Florida at 6,990–8,120 years ago based on their X2 genetic marker is broadly comparable on both sides of the Atlantic. So it seems to me that Lorenz's analysis is corroborated by DNA results of several different European studies. The bog people of Windover were Europeans who settled in the Americas from 8190 B.C. They came by sea in substantial numbers—in many ships.

A SOCIETY: THE SEAFARERS
WHO SETTLED IN FLORIDA

Like the later Minoan seafarers, the people of Windover were a kind and caring people—not savages. An examination of the remains of a fifty-year-old woman showed she had suffered multiple bone fractures several years before her death. She could not have lived without being cared for. In another case, a boy thirteen to fifteen years old had spina bifida, a crippling condition caused by failure of the vertebrae to grow together around the spinal cord. One of his feet was severely deformed and bones of the other leg indicated that a terrible—and probably fatal—infection had caused the loss of the foot and part of the leg. They must have cared for this boy almost all his life.

When the bog people died they were clothed in fabrics and

laid to rest reverently in this cemetery in Florida, together with their favorite tools and artifacts—as in the case of toys discovered alongside children. The fabric in which they buried their dead was made from local plants, using at least seven different complex weaves that required the use of a loom. The fabric would have taken quite some time to weave. It is thus apparent that they were not hunters always on the move, but a permanent society that gathered all sorts of plants, especially fruit and chestnuts, from trees that flourished in Florida nine hundred years ago, and gourds. They kept hunting dogs to hunt big game—horses and mastodons.

It is also evident that these Florida bog people were by no means the earliest European sailors to settle in the Americas thousands of years ago.

CONCLUSION

Who Discovered America?

One lesson is clear from our studies: Archaeologists should be cautious about dogmatically establishing estimates and theories concerning human migration to the New World. Not too long ago, the resident wisdom of the scholarly community did not accept the possibility that humans were present in either North or South America before 12,000 B.C. Then an archaeologist at the University of New Mexico, Frank Hibben, discovered Sandia Cave. There was clear evidence that the site had been occupied as early as 27,000 B.C., although some scientists refused to revise their views on the subject.

The reason for this refusal was that if the dating was correct, here was a site much older than the Clovis site—which archaeologists have used for centuries to substantiate the notion that the Americas were populated by crossing the Bering Strait. Clovis was near enough (15,000 B.C.) to the Bering Strait both physically and chronologically to support the Bering Strait myth. Now here was a much older site than Clovis—and much farther south, thousands of miles from the Bering Strait. Acceptance of the dating of Sandia Cave at 27,000 B.C. would deal a devastating blow to the Bering Strait/Clovis theory. As a result, archaeologists who participated in the Sandia cave dig were sometimes rejected and mocked for their studies.

As R. Cedric Leonard notes, sites discovered since the Sandia Cave have pushed back the reliable evidence on human habitation of the Americas to about 40,000 B.C. Here is some concluding information about that reality, focusing on Pedra Furada in northeastern Brazil, Monte Verde in Chile, and the Seaweed Trail. Details about these remarkable finds offer more than enough evidence individually to blow the Bering Strait theory to bits.

The first site, Pedra Furada, is currently the oldest known site in the Americas with reliable, accepted carbon dating that extends human habitation back to 48,000 to 32,000 B.C. The site has human remains and unique rock paintings. The leading archaeologist in exploring, dating, and propagating knowledge of this site is Niède Guidon, from Brazil.

Professor Guidon's team has used advanced dating techniques—accelerator mass spectrometry—devised by the Australian National University, Canberra, to date carbon found in hearths uncovered at Pedra Furada. Guidon has described the use of "prepared pigments" that enabled dating at least back to 29,000 B.C.

Serra da Capivara National Park, in which Pedra Furada is situated, is thousands of miles from the Pacific but may be reached via the 1,800-mile long San Francisco River, also known as "the River of National Unity" because it is a main transportation corridor from the sea to the west. The river flows eastward into the Atlantic Ocean between the states of Alagoas and Sergipe. The Canary and South Equatorial currents could carry boats from the Mediterranean to the mouth of the San Francisco.

The second site, Monte Verde, located near Puerto Montt in south-central Chile, was uncovered by archaeologist Tom Dillehay, who conducted his research along the Chinchihuapi Creek estuary. He reported finding housing made of wood and covered in animal hides, stone tools, twine, and other types of bindings, signs of cooking, and the remains of butchered mastodon bones. The discovery, later analyzed by a panel of archaeologists, challenges the theory that the Clovis were the first inhabitants of the hemisphere. Evidence of the Clovis civilization was found in New Mexico, where pieces of the carved spear points were uncovered.

Those who accept the theory of migrations across the icy land bridge from Siberia to Alaska avoid issues that are hard to resolve. The real question about the Bering Strait is succinctly stated by Jack Rossen, associate professor at Ithaca College and Native American studies coordinator in the Department of Anthropology: "Suppose you could find a corridor through a mile high wall of ice and follow it for a thousand miles," he asked. "What would you eat? Popsicles?"

The alternative to even venturing across the ice would have been to take advantage of a natural source of food, found beneath the belts of seaweed that extend along the Pacific coast from Alaska to Chile. Rossen describes the seaweed as a food source itself as well as a "canopy" for sea life that would have provided everything for human sustenance. "What would people rather do?" asks Rossen. "Try to find a meal in a world of ice or take a boat down the coast and help themselves to fish, oysters and greens?"

I think that Rossen is spot-on. The currents in the North Pacific flow in a great loop, carrying boats north from China, past Japan, then swinging east past the Aleutian and Kuril islands to Alaska, then south along the American coast to Central America (see the map at the front of the book). So sea travelers from Asia to North and Central America have a free ride and food along the way and can sail so they are only out of sight of land for three days. This great clockwise, nearly rectangular, flow of water takes place all year round.

It appears certain that man reached the Americas by sea at least forty thousand years ago. Doubtless this date will be continuously pushed back, probably to 100,000 B.C., which was when the first peoples sailed the Mediterranean to Crete and (separately) in the south from Asia to Australia.

Mariners sailed via the great currents, which gave them "free rides" across the Atlantic in a great circular loop from Europe to America, like those "free rides" across the Pacific from Southeast Asia to North and Central America. This is entirely consistent with the genetic studies of DNA described in chapter 6.

The settlers came in never-ending waves from 40,000 B.C. onward, settling initially along the coasts (Monte Verde and Pedra Furada), then migrating inland. In South America after 1600 B.C. there were more or less continuous journeys from Southeast Asia, as we have described in this book.

The first settlers in Brazil and Florida in 40,000 B.C. probably came from the eastern Mediterranean as signified by the X2 haplotype. The conquistadors came last—Columbus was forty thousand years too late to claim having discovered anything.

Between 3000 B.C. and 1400 B.C. there was continuous contact between the Minoans of the eastern Mediterranean (who came to the Great Lakes for copper) and North America. This is described in my book *The Lost Empire of Atlantis*.

This golden age was abruptly ended by the eruption of the Thera volcano, which also sent a huge tsunami across the Mediterranean. The combination of sunlight being blocked by the volcanic ash in the atmosphere and the tsunami not only smashed Minoan (and possibly Egyptian) fleets to pieces but also flooded northern Crete and probably the Nile delta. Plague followed. The Egyptian pharaoh lost control and a long night descended on the Mediterranean civilizations. Voyages to the Americas stopped, the Great Lakes mines ceased production, and contact between the New World and Europe largely ceased. The "sea peoples" took over and Mediterranean civilization disintegrated, until the emergence of Mycenae and then Athens around 500 B.C.

This left the field clear for the Chinese and Asian voyages of exploration, principally to Central and South America. They were carried to the New World by the Pacific currents. The Olmec and Maya civilizations of Central America were largely based on Chinese civilizations and culture, as we have described. Korean and Japanese ships joined Chinese fleets in voyages to the Pacific coasts of both North and South America from around 2000 B.C., as described in detail by Charlotte Harris Rees.

Chinese exploration peaked under the Emperor Zhu Di and his Admiral Zheng He. By then there were detailed Chinese maps of the Americas, created during the voyages of Kublai Khan and Zheng He. Chinese influence mostly evaporated after the death of Zhu Di in 1424. China retreated into isolation for more than five hundred years. This left the way clear for the European conquistadors.

America then is one incredibly rich continent—not just because of nature's bounty but on account of the talents brought by sailors on continuous voyages from Europe and Asia for the past forty thousand years. All of the great religions of the world were represented in wave after wave of exploration. Jains, Hindus, Buddhists, Taoists, Confucians, Jews, Christians, followers of Islam, Sikhs, and Parsis all have contributed to making the Americas the richest and most fascinating continents in the world.

Huge advances have been made in researching early America, as we have seen—discoveries of new documents and maps, archaeological material, studies of plants and animal organisms among them. Advances in the study of DNA, not least by the Human Genome Project, have allowed geneticists to devise human ancestry markers to assist in determining a person's heritage—whether Asian, Native American Indian, or European, and the percentage and mixture of each. Satellite photography and imaging has helped find more sites.

I am determined to invite skeptics along with me as I gather information, and have benefited from challenges and questioners of all or part of my earlier books. I have intended in this volume to update the evidence—which already was overwhelming—that demonstrates my description of these migrations. It will be an unending saga, I am sure, with new techniques and new generations of explorers setting off to deal rationally and logically with answers to who *really* discovered America. It has been a rewarding journey and we are not done yet.

Long live seafaring!

ACKNOWLEDGMENTS

GAVIN'S ACKNOWLEDGMENTS

Who Discovered America? should be my swan song, the culmination of my three previous books. All of these books have become international bestsellers. I am indebted to those who have bought copies of them and contributed to the everlasting stream of new evidence, which has resulted in this book. I thank all of these people, not only those who have helped in publishing it.

General Thanks

The three previous books are on sale in more than seventy-two editions, in more than one hundred countries and thirty languages. I left school at fifteen without formal qualifications and am not particularly clever, so it is I think legitimate to ask why anyone should read my books. My answer is that all of these books, not least *Who Discovered America?*, are the result of team efforts, of which I am proud to be a member. This can be illustrated by the way all four of the books have come about.

First, we are not alone in asserting that traditional history as currently taught is one long fairy story. Emeritus Professor John Sorenson and Emeritus Professor Carl Johannessen have devoted their lives to publishing bibliographies with descriptions of more than six thousand intercontinental journeys before Columbus. They have been joined by Emeritus Professor Carroll Riley and Emeritus Professor Betty Meggers. We have publicized their work in four popular history books—I am an unashamed popularizer.

Second, we have a golden stream of new evidence from the friends of our website, www.gavinmenzies.net (at our peak we had more friends than Oxford or Cambridge had undergraduates). This is the basis for all the books. "Professional" historians are patronizing about readers' contributions—in my view the critics' condescension is unwarranted now that the Web has arrived and enabled us all to become historians.

From the mass of new evidence we select the most interesting pieces and I write this up into a manuscript—which takes, on average, three months. I then show it to my literary agent, Luigi Bonomi, who advises me on what should be emphasized or deleted. My second draft is then given to Luigi, who decides to whom he can sell the proposal. Luigi is a genius at this—he has to date sold all four books to the first publisher he has approached. We then retain Midas, who have so brilliantly publicized all four books (they drew in twenty-two thousand press, radio, and TV mentions for the 1418 map). Midas devise a marketing campaign aimed to sell foreign rights at the London Book Fair each April. Selling foreign rights before the book is published helps the publishers sell it to bookstores in the principal markets.

The publishers—Bantam Press for *1421*, Orion for *The Lost Empire of Atlantis*, and HarperCollins for *1434* and *Who Discovered America?*—have all done a marvelous job in publishing, marketing, and selling these works. They are just like submariners—decent, pragmatic people, delightful to work with, and extremely clever. My books have been strongly disliked by "professional" historians who have accused my publishers of putting out fraudulent books. These wild accusations have been borne with great good nature and forbearance. I thank these publishers for standing by me.

Particular Thanks for Who Discovered America?

As mentioned, Luigi has worked his magic selling the manuscript to HarperCollins, his first choice.

HarperCollins have been wonderful publishers for the past twelve years. I should particularly like to thank Peter Hubbard (who is the publisher of record for all four of my books in America), Cole Hager (Peter's assistant), Liate Stehlik (publisher), Juliette Shapland (foreign rights director), and Camille Collins (publicist).

Peter has shown truly inspiring judgment in selecting and appointing Peter Eisner (a distinguished author in his own right) to restructure the book. Peter Eisner has greatly improved the structure so that it now contains a vast amount of information in a readable form. Peter has also documented the research of a considerable number of experts on whom we have relied—the notes reflect this.

I would also like to thank Ms. Moy for her fast, accurate, and good-natured word processing of the nine revisions of this book.

Ian Hudson has once again managed our team with great good nature and wise judgment. He is my joint author for *Who Discovered America?* and will, I hope, continue the revolution in future books he writes.

Finally, my heartfelt thanks to my beloved wife, Marcella, without whom there would have been no research and no book.

GAVIN MENZIES

June 19, 2013

IAN'S ACKNOWLEDGMENTS

First and foremost I would like to thank Gavin for giving me the amazing opportunity to write this book with him. I have known

Gavin from a very early age. He and Marcella have worked with my parents for many years, and their daughters are roughly the same age as my brothers and I. We spent many a happy time together in our childhood days with family trips to the pantomime, Bonfire Night parties, and the like. One outstanding memory was when Gavin and Marcella took us all to lunch in London's Chinatown, when I must have been all of eight years old. It was the first time that I had been exposed to the wonders of dim sum, and I remember being in awe of Gavin as he seemed to know exactly what he was doing, ordering deftly from the menu. So one might say that my initial interest in Chinese culture was sparked inadvertently by Gavin some twenty-five years ago!

I started working with Gavin in 2002, upon graduation from the University of Bristol. It was my first job as a graduate, and I haven't looked back. It has been a diverse, inspiring, and fascinating journey—a personal voyage of discovery that more than a decade ago I never would have dreamed of. Over the years, I have gained experience in all manner of fields—research, translation, editing, writing, lecturing, curating exhibitions, television documentary production—the list is endless, and I am eternally grateful to Gavin for trusting in me, and giving me the freedom to enhance and enrich my skill set. We have covered a great deal of ground over the years, seeing leaps in technology that have made our research work much easier, as well as increasing the speed and widening the breadth of dissemination of our finds around the world. It has been an honor and a pleasure to share this journey with Gavin, and I hope that there will be many more adventures to come.

I would also like to thank Frank Lee, who has worked tirelessly alongside Gavin and me, keeping us pointed in the right direction and enabling us to continue with our research projects. Gavin, Frank, and I formed a company in 2009 with a view to maintaining a sustainable business that could keep our website and research going for years to come. We would have found it incredibly hard to continue without Frank's support and advice over the years, and I hope that the steps that we have taken thus far will ensure our ongoing success in the future.

I would like to echo Gavin's words in thanking Luigi Bonomi and HarperCollins for all of their hard work over the years. It has been a pleasure working with so many diligent and inspiring people—long may it last!

The "1421 team" to me is now like a family, spread far and wide around the world. We are in touch with readers from almost every continent on a daily basis and it is a delight to be at the hub of this focal point for research and the sharing of knowledge. Our special thanks go to those whose ongoing research has contributed to this book. These contributors include, in no particular order, Cedric Bell and his son Dave, Dr. Rosanne Hawarden, Charlotte Harris Rees, Paul Chiasson, Dr. Siu-Leung Lee, Liu Gang, Dr. Gunnar Thompson, Jerry Warsing, Mark and Laurie Nickless, Emeritus Professor Carl Johannessen, and Emeritus Professor John Sorenson. They have all become friends to us along the way, and we are most grateful to them for sharing their knowledge and skills with us, inspiring us in our search for the truth. Their work embodies the brave, tireless spirit of the underdogs, rallying against the established paradigm of American discovery. We hope that this spirit shines through in our book and will continue to shine for many years to come.

IAN HUDSON
LONDON
June 26, 2013

NOTES

CHAPTER 1: A LAND BRIDGE TOO FAR

1. Here is our supplies list for the Bering Strait crossing we had planned:

Comprehensive kit of tools
Oil
Oil filters
Air filters
Fuel filters
Fuel shut-off valve
Bulbs
Brakes
Wipers
Starter
Alternator
Tires and wheels
Emergency puncture repair kits
Constant-velocity joint gaiters and fitting sleeve
Front wheel bearing kit
Rear wheel bearing kit
Driveshaft
Alternator belt
Cam belt
Diesel pump belt
Water jet belt
Water hoses
Inspection lamp (12 volt)
Powerful searchlight with own battery, preferably halogen
Jack and wheel brace and possibly four spare wheel nuts
12-volt tire compressor/pump
Brake fluid
Clutch cable
Throttle cable
Gasket set

Radiator fan
Radiator
Radiator fan switch
Fiberglass repair kit
Hand cleaner
Rubber gloves

Here are the provisions and essentials:
First-aid kit
Life jackets
Foghorn
Distress flares
Fire extinguishers
Rope
Winch
Waterproofs
Sleeping bags
Cooking utensils and cutlery
Stove
Gas
Water container
Insect repellent
Soap
Washing liquid
Condiments
Toilet paper rolls
Tissues
Small plastic washbowl
12-volt water heater
12-volt fridge/cooler/cooker
Spare heavy-duty battery (12-volt)
Small spade

CHAPTER 2: ALONG THE SILK ROAD

1. Gavin Menzies, *1421: The Year China Discovered America* (New York: William Morrow, 2003), 139.

CHAPTER 3: PLANTS BETWEEN CONTINENTS

1. Sorenson and Johannessen described *Biology Verifies Ancient Voyages* as "an expanded version of a presentation given at a conference, 'Contact and Exchange in the Ancient World,' held at the University of Pennsylvania, Philadelphia, May 5th, 2001. . . . Since our initial paper was submitted for inclusion in that volume, we made further discoveries. Some additions were included in an electronic version entitled *Scientific Evidence for Pre-Columbian Transoceanic Voyages to and from the Americas* (Sino-Platonic Papers No. 133, CD-ROM edition, April 2004), published by the Department of Asian and Middle Eastern Studies, University of Pennsylvania, Philadelphia. The present book incorporates further material. Because much of the literature that enters into our argument in this paper is interpreted in ways other than bi-

ologists conventionally do, for readers' convenience we give in Appendix 1 a précis of our reference materials on each species discussed. Appendix 2 summarizes the most salient types of evidence we have used. Selected illustrations and a bibliography for both the text proper and the appendices follow. . . ."

CHAPTER 4: EUROPEAN SEAFARING 100,000 B.C.

1. See John Noble Wilford, "On Crete, Evidence of Very Ancient Mariners," *New York Times,* February 15, 2010, http://www.nytimes.com/2010/02/16/science/16archeo.html?_r=0.
2. "Ataturk," Australian War Memorial Online-Encyclopedia, retrieved April 25, 2011.
3. http://countrystudies.us/turkey/3.htm.
4. Joseph Needham.

CHAPTER 5: MASTERY OF THE OCEANS BEFORE COLUMBUS

1. The evidence for this chapter comes from a number of distinguished archaeologists and historians to whom I am indebted. On the European front, Professor Stylianos Alexiou's *Minoan Civilization* gives an excellent summary of the development of Minoan civilization and in particular the part played by Minoan ships. The Uluburun shipwreck, which demonstrates how oceangoing ships were constructed in the fourteenth century B.C., was the subject of a special exhibition in the Metropolitan Museum of Art, New York City. The contents of this exhibition are described in *Beyond Babylon* (New Haven, CT: Yale University Press, 2008). I have relied heavily on this book, not least the chapter titled "The Uluburun Shipwreck and Late Bronze Age Trade," by Professor Cemal Pulak, whose devoted work has resulted in this extraordinary wreck being brought to the attention of the world. In a similar manner, the magnificent exhibition "The Dover Bronze Age Boat" in Dover Museum has been invaluable to my research. I am most grateful to the director, curator, and trustees. For Egyptian ships, my thanks to Maitland A. Edey for the beautifully produced book *Sea Traders* (New York: Time-Life Books, 1974).

   On the Chinese side I am indebted to Professor Joseph Needham for his monumental work *Science and Civilisation in China* (Cambridge: Cambridge University Press, 1954), and to Professor Robert Temple for *The Genius of China* (New York: Simon & Schuster, 1986), based on Needham's work. The development of Chinese shipbuilding technology is summarized in Gang Deng's excellent *Chinese Maritime Activities and Socioeconomic Development c. 2100 B.C.–1900 A.D.* (Westport, CT: Greenwood Press, 1997).

   There are many authors whose work on the Thera frescoes has advanced our knowledge of the ships, depicted c. 1450 B.C., in the fleet of eleven ships painted in the Admiral's House, Akrotiri, Thera. As well as those authors whom I have thanked in chapter 2 and 3, my gratitude to Raban Avner, for "The Thera Ships: Another Interpretation"; D. Gray in *Seewesen* for his analysis of seals showing Early Minoan ships; C. Tsountas, "Ships on Cycladic Frying Pans"; J. C. Gillmer, "The Thera Ships: A Re-analysis"; and P. F. Johnston, "Bronze Age Cycladic Ships." A full bibliography is given at the end of this book.
2. Gang Deng, *Chinese Maritime Activities and Socioeconomic Development: c. 2100 B.C.–1900 A.D.* (Westport, CT: Greenwood, 1997).
3. Ibid.

4. The thesis of an early African presence in the Americas was prominently advanced by Guyana-born anthropologist Ivan Van Sertima in his book *They Came Before Columbus* (1976; reprint, New York: Random House, 2003). Van Sertima argues that Africans reached the Americas in two stages.

CHAPTER 6: THE GENETIC EVIDENCE

1. Neither I nor any of our team has medical qualifications. We rely entirely on the generosity of many geneticists and virologists whose reports are noted in the bibliography. Without their painstaking work over the decades we would have gotten nowhere. All of the conclusions drawn in this chapter are mine and I take full responsibility for them. Inclusion or reference to a report does not in any way imply that the author(s) agree with my views or conclusions.
2. M. Hertzberg et al., "An Asian-Specific 9 of B.P. Deletion of Mitochondrial DNA Is Frequently Found in Polynesians," *American Journal of Human Genetics* 44, no. 4 (April 1989): 504–10. "One hundred and fifty Polynesians from five different island groups (Samoans, Maoris, Niueans, Cook Islanders and Tongans) were surveyed for the presence of an Asian-specific length mutation of mitochondrial (MT) DNA. . . . One hundred percent of Samoans, Maoris and Niueans . . . [had this DNA]."
3. Shinji Harihara and colleagues, "Frequency of a 9 B.P. Deletion in the Mitochondrial DNA among Asian Populations," *Human Biology* (April 1962). Harihara's Figure 2 has startling pie charts. It appears that inhabitants of Fiji, Samoa, Tonga, Nieu, the Cook Islands, and the Maori had ancestors from the Shizuoka prefecture of Japan.
4. Fuminaka Sugauchi et al., "A Novel Variant Genotype C of Hepatitis B Virus Identified in Isolates from Australian Aborigines," *Journal of General Virology* 82 (April 2001): "Variant C is found in Aborigines, genotype C in Japan, Korea, China, Thailand, New Caledonia and Polynesia."
5. Geoffrey K. Chambers et al., as published in BBC News, August 11, 1998: "World: Asia Pacific Maoris may have come from China. Using genes to reconstruct human history in Polynesia."
6. A. Arnaiz-Villena et al., "HLA Genes in Mexican Mazatecans, the Peopling of the Americas, and the uniqueness of Amerindians," *Tissue Antigens* 56 (November 2000).
7. The formal report by Professor Bruges-Armas and eight colleagues (including Professor Arnaiz-Villena) is published as "HLA in the Azores Archipelago: Possible Presence of Mongoloid Genes," *Tissue Antigens* 54 (1999): 349.
8. Ibid., 354.
9. Ibid., 357.
10. Ibid., 358.
11. "Parasitismoa migrações humanus pre-historicas," in *Estudos da pre-historia Geral a Brasiliera*, University of São Paulo, 1970.
12. http://onlinelibrary.wiley.com/doi/10.1002/ana.410410407/abstract.

CHAPTER 8: THE OLMEC: THE FOUNDATION
CULTURE OF CENTRAL AMERICA

1. H. Mike Xu, *Origin of the Olmec Civilization* (Edmond: University of Central Oklahoma Press, 1996) and Charlotte Harris Rees, *Secret Maps of the Ancient World* (Bloomington, IN: AuthorHouse, 2008).

2. Charlotte Harris Rees, *Secret Maps of the Ancient World* (Bloomington, IN: AuthorHouse, 2008).

3. Ibid.

4. Hernan Garcia, Antonia Sierra, and Gilberto Balam, *Wind in the Blood: Mayan Healing and Chinese Medicine* (Berkeley, CA: North Atlantic Books, 1999).

CHAPTER 9: PYRAMIDS IN MEXICO AND CENTRAL AMERICA

1. Jack E. Churchward, *Lifting the Veil on the Lost Continent of Mu: Motherland of Men* (Huntsville, AK: Ozark Mountain, 2011), 215.

2. Plans were obtained thanks to the kind assistance of Professor Thomas Bartlett of La Trobe University, Melbourne, Australia (where I had lectured).

3. With assistance again from Professor Bartlett

4. Private correspondence between Gavin Menzies and Prof. Bartlett.

5. Ibid.

6. Quoted in Robert M. Schoch, *Voyages of the Pyramid Builders* (New York: Penguin, 2004), 153.

7. Ibid.

8. For the information that follows I am indebted to James Q. Jacob's website, Mesoamerican Archaeoastronomy, http://www.jqjacobs.net/mesoamerica/meso_astro.html.

9. Frudakis speaking at Library of Congress Zheng He Symposium, 2006. See our website, www.gavinmenzies.net, for more information.

CHAPTER 10: PYRAMID BUILDERS OF SOUTH AMERICA

1. See Cynthia Lee, "Archaeologist Investigates Legend of Mythical Ruler of Ancient Peru," March 13, 2012, http://today.ucla.edu/portal/ut/archaeologist -sets-out-to-validate-230460.aspx.

2. Francisco A. Loayza, *Chinos llegaron antes de Colón* (Lima: D. Miranda, 1948).

3. Ibid.

4. Ibid.

5. Jorge E. Hardy, *Pre-Columbian Cities* (Buenos Aires: Ediciones Infinito, 1964).

CHAPTER 11: KUBLAI KHAN'S LOST FLEETS

1. http://en.wikisource.org/wiki/The_Travels_of_Marco_Polo/Book_3/Chapter_2.

2. *The Adventures of Marco Polo, the Great Traveler* (New York: D. Appleton, 1902), 133.

3. Gunnar Thompson, *Marco Polo's Daughters: Asian Discovery of the New World* (Seattle: Misty Isles Press, 2011).

4. Ibid., 6.

5. *Libre dels feits del rei en Jacme* (Book of the Acts of King James 1208–1276), http://www.cervantesvirtual.com/servlet/SirveObras/34697391092392752454679/index.htm.

6. Book III, Chapters LXXI and LXXIV, written in 1562. Translation courtesy of Carles Camp i Perez, e-mail correspondence from our website.

CHAPTER 12: THE 1418 CHINESE MAP OF THE WORLD

1. See Emeritus Professor Carol Urness: it has never been accused of being a forgery "and never will be."
2. Personal email correspondence with Library of Congress.
3. In Harris Rees, *Secret Maps of the Ancient World.*
4. http://www.gavinmenzies.net/?taxonomy=1421&s=1418+map.
5. See under Part I, iii, "Zheng He's Integrated Map of the World 1418," at http://www.gavinmenzies.net/china/book-1421/1421-evidence.
6. http://www.gavinmenzies.net/?taxonomy=1421&s=peru.
7. Professor Gabriel Novick and his colleagues.
8. María Rostworowski de Diez Canseco, *History of the Inca Realm* (Cambridge: Cambridge University Press, 1999), 211.
9. Justo Caceres Macedo, *Prehispanic Cultures of Peru: Guide of Peruvian Archaeology* (n.p.: Author, 2004).

CHAPTER 13: NORTH CAROLINA AND THE VIRGINIAS

1. James Mooney, *Myths of the Cherokee* from Nineteenth Annual Report of the Bureau of American Ethnology 1897–98, Part I.
2. George William Featherstonhaugh, *A Canoe Voyage up the Minnay Sotor; with an Account of the Lead and Copper Deposits in Wisconsin; of the Gold Region in the Cherokee Country; and Sketches of Popular Manners* (London: R. Bentley, 1847), ch. 59.

CHAPTER 14: THE EASTERN SEABORD

1. James and Melanie Bowles, Proud Spirit Horse Sanctuary, Personal email correspondence with authors.
2. Cherokee Cultural Society of Houston.
3. Hendon M. Harris, *Asiatic Fathers of America: Chinese Discovery & Colonization of Ancient America,* ed. Charlotte Harris Rees (Lynchburg, VA: Warwick House, 2006).
4. Please visit www.harrismaps.com for more information.
5. This account comes from Shinnick's "Digger's Diary: The Mysterious Ming Medallion."
6. Ibid.
7. Ibid.

CHAPTER 15: NOVA CATAIA: THE ISLAND OF SEVEN CITIES

1. Joseph Needham, *Science and Civilisation in China* (Cambridge: Cambridge University Press, 1954), Vol. 5, 13 at pages 356–69 and vol. 4, part 2, see 27, p. 390 ff.
2. *Annals of the Brothers Nicolo and Antonio Zeno* (London, 1898).
3. *Les voyages aventureux du Capitaine J. Alfonce.*

CHAPTER 16: THE PACIFIC COAST OF NORTH AMERICA

1. *Proceedings of the United States National Museum* 15, no. 899 (1892): 221 (with Plate XXIV).
2. Ibid.
3. See Gavin Menzies, *1434* (New York: William Morrow, 2008), esp. 257–67.

4. See http://www.cristobalcolondeibiza.com and Frank J. Frost, "The Palos Verdes Chinese Anchor Mystery," *Archaeology* 31, no. 1 (1982).
5. Paul Gallez, *Predescubrimientos de América* (Bahía Blanca: Instituto Patagonico, 2001).
6. *The Zuni Enigma. A Native American People's Possible Japanese Connection* (New York: W. W. Norton in 2000, Paperback 2001).
7. Belich, Mônica P., J. Alejandro Madrigal, William H. Hildebrand, Jacqueline Zemmour, Robert C. Williams, Roberta Luz, Maria Luiza Petzl-Erler, and Peter Parham. "Unusual HLA-B Alleles in Two Tribes of Brazilian Indians." *Nature* 357.6376 (1992): 326-29.
8. "Across Before Columbus? Evidence for Transoceanic Contact with the Americas prior to 1492" edited by Donald Y. Gilmore and Linda S. McElroy (NEARA Journal 1998:136).
9. University of Arizona Library, *Books of the South West*, chapter 1, "Indians of Arizona," http://southwest.library.arizona.edu/hav7/body.1_div.1.html.

CHAPTER 17: STONE AGE SAILORS: THE
"WINDOVER BOG" PEOPLE OF FLORIDA

1. The bog was the subject of a report on the PBS show *Nova*, http://www.pbs.org/wgbh/nova/ancient/americas-bog-people.html.
2. "The First Americans—Part 6—DNA of The Windover Bog People," http://www.youtube.com/watch?v=vbayBEbIEwc.
3. Gavin Menzies, *The Lost Empire of Atlantis* (New York: William Morrow, 2011), 303–8.
4. Maere Reidla et al., "Origin and Diffusion of Mt DNA Haplogroup X," *The American Journal of Human Genetics* 73000 (2003); and M. D. Brown et al., "Mt DNA Haplogroup X: An Ancient Link Between Europe/Western Asia and America?" *The American Journal of Human Genetics* 63 (1998): 90.

BIBLIOGRAPHY

This bibliography is structured to assist readers who wish to become experts in this particular subject or in a part of it—whether they are professional historians or not. The bibliography follows the chronology of the text:

Part A. Transcontinental Trade Before Columbus
Part B. China in the Americas
Part C. China's Explorations to the North
Each section is considered in more detail:
A1. Transoceanic Trade—General
A2. Atlantic Trade in the Bronze Age
A3. Sea Currents
A4. Trade on the Atlantic Coasts
A5. Tin and Copper
A6. Mediterranean Sea Trade in Prehistory
A7. Mycenae
A8. Chinese, Egyptian, and Minoan Ships and Their Trade
A9. Calculation of Longitude at Sea
A10. Ocean Navigation
A11. Maritime Trade in 100,000 B.C.
B1. DNA Evidence
B2. In Search of Lost Civilizations
B3. The Maya Compared with Peoples of the Ancient Near East
B4. Shang Dynasty and Olmec Art and Pyramids
B5. Pyramid Builders of South America and China
C1. Kublai Khan's Lost Fleets
C2. The Carolinas, Virginia, and the Eastern Seaboard
C3. Nova Cataia
C4. The Pacific Coast
C5. The Florida Bog People

SUGGESTED METHOD FOR FURTHER RESEARCH

1. After reading this book, study the notes and visit our website, www.Gavin Menzies.net. Then select your research topic.
2. Read this bibliography and decide generally which books interest you.
3. Read summaries of those books on a website like Goodreads or Amazon. Narrow your choice and purchase or borrow from a library those books you decide you should read. When at your local library, visit www.jstor.org and download all relevant papers (this excellent service is free in the British Library, and in countless libraries, museums, and educational institutions around the world).

   If you follow this advice you can become an expert within a month. In return, we ask that you contact us with the results of your investigations via email (zhenghe@gavinmenzies.net). With your permission, we will then place the conclusions on our website. This will spread the results quickly around the world, and in turn should help to further stimulate research on the topic. You will have joined a worldwide research group with an aim to rewriting "accepted" history.

GOOD LUCK!
GAVIN MENZIES AND IAN HUDSON

PART A. TRANSCONTINENTAL TRADE BEFORE COLUMBUS

Transoceanic Trade—General
Acosta, José de. *The Natural and Moral History of the Indies.* c. 1560; reprint, London: Hakluyt Society, 1880.
Alfieri, Anastase. *The Coleoptera of Egypt.* Cairo: Société Entomologique d'Egypte, 1976.
Allison, M. J., et al. "A Case of Hookworm Infestation in a Pre-Columbian American." *American Journal of Physical Anthropology* 41 (1974): 103–106.
Araujo, Adauto, et al. "Paleoepidemologia da Ancilostomose." *Paleoparasitologia no Brasil* (1988): 144–51.
Bagrow, Leo. "Maps from the Home Archives of the Descendants of a Friend of Marco Polo." *Imago Mundi* 5 (1948): 1–13.
Balabanova, S. "Tabak in Europa vor Kolumbus." *Antike Welt* 25, no. 3 (1994): 282–85.
Barthel, Thomas S. "Planetary Series in Ancient India and Pre-Hispanic Mexico: An Analysis of Their Relations with Each Other." *Tribus* 30 (1981): 203–30.
Barthel, Thomas S., et al. *Circumpacifica Festschrift für Thomas S. Barthel.* Frankfurt am Main: Peter Lang, 1990.
Buckland, P. C., and E. Panagiotakopulu. "Ramses II and the Tobacco Beetle." *Antiquity* 75 (2001): 549–56.
Burl, Aubrey. *From Carnac to Callanish.* New Haven, CT: Yale University Press, 1993.
Carter, G. F. *Pre-Columbiana: A Journal of Long-Distance Contacts* 2, no. 4 (2002).
Chadwick, R. E. "Toward a Theory of Trans-Atlantic Diffusion." Ph.D. diss., Tulane University, 1975.

Cunliffe, Barry W. *Facing the Ocean*. New York: Oxford University Press, 2001.
Diodorus Siculus. *Bibliotheca Historica*, 2.47 (quoting lost history of Hecataeus of Abdera).
Evenhuis, Neal L. "Charles Henry Townsend (1863–1944): Man of Wanderlust and Mystery." *Fly Times* 50 (2013): 15–24.
Guthrie, James L. "Observations on Nicotine and Cocaine in Ancient Egyptian Mummies." *Pre-Columbiana: A Journal of Long-Distance Contacts* 2, no. 4 (2002).
Harris, Hendon M., Jr. Edited and abridged by Charlotte Harris Rees. *The Asiatic Fathers of America*. Lynchburg, VA: Warwick House, 2006.
Harris Rees, Charlotte. *Chinese Sailed to America Before Columbus*. Bloomington, IN: AuthorHouse, 2011.
———. *Secret Maps of the Ancient World*. Bloomington, IN: AuthorHouse, 2008.
Heyerdahl, Thor. "Feasible Ocean Routes to and from the Americas in Pre-Columbian Times." *American Antiquity* 28 (1963), Bradshaw Foundation podcast.
Hosler, Dorothy. "Pre-Columbian American Metallurgy." Paper presented at 45th International Congress of Americanists, Bogotá, Colombia, 1985.
Hristov, Romeo, and Santiago Genovés. "Mesoamerican Evidence of Pre-Columbian Transoceanic Contacts." *Ancient Mesoamerica* 10 (1999): 207–13. See also http://www.unm.edu/~rhristov/.
Hutchinson, Sir Joseph B., R. A. Silow, and S. G. Stephens. *The Evolutions of Gossypium and the Differentiation of the Cultivated Cottons*. London: Oxford University Press, 1947.
Jairazbhoy, R. *Rameses III: Father of Ancient America*. London: Karnak House, 1992.
Jeffreys, M. D. W. "Pre-Columbian Maize in Africa." *Nature* 172 (1953): 965–66.
Johannessen, Carl L., and John L. Sorenson. *World Trade and Biological Exchanges Before 1492*. New York: iUniverse, 2009.
Landa, Fray Diego de. *Yucatan Before and After the Conquests*. Trans. William E. Gates. Baltimore: Maya Society, 1937. See also other Maya Society publications.
Landström, Björn. *The Ship*. London: Allen & Unwin, 1961.
Lui, Bao-Lin, and Alan D. Fiala. *Canon of Lunar Eclipses, 1500 B.C.–A.D. 3000*. Richmond, VA: Willmann-Bell, 1992.
MacNeish, R. S., and C. Earle Smith, Jr. "Antiquity of American Polyploid Cotton." *Science* 173 (1964): 675–76.
McGrail, Sean. *Ancient Boats and Ships*. Princes Risborough, UK: Shire, 2006.
———. Ancient Boats in Northwest Europe: The Archaeology of Water Transport to A.D. 1 500. London: Longman, 1998.
Mertz, Henriette. "The Pre-Columbian Horse." *Anthropological Journal of Canada* 10 (1972): 23–24.
Mookerji, D. N. "A Correlation of the Mayan and Hindu Calendars." *Indian Culture* 2, no. 4 (1935–36): 685–92.
Neugebauer, O. *A History of Ancient Mathematical Astronomy*. New York: Springer Verlag, 1975.
Parry, J. H. *The Discovery of South America*. New York: Taplinger, 1979.
Riley, Carroll L., et al., eds. *Man Across the Sea*. Austin: University of Texas Press, 1971.
Rydholm, Fred. *Michigan Copper—The Untold Story*. Marquette, MI: Winter Cabin Books, 2006

Sachan, J. K. S. "Discovery of Sikkim Primitive [Maize] Precursor in the Americas." *Maize Genetics Co-operative Newsletter* 60 (1986).

Sauer, Carl Ortwin. *Maize into Europe.* Vienna: Akten des 34. Internationalen Amerikanistenkongresses, 1962.

Smith, G. Elliot. *Elephants and Ethnologists: Asiatic Origins of the Maya Ruins.* London: Paul, Trench, Trubner, 1924.

Soper, Fred L. "The Report of a Nearly Pure *Ancylostoma Duodenale* Infestation in Native South American Indians and a Discussion of Its Ethnological Significance." *American Journal of Hygiene* 7 (1927): 174–84.

Sorenson, John L., and Martin H. Raish. *Pre-Columbian Contact with the Americas Across the Oceans: An Annotated Bibliography.* Provo, UT: Research Press, 1996.

Steffy, J. Richard. *Wooden Ship Building and the Interpretation of Shipwrecks.* 1994; reprint, College Station: Texas A&M University Press, 2011.

Tolstoy, Paul. "Transoceanic Diffusion and Nuclear Mesoamerica." In Shirley Gorenstein, ed., *Prehistoric America.* New York: St. Martin's Press, 1974.

Townsend, Charles H. T. "Ancient Voyages to America." *Brazilian American* 12 (1925).

———. 'Fly Times' No. 50, 2013.

Varshavsky, S. R. "Appearance of American Turkeys in Europe Before Columbus." *New World Antiquity* 8, no. 8 (1961). And ArchivesofCulturalExchanges.org.

Atlantic Trade in the Bronze Age

Almagro-Gorbea, M. "Ireland and Spain in the Bronze Age." In John Waddell and Elizabeth Shee Twohig, eds., *Ireland in the Bronze Age: Proceedings of the Dublin Conference, April 1995.* Dublin: Stationery Office, 1995.

Bradley, Richard. *The Prehistory of Britain and Ireland.* New York: Cambridge University Press, 2007.

———. *The Social Foundations of Prehistoric Britain.* London: Longman, 2004.

Butler, Jay J. "Bronze Age Connections Across the North Sea." *Paleohistoria* 9 (1963): 1–286.

Childe, V. Gordon. *The Bronze Age.* Cambridge: Cambridge University Press, 1930.

Clark, Peter. *Bronze Age Connections.* Oxford: Oxbow Books, 2009.

———. *The Dover Bronze Age Boat in Context: Society and Water Transport in Prehistoric Britain.* Oxford: Oxbow Books, 2004.

Cunliffe, Barry W. *Facing the Ocean.* New York: Oxford University Press, 2001.

———. *Mount Batten, Plymouth: A Prehistoric and Late Roman Port.* Oxford: Oxford University Committee for Archaeology, 1988.

Darvill, Timothy. *Stonehenge: The Biography of a Landscape.* Stroud, UK: Tempus, 2006.

Fitzpatrick, A. "The Amesbury Archer." *Current Archaeology* 184 (2003): 146–52.

Gonzalez-Ruibal, Alfredo. "Facing Two Seas: Mediterranean and Atlantic Contacts in the Northwest of Iberia in the First Millennium B.C." *Oxford Journal of Archaeology* 23, no. 3 (2004): 287–317.

Kristiansen, K. "Seafaring Voyages and Rock Art Ships." In Peter Clark, ed., *The Dover Bronze Age Boat in Context: Society and Water Transport in Prehistoric Britain.* Oxford: Oxbow Books, 2004.

Muckelroy, K. "Middle Bronze Age Trade Between Britain and Europe: A Maritime Perspective." *Proceedings of the Prehistoric Society* 47 (1981): 275–97.

Needham, S. "The Archer's Metal Equipment." Forthcoming.

———. "The Extent of Foreign Influence on Early Bronze Age Axe Development in Southern Britain." In M. Ryan, *The Origins of Metallurgy in Atlantic Europe: Proceedings of the Fifth Atlantic Colloquium, Dublin, 1978.* Dublin: Stationery Office, 1979.

Needham, S., and C. Giardino. "From Sicily to Salcombe." *Antiquity* 82, no. 315 (2008): 60–72. See also a number of works by Professor Needham relating to Bronze Age weapons.

Needham, S., et al. "An Independent Chronology for British Bronze Age Metalwork." *Archaeological Journal* 154 (1997): 55–107.

Needham, S., et al. "Networks of Contact, Exchange and Meaning: Beginning of the Channel Bronze Age." In S. Needham et al., eds., *The Ringlemere Cup.* London: British Museum, 2006.

Parker Pearson, Mike, et al., "The Age of Stonehenge." *Antiquity* 81 (2007): 617–39.

Rowlands, M. J. "The Production and Distribution of Metalwork in the Middle Bronze Age in Southern Britain." N.p.: *British Archaeological Reports,* 1976.

Scarre, Christopher, and Frances Healy. *Trade and Exchange in European Prehistory.* Oxford: Oxbow Books, 1993.

Sea Currents

Admiralty charts of North Atlantic.

Albert, HRH Prince, of Monaco. "A New Chart of the Currents of the North Atlantic." *Scottish Geographical Magazine* 8, no. 10 (1892).

Becher, A. B. "Bottle Chart of the Atlantic Ocean." *Nautical Magazine* 12 (1843): 181.

James, H. Guill. "Vila do Infante (Prince-Town), the First School of Oceanography in the Modern Era: An Essay." In Mary Sears and Daniel Merriman, eds., *Oceanography: The Past: Proceedings of the Third International Congress on the History of Oceanography.* New York: Springer-Verlag, 1980.

Richardson, P. L. "Drifting Derelicts in the North Atlantic 1883–1902." *Progress in Oceanography* 14 (1985): 463–83.

Trade on the Atlantic Coasts

Bannerman, Nigel V. C. "Bronze Age Smelting in North Wales: A Discussion Paper on Possible Smelting Sites for Great Orme Ore." *Journal of the Great Orme Exploration Society* 3 (1992): 7–16.

Briggs, C. S. *The Location and Recognition of Metal Ores in Pre-Roman and Roman Britain.* Bangor: University College of North Wales, 1988.

Chapman, D. "Great Orme, Smelting Site, Llandudno." *Archaeology in Wales* 37 (1997): 56–57.

David, G. "Great Orme, Bronze Age Mine, Llandudno." *Archaeology in Wales* 41 (2001): 118–19.

Dutton, L., and P. Fasham. "Prehistoric Copper Mining in the Great Orme, Llandudno, Gwynedd." *Proceedings of the Prehistoric Society* 60 (1994): 245–86. See also the bibliography to this article.

James, D. "Prehistoric Copper Mining on the Great Orme's Head." In J. Ellis Jones, ed., *Aspects of Ancient Mining and Metallurgy.* Bangor: University College of North Wales, 1988.

Lewis, C. Andrew. *Prehistoric Mining at the Great Orme*. Bangor: University College of North Wales, 1996.

Map of the Great Orme Country Park and Nature Reserve. Public Mapping Company, 2003.

Northover, Jeremy P. "Bronze in the British Bronze Age." In W. A. Oddy, ed., *Aspects of Early Metallurgy*, British Museum Occasional Paper 17, 1980. The paper also includes a catalog of Welsh Bronze Age metalwork.

O'Brian, William. *Ross Island: Mining, Metal, and Society in Early Ireland*. Galway: National University of Ireland, 2004.

Roberts, E. R. D. "The Great Orme Guide: The Copper Mine, The Prehistoric Period." 1993.

Robertson. "The Bronze Age—A Time of Change." 1994.

Taylor, Joan J. "The First Golden Age of Europe Was in Ireland and Britain." *Ulster Journal of Archaeology* 57 (1994): 37–60.

Tin and Copper

Gale, N. H. "Copper Oxhide Ingots: Their Origin and Their Place in the Bronze Age. In N. H. Gale, ed., *Bronze Age Trade in the Mediterranean*. Jonsered: P. Åströms Förlag, 1991.

Manning, Sturt, et al. "Chronology for the Aegean Late Bronze Age, 1700–1400 B.C." *Science* 312 (2006): 565–69.

Muhly, James D. "Mining and Metalwork in Ancient Western Asia." In Jack M. Sasson, ed., *Civilizations of the Ancient Near East*. New York: Scribner, 2000.

Mediterranean Sea Trade in Prehistory

Haldane, Cheryl W. "Direct Evidence for Organic Cargoes in the Late Bronze Age." *World Archaeology* 24 (1993): 348–60.

Knapp, A. *Copper Production and Divine Protection: Archaeology, Ideology, and Social Complexity on Bronze Age Cyprus*. Göteborg P. Åströms förlag, 1986.

———. "Island Cultures: Crete, Thera, Cyprus, Rhodes and Sardinia." In Jack M. Sasson, ed., *Civilizations of the Ancient Near East*. New York: Scribner, 2000. The Biblical Archaeologist Vol.55, No.2, 1992.

———. "Spice, Drugs, Grain, and Grog: Organic Goods in Bronze Age Mediterranean Trade." In N. H. Gale, ed., *Bronze Age Trade in the Mediterranean*. Jonsered: P. Åströms Förlag, 1991.

Bronze Age Seafaring in the Mediterranean

Bryce, Trevor. *The Kingdom of the Hittites*. Oxford: Oxford University Press, 2006.

———. *The Trojans and Their Neighbours*. London: Routledge, 2006.

Collins, Paul. *From Egypt to Babylon: The International Age 1550–500 B.C.* Cambridge, MA: Harvard University Press, 2008.

Curtis, John, et al. *Forgotten Empire: The World of Ancient Persia*. Berkeley: University of California Press, 2005.

Haldane, Cheryl [Ward]. "Organic Goods from the Uluburun Wreck." *INA Newsletter* 18 (1991): 11.

———. "Shipwrecked Plant Remains." *Biblical Archaeologist* 53, no. 1 (1990): 55–60.

Johnston, P. F. "Bronze Age Cycladic Ships: An Overview." Temple University Aegean Symposium, 1982.

Kantor, Helene J. *The Aegean and the Orient in the Second Millennium B.C.* Bloomington, IN: Principia Press, 1947.

Manning, Stuart W. *A Test of Time: The Volcano of Thera and the Chronology and History of the Aegean and East Mediterranean in the Mid-Second Millennium BC.* Oxford: Oxbow Books, 1999.

Merrillees, Robert S. "Aegean Bronze Age Relations with Egypt." *American Journal of Archaeology* 76 (1972): 281–94.

Moran, William L. *The Amarna Letters.* 1942; reprint, Baltimore: Johns Hopkins University Press, 2000.

Pulak, C. "As One Ship Is Unearthed, Another Is Reassembled." *INA Newsletter* 12 (1989): 4–5.

———. "The Balance Weights from the Late Bronze Age Shipwreck at Uluburun." In C. F. E. Pare, ed., *Metals Make the World Go Round.* Oxford: Oxbow Books, 2000.

———. "Cedar for Ships." *Archaeology and History in Lebanon* 14 (2001): 24–36.

———. "Paired Mortise and Tenon Joints of Bronze Age Seagoing Hulls." In *Boats, Ships, and Shipyards: Proceedings of the Ninth International Symposium on Ship Construction in Antiquity, Venice 2000.* Oxford: Oxbow Books, 2003.

———. "The Uluburun Hull Remains." In Harry Tzalas, ed., *Tropis VII: Proceedings of 7th International Symposium on Ship Construction in Antiquity.* Athens: Hellenic Institute for the Preservation of Nautical Tradition, 2002.

Raban, A. "The Siting and Development of Mediterranean Harbours in Antiquity." In Mary Sears and Daniel Merriman, eds., *Oceanography: The Past: Proceedings of the Third International Congress on the History of Oceanography.* New York: Springer-Verlag, 1980.

Rao, Shikaripur R., ed. *The Role of Universities and Research Institutes in Marine Archaeology: Proceedings of the Third Indian Conference on Marine Archaeology of Indian Ocean Countries, 1992.* Dona Paula, Goa, India: National Institute of Oceanography, 1994.

Reynolds, C. G. "Note: The Thera Ships." *Mariner's Mirror* 64 (1978): 124.

Roaf, Michael. *Cultural Atlas of Mesopotamia and the Ancient Near East.* New York: Facts on File, 1990.

Sandars, N. K. *The Sea Peoples: Warriors of the Ancient Mediterranean 1250–1150 B.C.* London: Thames & Hudson, 1978.

Shaw, Ian, ed. *The Oxford History of Ancient Egypt.* Oxford: Oxford University Press, 2003.

Shaw, M. C. "Painted 'Ikria' at Mycenae?" *American Journal of Archaeology* 84 (1980): 167–79.

Sølver, Carl V. "Egyptian Shipping of About 1500 B.C." *Mariner's Mirror* 22, no. 4 (1936).

Tilley, A. F., and Paul Johnstone. "A Minoan Naval Triumph?" *International Journal of Nautical Archaeology* 5 (1976): 285–92, published online February 22, 2007.

Tsountas, C. "Ships on Cycladic 'Frying Pans' " in Kykladika II, Arah Eph (1899) and Tsountas 1898 and *Hesperia* 72 (2003) (405–426).

Wachsmann, Shelley. *Seagoing Ships and Seamanship in the Bronze Age Levant.* College Station: Texas A&M University Press, 1998.

Mycenae
Schliemann, Heinrich. *Mycenae: A Narrative of Researches and Discoveries at Mycenae and Tiryns.* London: John Murray, 1878. See also article on Schliemann's Mycenae albums by Sinclair Hood. http://www.aegeussociety.org/images/uploads/publications/schliemann/Schliemann_2012_70–78_Hood.pdf.

Linear B
Ventris, Michael, and John Chadwick. *Documents in Mycenaean Greek.* Cambridge: Cambridge University Press, 1973.

Chinese, Egyptian, and Minoan Ships and Their Trade
Minoan
Astour, M. C. "Ugarit and the Aegean." *Alter Orient Und Altes Testament* 22 (1973): 17–27.

———. "Ugarit and the Great Powers." In Gordon Douglas Young, ed., *Ugarit in Retrospect: Fifty Years of Ugarit and Ugaritic.* Winona Lake, IN: Eisenbrauns, 1981.

Bass, G. F. "A Bronze Age Writing Diptych from the Sea of Lycia." *Kadmos Epigrafik* 29 (1990): 168–69. See also "Bronze Age Trade in the Mediterranean," paper delivered at Oxford University conference, December 1989.

———. "A Prolegomena to a Study of Maritime Traffic in Raw Materials to the Aegean in the 14th and 13th centuries B.C." In *Proceedings of 6th International Aegean Conference,* Temple University, Philadelphia, 1997.

———. "Nautical Archaeology and Biblical Archaeology." *Biblical Archaeologist* 53 (1990).

———. "Oldest Known Shipwreck Reveals Splendours of the Bronze Age." *National Geographic,* December 1987.

Bowen, R. L. "Egypt's Earliest Sailing Ships." *Antiquity* 34 (1960): 117. See many other articles by Bowen on this subject.

Brown, L. M. "The Ship Procession in the Miniature Fresco." In *Thera and the Aegean World.* London: Thera Foundation, 1978.

———. "Theran Awning and Stern Cabin." In *The Ship Procession in the Miniature Fresco.* London, 1978.

Bucaille, Maurice. *Mummies of the Pharaohs.* New York: St. Martin's Press, 1990.

Carter, Howard. "The Tomb of Tutankhamun 3." *Journal of Egyptian Archaeology* 26 (1940).

Casson, Lionel. *Ships and Seamanship in the Ancient World.* Princeton: Princeton University Press, 1971.

Castleden, Rodney. *Atlantis Destroyed.* London: Routledge, 1998.

Emanuele, P. Daniel. "Ancient Square Rigging with and Without Lifts." *International Journal of Nautical Archaeology* 6 (1977): 181–85.

Gibbins, D. "Bronze Age Wreck's Revelations." *Illustrated London News* 281 (1993): 72–73. See also numerous articles on wrecks by David Gibbins.

Gillmer, T. C. "The Thera Ships: A Re-analysis." *Mariner's Mirror* 64 (1978).

Uluburun Shipwreck

Bass, G. F., et al. "The Bronze Age Shipwreck at Uluburun: 1986 Campaign." *American Journal of Archaeology* 90, no. 3 (1986): 269–96.

Pulak, C. "The Cargo of the Uluburun Ship and Evidence for Trade with the Aegean and Beyond." In *Italy and Cyprus in Antiquity, 1500–450 BC: Proceedings of an International Symposium Held at the Italian Academy for Advanced Studies in America at Columbia University, November 16–18 2000.* Nicosia: Costakis & Leto Severis Foundation, 2001.

———. "Discovering a Royal Ship from the Age of King Tut: Uluburun Turkey. In George Fletcher Bass, ed. *Beneath the Seven Seas.* London: Thames & Hudson, 2005.

———. "The Late Bronze Age Shipwreck at Uluburun: Aspects of Hull Construction." In W. Phelps, Y. Lolos, and Y. Vichos, eds., *The Point Iria Wreck: Interconnections in the Mediterranean ca. 1200 B.C.: Proceedings of the International Conference, Island of Spetses, 19 September 1998.* Athens: Hellenic Institute of Marine Archaeology, 1999.

———. "The Uluburun Shipwreck." In *Res Maritimae: Cyprus and the Eastern Mediterranean from Prehistory to Late Antiquity: Proceedings of the Second International Symposium "Cities on the Sea," Nicosia, Cyprus, October 18–22, 1994.* Atlanta: Scholars Press, 1994.

Egyptian Ships

Barton, George A. *Archaeology and the Bible.* 3rd ed. Philadelphia: American Sunday-School Union, 1920 (for Akkad besieging Crete). See many articles by Barton on disasters.

Bietak, Manfred. "Egypt and Canaan During the Middle Bronze Age." *Bulletin of the American Schools of Oriental Research* 281 (February 1991): 27–72.

———. "Servant Burials in the Middle Bronze Age Culture of the Eastern Nile Delta." *Eretz Israel* 20 (1989): 30–43.

Building Pharaoh's Ship. WGBH, Boston, January 2010.

Clagett, Marshall. *Ancient Egyptian Science: A Source Book.* Philadelphia: American Philosophical Society, 1989.

Clayton, Peter A. *Chronicle of the Pharaohs: The Reign-by-Reign Record of the Rulers and Dynasties of Ancient Egypt.* London: Thames & Hudson, 1994.

Dever, William G. "Tell el Dab'a and Levantine Middle Bronze Age Chronology: A Rejoinder to Manfred Bietak." *Bulletin of the American Schools of Oriental Research* 281 (1991): 73–79.

Dodson, Aidan, and Dyan Hilton. *The Complete Royal Families of Ancient Egypt.* London: Thames & Hudson, 2004.

Grajetzki, Wolfram. *The Middle Kingdom of Ancient Egypt: History, Archaeology and Society.* London: Duckworth, 2006.

Holladay, John S., et al. *Cities of the Delta, Part III, Tell el-Maskhuta: Preliminary Report on the Wadi Tumilat Project 1978–1979.* American Research Center in Egypt Reports, vol. 6. Malibu, CA: Undena, 1985.

Landström, Björn. *Ships of the Pharaohs.* London: Allen & Unwin, 1970.

Linder, E. "Naval Warfare in the El-Amarna Age." In David J. Blackman, ed., *Marine Archaeology.* Colston Papers 23. London: Butterworths, 1973.

Redmount, Carol A. "Ethnicity, Pottery and the Hyksos at Tell El-Maskhuta in the Egyptian Delta." *Biblical Archaeologist* 58 (1995): 182–90.

———. "On an Egyptian/Asiatic Frontier: An Archaeological History of the Wadi Tumilat." Ph.D. diss., University of Chicago, 1989.

Ryholt, K. S. B. *The Political Situation in Egypt During the Second Intermediate Period c. 1800–1500 B.C.* Copenhagen: Museum Tuscolanum Press, 1997.

Shaw, Ian, ed. *The Oxford History of Ancient Egypt*. Oxford: Oxford University Press, 2000.

Tufnell, Olga, and William F. Ward. *Relations Between Byblos, Egypt and Mesopotamia at the End of the Third Millennium B.C. A Study of the Montet Jar*. Paris: Librairie Orientaliste Paul Geuthner, 1966.

Ward, Cheryl. "Building Pharaoh's Ships: Cedar, Incense and Sailing the Great Green." *British Museum Studies in Ancient Egypt and Sudan* 18 (2012): 217–32.

Translation/Deciphering Minoan Linear A

Tsikritsis, Minas. Continued on Gavin Menzies's website. http://www.gavinmenzies.net/Evidence/chapter-40-%E2%80%93-a-return-to-crete.

Material Evidence of Trade

Betancourt, Philip P. "Dating the Aegean Late Bronze Age with Radiocarbon." *Archaeometry* 29 (1987): 45–49.

———. *The History of Minoan Pottery*. Princeton: Princeton University Press, 1985.

Kenna, Victor E. "Cretan and Mycenaean Seals in North America," *American Journal of Archaeology* 68 (January 1964): 1–12.

Panagiotaki, M. "Crete and Egypt: Contacts and Relationship Seen Through Vitreous Materials." In Alexandra Karetsou, ed., *Krete-Aigyptos: Politismikoi Desmoi Trion Chilietion*. Athens: Herakliou, 2000.

Calculation of Longitude at Sea
General

Levy, David H. *The Sky: A User's Guide*. Cambridge: Cambridge University Press, 1991. See also many guides by Levy.

Moore, Patrick. *Naked Eye Astronomy*. New York: Norton, 1965. See also many other useful books by Sir Patrick Moore.

Rawlinson, Henry Creswicke. "The Assyrian Canon Verified by the Record of a Solar Eclipse BC 763." *Athenaeum: Journal of Literature, Science, and the Fine Arts*, no. 2064 (May 18, 1867): 660–61.

Toulmin, Stephen, and June Goodfield. *The Fabric of the Heavens*. Chicago: University of Chicago Press, 1999.

Van der Waerden, B. *Science Awakening II: The Birth of Astronomy*. New York: Oxford University Press, 1975. See also many articles by the same author.

Wagner, Jeffrey K. *Introduction to the Solar System*. Philadelphia: Saunders College Publishing, 1991.

Water Clocks

Brown, D., J. Fermor, and C. B. F. Walker. "The Water Clock in Mesopotamia." *Archiv für Orientforschung* 46 (1999): 141–48.

Englund, R. K. "Administrative Timekeeping in Ancient Mesopotamia." *Journal of the Economic and Social History of the Orient* 31 (1988): 121–85.
Fermor, John. "Timing the Sun in Egypt and Mesopotamia." *Vistas in Astronomy* 41 (1997): 157–67.
Michel-Nozières, C. "Second Millennium Babylonian Water Clocks: A Physical Study." *Centaurus* 42, no. 3 (2000): 180–209.
Steele, John M. "The Design of Babylonian Waterclocks." *Centaurus* 42 (2000): 210–22.
Walker, C., and J. Britton. "Astronomy and Astrology in Mesopotamia." In C. B. J. Walker, ed., *Astronomy Before the Telescope*. London: British Museum Press, 1996.
The Babylonian World. New York: St. Martin's Press, 1996.

Ocean Navigation
Babylonian Lunar Theory
Aaboe, Asker H. *A Computed List of New Moons for 319 B.C. to 316 B.C. from Babylon*. Copenhagen: Munksgaard, 1969.
———. *Contributions to the Study of Babylonian Lunar Theory*. Copenhagen: Munksgaard, 1979. See also review by N. M. Swerdlow in *Journal of Cuneiform Studies* 32 (1980).
———. *Lunar and Solar Velocities and the Length of Lunation Intervals in Babylonian Astronomy*. Copenhagen: Munksgaard, 1971.
———. *Some Lunar Auxiliary Tables and Related Texts from the Later Babylonian Period*. Copenhagen: Munksgaard, 1968.
———. "Two Lunar Texts of the Achaeminid Period from Babylon." *Centaurus* 14 (1969): 1–22.
Brack-Bernsen, Lis. "On the Babylonian Lunar Theory: A Construction of Column Φ from Horizontal Observations." *Centaurus* 33 (1990): 39–56.
Brack-Bernsen, Lis, and H. Hunger. "A Collection of Rules for the Prediction of Lunar Phases and of Month Length." *SCIAMUS* 3 (2002): 3–90. See several other papers by Lis Brack-Bernsen.
Fatoohi, L. J., F. R. Stephenson, and S. S. Al-Dargazelli. "The Babylonian First Visibility of the Lunar Crescent: Data and Criterion." *Journal for the History of Astronomy* 30 (1999): 51–72.
Goldstein, Bernard R. "On the Babylonian Discovery of the Periods of Lunar Motion." *Journal for the History of Astronomy* 33 (2002): 1–13.
Hubor, Peter J. "Babylonian Short-Time Measurements: Lunar Sixes." *Centaurus* 42 (2000): 223–34.
Neugebauer, O. E. "On Babylonian Lunar Theory." *Sky and Telescope* 4 (1944): 3.
Steele, J. M. "Babylonian Lunar Theory Reconsidered." *Isis* 91 (2000): 125–26.
———. "Miscellaneous Lunar Tables from Babylon." *Archive for History of Exact Sciences* 60 (2006): 123–55.
Swerdlow, N. M., ed. *Ancient Astronomy and Celestial Divination*. Cambridge, MA: MIT Press, 1999.

Maritime Trade in 100,000 B.C.
General
Aksit, Ilhan. *Anatolian Civilisations and Historical Sites*. Ankara: Turkish Ministry of Culture, 2009.

"Aspendos" by M. Edip Ozgur, Ankara. ISBN 978-975-387-107-5.

Ayabakan, Cumali. *All of Aphrodisias Step by Step.* Kartpostal ve Turistik Yayincilik. Antalya: Güney, n.d.

Cimok, Fatih. *The Hittites.* Ankara: A Turizm Yayinlari, 2011.

Clark, Peter. *Bronze Age Connections: Cultural Contact in Prehistoric Europe.* Oxford: Oxbow Books, 2009.

Demirer, Unal, and Antalya Müzesi. *Antalya Museum.* Antalya: Curators of Antalya Museum, 2005.

Ephesus Museum. Selcuk, Pub 3KG. ISBN 786055 488017.

Eracun, Selçuk. *Ephesus.* Istanbul: Hitit Color Yayinlari, n.d.

Korfmann, Manfred. *Troia/Wilusa: Guidebook.* N.p.: Canakkale, 2005.

Kunar, Serhat. *All of Antalya and Mediterranean Coast.* Istanbul: Turistik Yayinlari, 2004.

Macqueen, J. G. *The Hittites.* London: Thomas & Hudson, 1986.

———. *The Hittites and Their Contemporaries.* London: Thames & Hudson, 1998.

The Museum of Anatolian Civilisations. ISBN 975-17-2498-9.

"Pergamon" Pub Mert. Istanbul, 2004. ISBN 9-789752850583.

Seeher, Jürgen. *Hattusa Guide: A Day in the Hittite Capital.* Istanbul: Ege Yayinlari, 2005.

Sözen, Zeynep. *Perge: Guide.* Istanbul: Kultur Sanat Yayincilik, 2009.

Guidebooks of Museums in Anatolia
Ephesus
Turkey—Lonely Planet, 1996
Aphrodisias—"Step by Step"
Aspendos—"A Travel Guide"
Aspendos Orenyeri—Antalya Museum
"The Ruins in Arkanda"—Antalya Museum
Turkey Pocket Map—Duru
Pergamon—Mert Istanbul 2004
Ephesus Museum—3KG Publications
Perge—BKG Publications
Antalya Museum—Curator Antalya Museum 2005, Ankara

PART B. CHINA IN THE AMERICAS

DNA Evidence

Brown, M. D., et al. "mtDNA Haplogroup X: An Ancient Link Between Europe/Western Asia and America?" *American Journal of Human Genetics* 63, no. 6 (1998): 1852–61.

King, R. J., et al. "Differential Y Chromosome Anatolian Influences on the Greek and Cretan Neolithic." *Annals of Human Genetics* 72, no. 2 (2008): 205–14.

Reidla, Maere, et al. "Origin and Diffusion of mtDNA Haplogroup X." *American Journal of Human Genetics* 73, no. 5 (2003): 1178–90.

Mercier, G., F. Diéterlen, and G. Lucotte. "Y-Haplotype X in the Balkans." *International Journal of Anthropology* 21, no. 2 (2006): 111–16.

Novick, Gabriel, et al. "Polymorphic Alu Insertions and the Asian Origin of Native American Populations," *Human Biology: The International Journal of Population Genetics and Anthropology* 70, no. 1 (1998): 32.

Richards, M., et al. "Tracing European Founder Lineages in the Near East mtDNA Pool." *American Journal of Human Genetics* 67, no. 5 (2000): 1251–76.

Schurr, Theodore G. "Mitochondrial DNA and the Peopling of the New World." *American Scientist* 88 (2000): 246–53.

Shlush, Liran I., et al. "The Druze: A Population Genetic Refugium of the Near East." *PLoS ONE* 3, no. 5 (2009): e2105.

Torroni, A., et al. "Mitochrondrial DNA 'Clock' for the Amerinds and Its Implications for Timing Their Entry into North America." *Proceedings of the National Academy of Sciences of the United States of America* 9 (1994): 1158–62.

In Search of Lost Civilizations

Gallenkamp, Charles. *Maya—The Riddle and Rediscovery of a Lost Civilisation.* London: Penguin, 1987.

Mookerji, D. N. "A Correlation of the Maya and Hindu Calendars." *Indian Culture* 2, no. 4 (1935–36): 685–92.

Neugebauer, O. *A History of Ancient Mathematical Astronomy.* New York: Springer-Verlag, 1975.

Newcomb, R. M. *Plant and Animal Exchanges Between the Old and the New Worlds.* Privately printed 1963.

Parry, J. H. *The Discovery of South America.* New York: Taplinger, 1979.

Riley, Carroll L., et al., eds. *Man Across the Sea.* Austin: University of Texas Press, 1971.

Sachan, J. K. S. "Discovery of Sikkim Primitive [Maize] Precursor in the Americas." *Maize Genetics Co-operative Newsletter* 60 (1986).

Sauer, Carl Ortwin. *Maize into Europe.* Vienna: Akten des 34. Internationalen Amerikanistenkongresses, 1962.

Smith, G. Elliot. *Elephants and Ethnologists: Asiatic Origins of the Maya Ruins.* London: Paul, Trench, Trubner, 1924.

Soper, Fred L. "The Report of a Nearly Pure *Ancylostoma Duodenale* Infestation in Native South American Indians and a Discussion of Its Ethnological Significance." *American Journal of Hygiene* 7 (1927): 174–84.

Steffy, J. Richard. *Wooden Ship Building and the Interpretation of Shipwrecks.* 1994; reprint, College Station: Texas A&M University Press, 2011.

Townsend, Charles H. T. "Ancient Voyages to America." *Brazilian American* 12 (1925).

Varshavsky, S. R. "Appearance of American Turkeys in Europe Before Columbus." *New World Antiquity* 8, no. 8 (1961).

The Maya Compared with Peoples of the Ancient Near East

Aveni, Anthony, and Owen Gingerich. *Skywatchers of Ancient Mexico.* Austin: University of Texas Press, 1980.

Bork, Ferdinand. *Amerika und Westasien.* Leipzig: Karl W. Hiersemann, 1912.

Charencey, Hyacinthe de Comte. "Les Noms de Métaux Chez Differents Peuples de la Nouvelle Espagne." In *Congres Internacional des Americanistes, Compte-Rendu, Paris 1890.* Paris: Ernest Leroux, 1892.

Chatelain, Maurice. *Nos Ancêtres Venus du Cosmos.* Paris: Laffont, 1975.

Clarke, Hyde. *Researches in Prehistoric and Protohistoric Comparative Philology and Mythology.* London: Trübner, 1875.

Coe, M. D. "Native Astronomy in Mesoamerica." In A. F. Aveni, ed., *Archaeoastronomy in Pre-Columbian America.* Austin: University of Texas Press, 1975.

———. "The Funerary Temple of the Classic Maya." *Southwestern Journal of Anthropology* 12 (1956): 387–94.

Durbin, Marshall. "The Evolution and Diffusion of Writing." *American Anthropologist* 73 (1971): 299–304. Published online October 28, 2009.

Fraser, D. "Theoretical Issues in the Trans-Pacific Diffusion Controversy." *Social Research* 32 (1965): 452–77.

Freed, Stanley A., and Ruth S. Freed. "Swastika: A New Symbolic Interpretation." In Christine M. Sakumoto Drake, ed., *The Cultural Context: Essays in Honor of Edward Norbeck,* Rice University Studies, No. 66. Houston: William Marsh Rice University, 1980.

Gingerich, Owen. "Summary: Archaeoastronomy in the Tropics." In Anthony F. Aveni and Garu Urton, ed., *Ethnoastronomy and Archaeoastronomy in the Tropics,* Annals of the New York Academy of Sciences, vol. 385. New York: New York Academy of Sciences, 1982. See also many essays by Gingerich on related subjects.

Gordon, Cyrus H. "The Metcalf Stone." *Manuscripts* 21, no. 3 (1969).

Gordon, G. B. "The Serpent Motive in the Ancient Art of Central America and Mexico." *Transactions of the University of Pennsylvania* 1, no. 3 (1905). Spanish ed. published in 2013 by Hardpress.

Guitel, Geneviève. "Comparaison entre les numérations Aztèqe et Egyptienne." *Annales* 13, no. 4 (1958): 687–705.

Hagar, Stansbury. "The Bearing of Astronomy on the Subject." *American Anthropologist* 14 (1912): 32–48.

Holden, E. S. "Studies in Central American Picture Writing." In *First Annual Report of The Bureau of Ethnology to the Secretary of the Smithsonian Institution, 1879–80.* Washington, DC: Smithsonian Institution, 1879.

Holmes, William H. "Bearing of Archaeological Evidence on the Place of Origin." *American Anthropologist* 14 (1912): 30–36.

Howey, M. Oldfield. *The Encircled Serpent: A Study of Serpent Symbolism in All Countries and Ages.* 1955; reprint, Whitefish, MT: Kessinger, 2005.

Kelley, David H. "Calendar Animals and Deities." *Southwest Journal of Anthropology* 16 (1960): 317–37.

———. "The Nine Lords of the Night." In J. Graham, ed., *Studies in the Archaeology of Mexico and Guatemala, University of California Archaeology Research Facility Contributions* 16 (1972): 58–68. See also many articles by D. H. Kelley.

Luyties, O. *Egyptian Visits to America: Some Curious Evidence Discovered.* New York: N.p., 1922.

Marti, Samuel. "Mudra: Manos Simbólicas en Asia y América." *Cuadernos Americanos* 69 (1970).

Medvedov, Daniel. "Anatomia Maya." *Abstracts of Papers: 44th International Congress of Americanists.* Manchester: University of Manchester Press, 1982.

Moran, H. A., and David H. Kelley. *The Alphabet and the Ancient Calendar Signs.* Palo Alto, CA: Daily Press, 1969.

Nachitgall, V. Von. "On the Origin of American Advanced Cultures." *Paideuma* 7 (1960).

Nichols, Dale. *The Pyramid Text of the Ancient Maya.* Antigua, Guatemala: Mazdan Press, 1969.

Rands, Robert L. "The Water Lily in Maya Art: A Complex of Alleged Asiatic Origin." *Smithsonian Bulletin* 151 (1953).

Rejón García, Manuel. "Los Mayas Primitivos." In *Imprenta de la Lotería del Estado Merida.* Yucatan, 1905.

Reko, B. P. "Star Names of the Chilam Balam of Chumayel." *El Mexico Antiguo* 4 (1935–38): 95–129.

Smith, Joseph Lindon. *Tombs, Temples, and Ancient Art.* Norman: University of Oklahoma Press, 1956.

Sorenson, John L. *An Ancient American Setting for the Book of Mormon.* Salt Lake City: Deseret, 1996.

———. "The Significance of an Apparent Relationship Between the Ancient Near East and Meso America." In Carroll L. Riley et al., eds., *Man Across the Sea.* Austin: University of Texas Press, 1971.

———. "Some Mesoamerican Traditions of Immigration by Sea." *El Mexico Antiguo* 8 (1955): 425–38.

Soto-Hall, Máximo. *Los Mayas.* Coleccion Labor, Biblioteca Ciencias Histroicas, No. 403. Barcelona: Editorial Labor, 1937.

Stewart, D. N. "Geometric Implications in Construction of the Caracol: Greek Measures in Maya Architecture." *El Palacio* 59, no. 6 (1952): 163–74.

Thompson, J. Eric S. *Maya History and Religion.* Norman: University of Oklahoma Press, 1970. See also review in *American Anthropologist* 73, no. 4 (1971): 915–17.

Van Blerkom, Linda Miller. "A Comparison of Maya and Egyptian Hieroglyphics." *Katunob* 11, no. 3 (1979): 1–8

Winzerling, E. O. *Aspects of the Maya Culture.* New York: North River, 1956.

Wolff, Werner. *Déchiffrement de l'écriture Maya et traduction des codices.* Paris: Librairie Orientaliste Paul Geuthner, 1938.

Shang Dynasty and Olmec Art and Pyramids
General

Xu, H. Mike. *Origin of the Olmec Civilization.* Edmond: University of Central Oklahoma Press, 1996. See also http://www.chinese.tcu.edu/www_chinese3 _tcu_edu.htm.

Mexico

Bahn, Paul G. *Lost Cities.* London: Weidenfeld & Nicolson, 1997.

Diaz, Edith Ortiz. "Salamaya." *Arqueología Mexicana*, Especial 15.

"La Mixteca." *Arqueología Mexicana*, Especial 15, no. 9.

"La Navegacion entre Los Mayas." *Arqueología Mexicana* 6, no. 33.

"Los Tesoros de Palenque." *Arqueología Mexicana*, Especial 18.

Marin, Carlos Martinez. *National Museum of Anthropology.* Instituto Nacional de Antropología, 1967.

Caral-Supe
Solís, Ruth Shady. *The Caral Supe Civilisation: 5,000 Years of Cultural Identity in Peru*. Lima: Instituto Nacional de Cultura, 2005.

Monte Alban
Robles García, Nelly M. *Monte Alban*. Mexico: Monclem Ediciones, 2004.

Chichen Itza
Chan, Román Piña. *Chichen Itza: La Ciudad de Los Brujos del Agua*. Mexico: Fondo de Cultura Económica, 1980.
Lothrop, S. Kirkland. *Metals from the Cenote of Sacrifice: Chichen Itza, Yucatan*. Vol. 10 of *Memoirs*, Peabody Museum of Archaeology and Ethnology, Harvard University, Cambridge, MA, 1952.
Martinez, Hector Perez. *Relacion de los Cosas de Yucatan*. Mexico, 1938.
Stephens, John Lloyd. *Incidents of Travels in Yucatan*. London: Author, 1843.
Willard, Theodore Arthur. *The City of the Sacred Well*. New York: Grosset & Dunlap, 1926

Paracas
Pierantoni Campora, Antonio. *La Cultura Paracas: Treinta Siglos de Arte Textil* (The Paracas Culture: Thirty Centuries of Textile Art). Lima: Editora Diskcopy, 2005.

Machu Picchu
Frost, Peter, et al. *Machu Picchu Historical Sanctuary*. Lima: Nuevas Imágenes, 1995.

Uxmal
Casanova, J. P. *Uxmal and the Puuc Region*. Mérida, Mexico: Editorial Dante, 1992.

Cholula
Solís Olguín, Felipe, et al. *Cholula: The Great Pyramid*. Mexico City: Grupo Azabache, 2006.

Chavin
Burger, Richard L. *Chavin and the Origins of Andean Civilization*. London: Thames & Hudson, 1995.

Maya
Hughes, Nigel. *Maya Monuments*. Woodbridge, UK: Antique Collectors Club, 2000.

Pyramid Builders of South America and China
Alva, Walter, and Christopher B. Donnan. *Royal Tombs of Sipan*. Los Angeles: Fowler Museum of Cultural History, University of California, 1993.
Burger, Richard L. *Chavin and the Origins of Andean Civilization*. London: Thames & Hudson, 1992.
Gurney, O. R. *The Hittites*. Rev ed. New York: Penguin, 1990.

Heyerdahl, Thor. *The Pyramids of Tucume: The Quest for Peru's Forgotten City.* London: Thames & Hudson, 1995.

Kolata, Alan L. *Tiwanaku: Portrait of an Andean Civilization.* Cambridge, MA: Blackwell, 1993.

Markham, Sir Clement. *The Incas of Peru.* New York: AMS Press, 1969.

Moseley, Michael E. "The Batan-Grande." In *The Northern Dynasties: Kingship and Statecraft in Chimor.* Washington, DC: Dumbarton Oaks Research Library and Collection, 1990.

Moseley, Michael E., and Kent C. Day. *Chan Chan: Andean Desert City.* Albuquerque: University of New Mexico Press, 1982.

Pozorski, Sheila, et al. *Early Settlement and Subsistence in the Casma Valley, Peru.* Iowa City: University of Iowa Press, 1987. And *Andean Archaeology* (2002) 21–51.

Reinhard, Johan. "Peru's Ice Maidens: Unwrapping the Secrets." *National Geographic,* June 1996.

Rostworowski, María de Diez Canseco. *Historia del Tahuantinsuyu.* Lima: Instituto de Estudios Peruanos, Ministerio de la Presidencia, Consejo Nacional de Ciencia y Tecnología, 1988.

Rostworowski, María de Diez Canseco, et al. *The Northern Dynasties: Kingship and Statecraft in Chimor.* Washington, DC: Dumbarton Oaks Research Library, 1990.

Shimada, Izumi. *Pampa Grande and the Mochica Culture.* Austin: University of Texas Press, 1994.

Trazegnies, Fernando de. *China y el Perú precolombino.* In "La inmigración China al Perú. Arqueología Historia y sociedad." Richard Chuhue, Li Jing Na y Antonio Coello, compiladores. Instituto Confucio. Universidad Ricardo Palma. Lima, Perú, 2012.

Velikovsky, Immanuel. *Worlds in Collision.* London: Abacus, 1972.

Von Hagen, Adriana, and John Hyslop. *The Cities of the Ancient Andes.* London: Thames & Hudson, 2008.

PART C. CHINA'S EXPLORATIONS TO THE NORTH

Kublai Khan's Lost Fleets
Thompson, Gunnar. *American Discovery.* Raleigh, NC: Lulu.com, 2013.
———. *Marco Polo's Daughters.* Raleigh, NC: Lulu.com, 2011.

The Carolinas, Virginia, and the Eastern Seaboard
Baldwin, William P. *Lowcountry Day Trips.* 2nd ed. Greensboro, NC: Legacy, 2010.

Byrd, William. *The Secret Diary of William Byrd of Westover, 1709–1712.* New York: Arno Press, 1972.

De Gast, Robert. *Five Fair Rivers.* Baltimore: Johns Hopkins University Press, 2000.

Edgar, Walter B. *South Carolina: A History.* Columbia: University of South Carolina Press, 1999.

———. *South Carolina: The WPA Guide to the Palmetto State.* Columbia: University of South Carolina Press, 1988.

Fleming, Kevin, et al. *Delaware Discovered*. Annapolis, MD: Portfolio Press, 1992.

Jolley, Harley E. *The Blue Ridge Parkway*. Knoxville: University of Tennessee Press, 1969.

Lee, Siu-Leung. 2006. http://www.asiawind.com/zhenghe.

———. *Deciphering the Kunyu Wanguo Quantu, A Chinese World Map—Ming Chinese Mapped the World Before Columbus* (in Chinese). Taipei: Linking Publishing Company, 2012.

Leifermann, Henry. *South Carolina*. Oakland, CA: Compass American Guides, 2006.

Lonely Planet. *Great Smoky Mountains & Shenandoah National Parks*. Oakland, CA: Lonely Planet, 2005.

———. *Virginia and the Capital Region*. Oakland, CA: Lonely Planet, 2000.

Scott, Jane. *Between Ocean and Bay: A Natural History of Delmarva*. Centreville, MD: Tidewater, 1991.

Smith, Captain John. *The Generall Historie of Virginia, New England, and the Summer Isles*. Edited by Philip Barbour. New York: Wisconsin Historical Society/Scribner's, 2003.

Twining, Mary Arnold, and Keith E. Baird. *Sea Island Roots: African Presence in the Carolinas and Georgia*. Trenton, NJ: Africa World Press, 1991.

Nova Cataia

Chiasson, Paul. *The Island of Seven Cities: Where the Chinese Settled When They Discovered America*. Toronto: Random House Canada, 2008.

The Pacific Coast

Davis, Nancy Yaw. *The Zuni Enigma*. New York: Norton, 2002.

Mertz, Henriette. *Gods from the Far East: Two Ancient Records of Chinese Exploration in America*. 1975; reprint, n.p.: Forgotten Books, 2008.

———. *Pale Ink*. Self-published, 1953.

———. *The Wine Dark Sea: Homer's Heroic Epic of the North Atlantic*. Chicago: Author, 1964.

Needham, Joseph. *Science and Civilisations in China*. 34 vols. Cambridge: Cambridge University Press, 1954–2008.

Also please refer to www.gavinmenzies.net for further bibliographies and books relating to the Pacific coast of North America.

The Florida Bog People

Brown, M. D., et al. "mtDNA Haplogroup X: An Ancient Link Between Europe/ Western Asia and America?" *American Journal of Human Genetics* 63, no. 6 (1998): 1852–61.

"The First Americans—Part 6—DNA of the Windover Bog People." http://www .youtube.com/watch?v=vbayBEbIEwc.

Ice Age Columbus. Discovery Channel, 2005.

Places to Go and Things to Do. Titusville Community Guide. http://www.nbbd .com/godo.

Reidla, Maere, et al. "Origin and Diffusion of mtDNA Haplogroup X." *American Journal of Human Genetics* 73, no. 5 (2003): 1178–90.

Schurr, Theodore G. "Mitochondrial DNA and the Peopling of the New World."
    American Scientist 88 (2000): 246–53.
Secrets of the Bog People. Learning Channel, 2003.
Stone Age Columbus. BBC 4, 2002.
"Stone Age Sailors Beat Columbus to America." *Observer*, November 28, 1999.
Tracing the Genes. PBS, 2004.

PERMISSIONS

We would like to acknowledge the following for their kind permission in allowing us to use their photographs, diagrams, and illustrations:

COLOR INSERT 1

Bering Strait © Crissi
Diomede Island courtesy of Meredith Beck
Silk Road and Silk Road horse © Gavin Menzies
Zea mays, public domain
Tobacco © Kevin Bercaw
Hookworm, courtesy of the Rockefeller Archive Center
Tomb of the General (Jian Jun Ten or the Pyramid of the East) located in Jian, China, by Kevin Felt
Stepped pyramid at Chichen Itza, Mexico © Gavin Menzies
The Wrestler © DeLange
Las Limas monument 1 © Olga Cadena
Mochica ceramics © Museo Larco, Lima, Peru, http://www.museolarco.org
Chinese prisoner © George L. Parrott, Ph.D. Professor of Psychology, emeritus, California State University, Sacramento
Juanita, Inca Ice Maiden © Gavin Menzies
Chinese lion in the shape of a pillow, acquired by Henry Walters, 1916 © Walters Art Museum
Aztec jaguar sculpture, Cuauhxicalli © Xuan Che
Chinese lion, Baoding's tomb; Mesoamerican jaguar; jade bear; and jade jaguar © Gavin Menzies
Aztec calendar courtesy of Library of Congress
Nova Cataia terrace remains and cut stone © T. C. Bell
Palos Verdes stone anchor © Ian Hudson
Cave art at Pedra Furada © Jean-Marc Lamotte

COLOR INSERT 2

Harris World Map 5, from the Dr. Hendon M. Harris Jr. Map Collection © 2010
    Harris Maps, Charlotte Harris Rees
David Deal's interpretation of Harris Map © David Deal
Venice map © Doge's Palace Museum, Venice
"Map with Ship" from Rossi Collection, and Waldseemüller map, Library of Con-
    gress, Geography and Map Division, Washington, D.C., United States
Kangnido map, Ryukoku University Library, Japan
1418/1763 Liu Gang map, 2007 © Liu Gang
Waldseemüller "Green Globe" © Bibliotheque Nacionale de France, Paris

DIAGRAMS/ILLUSTRATIONS THROUGHOUT

Site plan showing the Emperor Qin's Mausoleum from Bevan, A, Kun, Z, Li, X.J.,
    Martinón-Torres, M, Rehren, T and Xia, Y 2011
Maximum-likelihood tree illustrating human phylogenetic relationships, re-
    printed from Figure 2 from "Polymorphic Alu Insertions and the Asian Or-
    igin of Native American Populations" by Gabriel Novick et al., in *Human
    Biology: The International Journal of Population Genetics and Anthropol-
    ogy* 70, no. 1. Copyright © Wayne State University Press, with the permis-
    sion of Wayne State University Press.
Minoan seals depicting ships with masts and rigging: Andrea Salimbeti, http://
    www.salimbeti.com/micenei/ships.htm
Plan of La Venta Ceremonial Center by Map Master
Analysis by Dr. Mike Xu of engraved writings on excavated stones found at La
    Venta: http://www.chinese.tcu.edu/www_chinese3_tcu_edu.htm
Points and meridians in traditional Chinese medicine compared with points
    and wind channels in Mayan medicine. From *Wind in the Blood: Mayan
    Healing and Chinese Medicine* by Hernán García, Antonio Sierra, and
    Gilberto Balám. English translation by Jeff Conant, published by North
    Atlantic Books, copyright © 1999 by Hernán García, Antonio Sierra, and
    Gilberto Balám. Reprinted by permission of publisher.
Precession of the Earth's axis © Hui Chieh, www.mydarksky.org
Reproduction of Oriental horseman described by Father Antonio de la Calancha,
    from a huaca in Trujillo, Peru. From Francisco A. Loayza (*Chinos llegaron
    antes de Colón*, Lima, D. Miranda 1948)
Map of the Ancash province in Peru containing a plethora of villages and small
    towns with Chinese names, from Francisco A. Loayza (*Chinos llegaron
    antes de Colón*, Lima, D. Miranda 1948)
Map of Peru—the dots on this map show Peruvian names that correspond with
    geographical names of China, from Francisco A. Loayza (*Chinos llegaron
    antes de Colón*, Lima, D. Miranda 1948)

INDEX

About the Authors

About the Book

Insights,
Interviews
& More ...

Read on

Meet Gavin Menzies and Ian Hudson

Photograph by Heathcliff O'Malley

GAVIN MENZIES is the bestselling author of *1421: The Year China Discovered America*, *1434: The Year a Magnificent Chinese Fleet Sailed to Italy and Ignited the Renaissance*, and *The Lost Empire of Atlantis: History's Greatest Mystery Revealed*. His ideas have been profiled in the *New York Times Magazine* and the *Wall Street Journal*, and he has lectured at the Library of Congress, Royal Geographical Society, National Maritime Museum, and other prestigious venues. He served in the Royal Navy between 1953 and 1970. His knowledge of seafaring and navigation sparked his interest in the epic voyages of Chinese Admiral Zheng He. Menzies lives in London.

www.gavinmenzies.net

Photograph by Oliver Blackwell

Ian Hudson was educated at Eton College and the University of Bristol. He started working with Gavin Menzies in 2002 and has been involved with all of his book projects since the publication of *1421*. Ian established the website www.gavinmenzies.net and has managed the research team in London since then. He divides his time between London and his farm in Melchbourne, Bedfordshire.

Introduction

AS WITH OUR PREVIOUS BOOKS, our publisher has kindly allowed us to write a P.S. section to accompany the paperback edition, enabling us to give readers an insight into what has happened in the months since publication of the hardcover. As readers will most likely know by now, our website, www.gavinmenzies.net, acts as a hub for ongoing research into pre-Columbian global exploration, and is witness to a constant stream of new information and ideas. Therefore, it came as no surprise for us to receive a barrage of e-mails from readers around the world who had read *Who Discovered America?* and wanted to weigh in with their comments and suggestions. This P.S. section aims to give a general synopsis of the developments since publication, and is split into two parts: new evidence to support the theory of pre-Columbian transoceanic voyages, and information on suggested further reading and research. ∾

New Evidence

Earthworms in the Americas

After publication, some of the most exciting moments come in the form of tangible supporting evidence. One such example was suggested to us by a reader who had been studying the presence of earthworms in the Americas in the 1980s. Hubert Timmenga e-mailed us after reading *WDA?* with details concerning species of earthworms that were discovered on Vancouver Island and along the coastal forests of British Columbia, Canada.[1]

We know that, like the plants and animals studied in Emeritus Professors Sorenson and Johannessen's great body of research, earthworms are not able to travel long distances, and require human assistance if they are to do so. Research in the 1980s suggested that the majority of earthworms present in the area of study had been introduced by European immigrants—European species of earthworm had been arriving since the 1600s with plants and farm animals. A minority of the earthworms were indigenous to parts of the southern United States where the last ice age did not extend. A smaller minority of earthworms that were discovered in the deep organic soils along the west coast of British Columbia, however, were categorized as Megascolecidea. Megascolecidea are Asian worms and ▸

---

1 http://www.cfs.nrcan.gc.ca/pubwarehouse /pdfs/5102.pdf.

could not have arrived in the Americas without human assistance. Did early explorers from Asia bring earthworms with them, as they did other plants and animals? Sorenson and Johannessen agreed in e-mail correspondence that this is an interesting subject for discussion, and something worth investigating further.

The Oldest Globe to Depict the New World

The finding of the oldest globe to depict the New World[2] was of huge interest to us. This globe, engraved on two conjoined shells of ostrich egg, was purchased by an anonymous private institution at the London Map Fair in 2012 and has been studied by an independent Belgian researcher named Stefaan Missinne. The globe exhibits a high level of cartographic skill, depicting the world with flair and clarity, but with some significant errors. The content on the globe is similar to Waldseemüller's green globe of 1506 (see second color insert of *WDA?*) and it is said to have been used to cast the Lenox globe, circa 1510. Missinne infers that he has evidence that the ostrich egg globe is connected to Leonardo da Vinci's workshop in Florence, Italy. If this can be proved, it would reinforce the theory put forward in Gavin's book *1434* that Leonardo had been privy to cartographic data passed to Europeans by a Chinese delegation that had a 1434 audience with Pope Eugenius IV in Florence. Paolo Toscanelli, the Florentine polymath who described the encounter with this delegation, was later to provide Columbus with the geographical information that guided him to his "discovery" of the New World.

The Vatican's recent announcement[3] that it has embarked on the process of digitizing its archives—at a cost of some $20 million—has raised the possibility of uncovering many interesting documents related to this delegation, and we await the project's completion with great anticipation!

---

2 http://www.history.com/news/ostrich-egg-globe-may-be-oldest-to-depict -new-world.
3 http://www.bbc.co.uk/news/world-europe-26676909.

The Great Dismal Swamp Junk: Some Professional Feedback from a Retired Naval Aviator

Visitors to our website come from all walks of life. Gavin is particularly pleased to hear from fellow submariners, and others who have shared similar experiences when serving with the armed forces. So, we were intrigued to hear from Simon Askins, a retired naval aviator who had read *WDA?* and was keen to help us try to solve the mystery of the Great Dismal Swamp junk. He wrote to us with firsthand experience as a navigator, saying "You say that you searched along the runway heading of 280° for some miles. As an ex–Royal Navy aviator, I would guess that a 1943 fighter bomber would be a bit like a Hellcat—which probably climbed out at 120 knots—so in 7 minutes would go about 15 miles ±5 miles. I know of airfields in the UK where, between when I first flew in 1959, and now, there has been a change in variation, altering the magnetic runway heading on some airfields by 10 degrees. If this same variation change applies in Virginia, this over some 15 to 20 miles range would give a sideways error of about 2 miles per degree. Could this have affected your search? In addition you would need to consult an American aviator who is familiar with the ground there and ask how the topography would affect his choice of emergency landing area. It sounds as though it is probably 'Virginia jungle' in which case his choice would probably be to ditch in the river, rather than into trees in an aircraft still full of Avgas. In which case, he would have selected the river direction most into wind . . ."

Although we don't currently have anyone "on the ground" in Virginia to see how this will affect the search area for the elusive junk, this recent correspondence emphasizes the practical and multidisciplinary focus of the circle of researchers who advise us from around the world—for which we are extremely grateful. ∾

Further Reading and Research

Celia Heil, *Lacquer Across the Oceans: Independent Invention or Diffusion?*[4]

In early 2014 we were made aware of a book written by cultural anthropologist Celia Heil. Her book is cited as bringing to light "new information on the lacquer technology of Mexico and its direct link to Asian lacquerware, technology, materials, and decorative styles."

We were understandably interested in this work, especially since the similarities in lacquer technology used in Mexico and China had been alluded to previously in *1421*. The likeness was central to the theory that Mesoamerica had been witness to an exchange of scientific and technical knowledge with China before the European arrival in the area. The detailed history of lacquer production in the Old and New Worlds that Heil has accumulated on her travels brings us to the inescapable conclusion that there was a sustained and significant interaction between Asia and Mexico before Columbus set sail in 1492.

---

4 http://www.prweb.com/releases/CeliaHeil /LACQUERAcrosstheOceans/prweb11241516 .htm.

John Ruskamp, *Asiatic Echoes: The Identification of Ancient Chinese Pictograms in pre-Columbian North American Rock Writing* **(2nd edition)**[5]

We have been following with interest the ongoing research of John A. Ruskamp Jr. for some time now. In 2009 he published a paper titled "Found: An Ancient Chinese Ideograph Integrated into Native American Rock Writing." This paper charted his interpretation of ancient petroglyphs found in Arizona, New Mexico, and California. He followed up the paper in 2011 with publication of his book, *Asiatic Echoes: The Identification of Chinese Pictograms in North American Rock Writing,* which incorporated a more substantial body of work. The second edition of the book was published in 2013.

In his own words, John's research "evaluates previously unrecognized ancient rock writing evidence that in pre-Columbian times, multiple intellectual exchanges took place between Asiatic and North American populations. Using the novel integration of the legal construct of substantial similarity with the comparative statistical tool of Jaccard's Index of Similarity, the Chinese origin of fifty-three North American petroglyphs and pictographs is established. Collectively, independent experts with knowledge of ancient Chinese calligraphy and the determination of Native American ▶

---

5 http://asiaticechoes.org/.

tribal rock art affiliations, dating, and styles have confirmed the study's most significant findings."

DNA Studies

The results of several noteworthy DNA studies were released in the months following publication of *WDA?*. I have attempted to give simplified synopses of their conclusions below:

"Ancient DNA from Siberian Boy Links Europe and America"[6]

The first genetics study of importance relied on the extraction of DNA from a young boy who had died in south-central Siberia some 24,000 years ago. The body had been found in the 1920s at a dig near the Russian town of Mal'ta. From the remains of this four-year-old, scientists were able to sample and sequence what is said to be the oldest modern human genome to date. Significantly, the results of various tests showed that up to one-third of Native American ancestry stemmed from an ancient population connected to Europeans. According to Eske Willerslev, one of the scientists conducting the research: "When we sequenced this genome, something strange appeared. . . . Parts of the genome you find today in western Eurasians, other parts of the genome you find today in Native Americans— and are unique today to Native

---

6 http://www.bbc.co.uk/news/science -environment-25020958.

Americans. . . . But the most puzzling part of this finding was that the boy showed no clear affinities with East Asian populations such as the Chinese, Koreans or Japanese. . . ."

The appearance of "European" DNA was of relevance to our research, not least as it seemed to echo the results of the DNA tests carried out on the "Windover bog people" described in chapter 17 of *WDA?*, emphasizing yet again that the Beringia migration theory was not as clear-cut as previously imagined.

Across Atlantic Ice

The controversial Solutrean theory, which hypothesizes that the founding populations of the Americas came from Europe, was brought to a global audience with the publication of *Across Atlantic Ice* by coauthors Bruce Bradley and Dennis Stanford. In their book, the authors find an array of similarities between flint tools and arrowheads in North America and Western Europe, but which display little resemblance to the artifacts found at Clovis sites on the west coast of the Americas. The Solutrean hypothesis, as a result of this, suggests that early explorers to the eastern seaboard of the Americas traveled in wooden and animal-skin boats from France and Spain. It advocates a passage by sea along the ice margins in the North Atlantic, with ancient man's arrival in the New World dated to 18,000–25,000 years ago. ▶

Further Reading and Research *(continued)*

A significant find that supported this theory was a tapered stone blade found with a mastodon tusk that had been hauled up out of the sea by a scallop trawler in Chesapeake Bay in 1970. The tusk was dated to being 22,760 years old. Dennis Stanford firmly believes that the blade was used to butcher the mastodon, thus providing proof of pre-Clovis human habitation in the United States.

In an essay on the subject Stanford and Dennis summarize things succinctly: "The ultimate test of this hypothesis may be found in genetic research on ancient human remains. Michael Brown and colleagues reported in 1998 that mitochondrial-DNA haplogroup X (a genetic marker of population groups) is found in low frequencies in both European and Native American populations, but not among Asians. This indicated to them that some of the American founders may have come from Europe between 36,000 and 12,000 years ago. . . . Regardless of whether a Solutrean-Clovis link is eventually proven, exploring this hypothesis should increase our understanding of the development of technological innovations and broaden our knowledge of early peoples of the New World. . . ."[7]

---

7 http://www.cabrillo.edu/~crsmith/solutrean_solution.html.

"Native Americans Descended from Ancient Montana Boy" [8]

In February 2014 we were notified of a DNA study that purported to be the "final nail in the coffin" for the Solutrean hypothesis, coming in the form of DNA from a young boy found at an ancient burial site in Montana. The results were discussed on the *Science* website as follows:

> The skull of a young boy which has been examined and dated to c. 12,700 years old. . . . The 1- to 2-year-old Clovis child, now known to be a boy, is directly ancestral to today's native peoples from Central and South America. "Their data are very convincing . . . that the Clovis Anzick child was part of the population that gave rise to North, Central, and Southern American groups," says geneticist Connie Mulligan of the University of Florida in Gainesville. . . . The child's DNA more closely resembles that of Central and South Americans than Native Americans from the far north, although the relationship is still very close. Comparing the Anzick genome with that of a 24,000-year-old Siberian boy and a 4,000-year-old Paleo-Eskimo from Greenland ▶

---

8 http://news.sciencemag.org/archaeology /2014/02/native-americans-descend-ancient -montana-boy.

confirms that Native Americans originally come from Northeast Asia. . . ."

Nonetheless, subscribers to the Solutrean hypothesis stand firm in their beliefs. Bruce Bradley, author of *Across Atlantic Ice*, argues: "This is a single individual and can in no way represent all that was happening."

Pedra Furada

We are often been blessed with great serendipity during the writing process. The stream of new information that comes to us via our website is never-ending, and we frequently find it hard to stop adding new evidence and draw the line in time for publication deadlines. (Our publishers, quite rightly, get tired of having to chase our "moving targets"!) Never before has providence come into play so evidently as on the weekend just passed, when, while I was striving to put pen to paper to write this P.S. section, an e-mail flashed up on my computer screen alerting me to a new article in the *New York Times*. The story that "Jay" had sent us in a link was titled "Discoveries Challenge Beliefs on Humans' Arrival in the Americas." It was written by Simon Romero and appeared on March 27, 2014.[9]

The piece started off by describing

---

9 http://www.nytimes.com/2014/03/28/world /americas/discoveries-challenge-beliefs-on -humans-arrival-in-the-americas.html.

Serra da Capivara National Park in northeastern Brazil, which is home to the Pedra Furada site. The park houses hundreds of ancient archaeological sites, and thousands of rock art images and glyphs etched and painted on the cliff walls depict epic scenes of human interaction with nature. Some of these painted images have been dated to circa 10,000 years ago. However, even more significant are finds of handmade stone tools and implements found in situ among evidence of human habitation, which have been dated to as early as 22,000 years ago. We were of course aware of the Pedra Furada site and the substantial impact that it had in demolishing the "Clovis-first" theory— not least as it is described in the final chapter of *WDA?* as a "game-changer."

The article was significant primarily in that it brought an otherwise largely unknown site and ongoing debate to a global audience. Furthermore, it echoed the conclusion of *WDA?*, which was that dates for human habitation in the Americas are constantly being pushed back. We had suggested that the evidence might go back as far as 100,000 years ago, and Dr. Guidon, the eighty-one-year-old archaeologist who first laid eyes on Pedra Furada in the 1970s, believes in a similar date, theorizing that travelers arrived in Brazil from Africa by boat. According to the French archaeologist Eric Boëda, who leads the excavations at Pedra Furada, "The Clovis paradigm is finally buried." ⌒

Conclusion

THERE IS A HUGE AMOUNT of contradictory research concerning early human migration patterns to the New World, with reliable dates for primitive human habitation deviating from as far back as 48,000 years ago to as recently as 11,000 B.C. In spite of all the advances in scientific data collection and analysis, there remains a considerable amount of uncertainty regarding the minutiae, although the basic patterns are delineated with ever-growing certainty. What is strikingly obvious, however, is that the peopling of the Americas was a process that was far more complex than the Beringia and "Clovis-first" theories would allow us to believe. Ancient man's harnessing of the power of wind and water clearly also played a much more important role.

Ian Hudson
London
March 31, 2014 ∾